Islam in Performance

Contemporary Plays from South Asia

At the Sound of Marching Feet
Life of Araj
The Djinns of Eidgah
The Far-reaching Night
We Shall Resist
Watch the Show and Move on

Edited by
ASHIS SENGUPTA

Bloomsbury Methuen Drama
An imprint of Bloomsbury Publishing Plc

B L O O M S B U R Y
LONDON · OXFORD · NEW YORK · NEW DELHI · SYDNEY

Bloomsbury Methuen Drama

An imprint of Bloomsbury Publishing Plc

Imprint previously known as Methuen Drama

50 Bedford Square	1385 Broadway
London	New York
WC1B 3DP	NY 10018
UK	USA

www.bloomsbury.com

BLOOMSBURY, METHUEN DRAMA and the Diana logo are trademarks of Bloomsbury Publishing Plc

This collection first published 2017 and the following plays are published for the first time in the English language in this volume.

At the Sound of Marching Feet / Payer Awaj Pawa Jai © Syed Shamsul Haq 2017
Life of Araj / Araj Charitamrita © Masum Reza; trans. Bina Biswas, Sayantan Gupta 2017
The Far-reaching Night / Bahut Dur Tak Raat Hogi © Zahida Zaidi; trans. Ameena Kazi Ansari 2017
We Shall Resist / Hum Rokaen Gae © Anwer Jafri; trans. Sheema Kermani
Watch the Show and Move on / Dekh Tamasha Chalta Ban © Shahid Nadeem; trans. Shuby Abidi

The following play has been reproduced by kind permission of Oberon Books Ltd.
The Djinns of Eidgah © Abhishek Majumdar 2013
First published by Methuen Drama in this volume in 2017

Introduction copyright © Bloomsbury Methuen Drama 2017

The authors have asserted their right under the Copyright, Designs and Patents Act, 1988, to be identified as author of this work.

British Library Cataloguing-in-Publication Data
A catalogue record for this book is available from the British Library.

ISBN:	HB:	978-1-4742-5071-9
	PB:	978-1-4742-5070-2
	EPDF:	978-1-4742-5072-6
	EPUB:	978-1-4742-5073-3

Library of Congress Cataloging-in-Publication Data
A catalog record for this book is available from the Library of Congress.

Typeset by Fakenham Prepress Solutions, Fakenham, Norfolk NR21 8NN
Printed and bound in Great Britain

we sit on a fence,
on another they;
we shoot at them,
at us they do;
like aiming stones
at a pole, sitting in
a balcony sipping tea.
we remain us
they, they –
with no knowledge
of the self or other,
like weapons of the same
stock, parroting each other,
in a crossfire.

a Child pops its head
in between, from
a heap of bodies,
a body of anonymity –
but claimed as
trophies by both sides –
and asks the livid living:
"where do I belong?"
Silence shoots all.

A.S.

Note on the Volume

The plays collected in this volume are works of fiction. Names, characters, businesses, places, events, and incidents appearing in them are either the products of the playwrights' imagination or are used in a fictitious manner. The anthology does not intend to outrage the faith/religious beliefs of any community or to cause any kind of damage or loss to any person/party. The publisher, the volume editor, playwrights, and translators do not assume any responsibility to anyone or to any party for any unintended hurt or damage or loss in this regard.

Contents

Acknowledgments

I sit at my desk on a slow Sunday morning, savoring the flavors of my Darjeeling cuppa, and of Bengal's autumn. A plethora of emails, marked "unread," demand immediate replies. The first I click open is from a former student who thanks me lavishly for what I would call a little something that I did for him years ago. I begin to wonder, reading his lines for a second time, about the strange alleys of the human mind that can suddenly choke with memories at the slightest "provocation." A book that *his* student gifted him the other day made him remember me somehow. I reply with a "thanks—so nice of you." His was an acknowledgment, a compliment; mine—an appreciation, reciprocation. This sets me wondering if an acknowledgment, when put to words from a state of pure feeling, may ever lose its fullness and sound formulaic. The idle musings around the email soon turn into a reminder of sorts, of the "Acknowledgments" that I have long been meaning to write for this volume! Words often fail us; yet, in words alone, can I ever give credit to those people who have made this work possible. I sign out of email and start typing over a virtual space—lines that I imagine my benefactors (and others) will read one day in print.

The mixed feeling of accomplishment ("Ah, I can finish the book finally!") and dissatisfaction ("Um, it *could* have been better"), as I begin to draft these lines, is taken over by an overwhelming sense of gratitude to all whose book it basically is. First, I would thank the playwrights who trusted me with their manuscripts (I also silently remember those whose works I have read with great admiration, but cannot, unfortunately, include here due to space, and who, I hope, will forgive me on this count). Many thanks to the late Syed Shamsul Haq, Anwer Jafri, Abhishek Majumdar, Shahid Nadeem, Masum Reza, and the late Zahida Zaidi. I wish Professor Zaidi had lived to see her play in translation.

The translators have done a commendable job, indeed. While they have tried hard to maintain lexical fidelity to the original, they have been no less creative in making the play texts eminently readable in another language, as well as performable across cultures. Thanks so much— Shuby Abidi, Ameena Kazi Ansari, Bina Biswas, Sayantan Gupta, and Sheema Kermani. I thank all of you also for your unwaivering cooperation during the multiple stages of editing.

Special thanks are due to Oberon Books for permission to reprint *The Djinns of Eidgah*, as well as to Zoya Zaidi, for permission to publish the translation of *Bahut Dur Tak Raat Hogi*.

Honestly, I was not sure—even after I had spent a whole year on the project—about its feasibility. Collecting some of the play texts for the volume—and finding eminent translators, of course—seemed an insurmountable task then. Friends, who had extended unforgettable help at the time by putting me in touch with the right people, need special mention here. A big "thank you" to Syed Jamil Ahmed, Fakrul Alam, Syed Humayoun, Ramendu Majumdar, Anisur Rahman, and Sumana.

Many thanks to the anonymous readers of my book proposal for their significant suggestions for improvement. I also deeply appreciate Ayesha Jalal's invaluable comments on my draft Introduction. Thank you, Janelle Reinelt, for your very kind encouragement at the formative stage of the project. I appreciate the great care, Anna Brewer, which you took all along to see this volume through. Pinaki, I can never forget your continuous effort to help me find more time for this project.

Thanks are also due to Ajoka Theatre Pakistan and MELOW–India for the opportunities to discuss some of my ideas at their conferences, in 2015 and 2016, respectively. I am also thankful to the University of North Bengal for awarding me a modest research grant for the project.

And, without your significant support and boundless love, Mitra and Pipli, I could not have been here.

As regards my Introduction to this volume, I would like to note that Sections I and IV partly draw on my Introduction to *Mapping South Asia through Contemporary Theatre: Essays on the Theatres of India, Pakistan, Bangladesh, Nepal and Sri Lanka* (Palgrave Macmillan, 2014), and that Section II borrows a couple of lines from my article, "Of Race/Religion, Nation and Violence," *Comparative American Studies* 8.3 (2010).

Lastly, my sincere apologies if there are any inadvertent factual errors, oversights, or omissions of any kind in the book. My publisher and I look forward to the earliest opportunity for correction.

Introduction: Performing Islam in South Asia

I
Why This Book?

Islam—especially since the Iranian Revolution of 1978–9, the US-led Talibanization of Afghanistan to end its occupation by the Soviet forces in 1979, and, more recently, the 9/11 attack on the World Trade Center in 2001, and the emergence of ISIS in 2013—has become in the Western perception synonymous with violence and that has significantly affected the attitude of the rest of the world toward that religion. Closer home, the political chemistry around Islam, which is not totally unconnected from any of the above events, has much influenced the making of contemporary South Asia in both tangible and intangible ways. For global, as well as regional reasons, Islam (which etymologically means "submission to [the Will of] God") evokes today a strange and negative range of emotions and reactions, from suspicion to disdain. "Islamic fundamentalism," and the militancy/atrocities it encourages, does remain an unpleasant, if not gruesome, reality in the subcontinent as elsewhere. However, a biased, lopsided understanding of Islam as a source of all political malaise in our times appears as a conspiracy to wink at the other forms of (religious) fundamentalism which not only threaten and provoke the minorities, overtly or covertly, but also conduct moral policing of the so-called "deviants" within majority communities. The demolition of the Babri Masjid (mosque) in 1992,[1] and the post-Godhra carnage of 2002[2]—not to speak of the anti-Sikh riot of 1984[3], and the violent Buddhism in Sri Lanka and Myanmar—are examples of grisly incidents from the recent past that should substantiate this claim with specific regard to South (east) Asia. The Islamophobia permeating our times, for all the real dangers from Islamism's changing incarnations, is also symptomatic of a cocktail of confusion, fear, and irrationality that has come to grip the seemingly secular and non-secular spaces alike, both in thought and reality. And this applies to Islam as faith, as well as identity.[4]

This volume is a collection of plays from South Asia which deal with the social and political performance of Islam in the region post-1947. The first of its kind, the anthology puts together play texts from Bangladesh, India, and Pakistan which offer insights into a situation where the *performance* of political Islam refers both to the construction of myths about the religion, and their deconstruction through a variety of theatrical modes. It presents the plays in conversation with one another in contexts of competing nationalist narratives predicated on Islam in South

Asia, and ferrets out their working through abuses of state power that include unleashing violence on the religious Other. The playwrights may or may not be much aware of one another's works, although their plays sometimes cross borders to take part in the region's annual theater festivals and seminars. The book hopes to establish a connection between them, creating a complex framework of South Asian theater around the narrative of Islam—a pattern that broadly hinges on the plays' abiding as well as changing contours of relationship with society and politics.

Each of the plays collected here creates in its own style a reciprocal loop of "fact" and "fiction" in the performance space. Reality in drama or theater as a work of *fiction* is an aesthetic representation of something outside the text or its performance that may not have the stake to prove the authenticity of that "something," whereas a historical representation is always anxious about such stake and also challenged by other historical articulations of the reality in question.[5] The selected plays, through their explicit performativity, enjoy a unique freedom by engaging with the regional "reality" of Islam and, by extension, Islamism at different levels of affirmation and interrogation, intervention, and reinscription when history with its institutional discipline would need a set of tools to ascertain the veracity of facts (even as one argues that facts are but products of performance). The plays hardly indicate a fixed referent or a determinate position of the object represented; they are strategic, exploring, interpretive, creative, and redefining instead. This anthology demonstrates how theater in its different forms supplements conventional history which cannot often help leaving out of its purview the intangibles of the past—such as feeling, belief, and memory—and thus betrays its own inadequacies and erasures.

The social relevance of plays, as well as their aesthetic appeal, depends largely on the intersection of several factors, such as issues of address, dynamics of representation, and the historical time and locus of performance. Most of the pieces collected here have an active intent and a dynamic relationship with the audience, since they play with the line separating life from theater. Their social effectiveness is considerably determined by the space between "the interests of writing"/production and "those of reading"/viewing,[6] while the playwright's or the director's own ideological orientation may no less influence their construction and reception. The plays in this volume may or may not bring about any immediate or visible change to the existing political or social order in South Asia where Islam is a prominent religion which influences state policies in one way or another. But they can certainly have a lasting impact on people's attitudes and their ways of thinking by delineating in a theater idiom, more direct and persuasive than seductive and metaphorical, serious sociopolitical issues emanating from present contestations over Islam.

Given the vastness and complexity of the subject the anthology broaches, and the space constraints associated with any such publication, I had no option but to let go of several South Asian plays, even though they deal with issues of religious politics directly or indirectly affecting the polity and quality of life in the subcontinent. Yet this book seeks to maintain a balance by selecting genres and subgenres from across mainstream and parallel theaters, which together provide a revealing window into the construction and performance of the "Muslim" subject in contemporary South Asia. The volume contains plays written and performed over the past four decades or so, and by no means claims to be comprehensive in its representation of Islam in the region or in its theaters.

Islam in Performance distinguishes, in keeping with the themes of the plays collected here, between Islam as faith and Islam as political ideology, however connected the two might be in the constantly evolving narrative of jihad at home and abroad. It focuses more on the latter to understand historically the politicization of the faith, particularly in South Asia, and critique its contemporary excesses that do not, however, preclude the abuse of Islam for purely secular and even personal gains. The ongoing discourse on the "Muslim" subject (which in a way also constructs it) is not only contingent upon the fundamentalist interpretation of Islamic texts and its recent non-liberal ramifications in the political–legist praxis, but also informed by right-wing Hindutva politics in the region, and the Western projection of the Islamic community as suspect. Here, it also becomes necessary to see what place religious nationalism has in the supposedly post-religious secular space of the modern nation-state.

Islam, as a spiritual worldview, is, therefore, less the theme of any of the plays here, and more a trope which, tempered within the crucible of divisive politics in colonial and postcolonial South Asia, has been used to breed and foster narratives of nation-making that continue to largely affect the state of affairs in South Asia. On the other hand, the targeting of Islam, or unequal treatment of its followers in places where they are the minority, becomes an equally significant aspect of the anthology. The concerns addressed in the plays in this book go beyond the clichéd frame of communalism to incorporate much wider patterns of life woven circuitously around the political and personal exploitation of a faith, as much by its professed followers as by its detractors. The plays invite comparison with one another, engaging with this situation from perspectives of the three countries concerned: the idea of *azadi*[7] countering the performance of state-sponsored nationalism and the predicament of life in the Kashmir Valley today (*The Djinns of Eidgah*, 2012); Hindutva politics shaking the long-held principles of a plural India, and often threatening to erase the religious "Other" (*The Far-reaching Night*, 2006); sectarian violence and abuse of Pakistan's blasphemy laws by self-professed guardians of Islam (*We Shall Resist*, 2009); Islamization of Pakistan at the expense of political governance, and persecution of non-Muslim minorities (*Watch the Show and Move on*, 1992); the clash between ethno-linguistic and religious nationalism, culminating in Bangladesh's Liberation War (*At the Sound of Marching Feet*, 1976); and censorship of production/dissemination of scientific knowledge and threat to the lives of secular liberals in the country (*Life of Araj*, 2001). As nation-building in South Asia remains a continuous, unfinished project, trouble keeps brewing around the contestatory constructions of the "Muslim" subject by Muslims as well as non-Muslims of a geopolitical and cultural space that they have co-inhabited historically. The plays also underscore the need, through a spectacle of triumph or of defeat, to resist violence in the name of faith, and uphold the ideals of plurality and hospitality across the region.

II
Religious and Secular Nationalism/Religion and Scripture

Before we attempt a deeper probe into the historical role of Islam in the making of modern South Asia—how it influenced the bloody formation of two separate nation-states in 1947, and then the subcontinent's further fragmentation in 1971, it is important to understand the common possible reasons for the resurgence of religious nationalism in our times, its paradoxical use of the modern state apparatus to consolidate its power, and the danger this lethal combination of religion and politics spells for a whole region, if not for the entire world.

If religious nationalism can be considered an anachronism in a globalized space and an irrational/unjust challenge to the secular (and supposedly universal) world order, then its resurgence can also be accounted for against the backdrop of the failures of modern secularism. Religious nationalism as "a culturally liberating force" gained ground mainly due to secularism's failure to fulfill "its own promises of political freedom, economic prosperity, [...] social justice," and security ever since the end of the Second World War, disenchanting many secular nationalists eventually.[8] This narrative of religious nationalism grows out of a deep sense of deprivation and exploitation within a community that, in turn, produces "a feeling of insecurity," and may also seek revenge against the perceived exploiters. Secularism lacks moral idealism in this perspective, and religious nationalism can supposedly cure the moral ills that secularism may engender, and thus also improve material living conditions. Religious nationalism can thus be "inspired by a reformist zeal" that may be inseparable from "a quest for power."[9]

Modern secularism is not always tolerant either and may even bear in its cultural nationalism what Robert Bellah calls "civil religion" (quasi-religious national values that gain occasional visibility through the secular state's public rituals and symbols).[10] Resulting from the rationalist secularism of the Enlightenment, the concept of modern nation did not evidently supersede religion. In fact, many nationalists borrowed the language of "relativization" and "territorialization" from the theocrat's unselfconscious description of a particular faith as "truest" rather than "true." Such "relativization"/"territorialization" became "selfconscious and political in intent" over time,[11] leading to wars between states, as well as intra-national group hostilities. Toleration, or acceptance, of ethnic/religious difference, is, in such circumstances, replaced by "a drive toward unity and singularity."[12] This brings a split in the "deep, horizontal comradeship" that the nation is envisioned to be despite all actual inequality prevalent in it, and paves the way for ethnic cleansing that thrives on *killing*, rather than *dying willingly*, for "an imagined political community."[13] Moreover, if secularism's "prohibition" model (European) can be pulled up for its failure to check social injustice and corruption, secularism's "neutrality" model (South Asian/Indian) can also be critiqued for its practical inability to maintain true neutrality toward all religions in a multiethnic, plural society.[14] Any model of nationalism, for its possible or relative success in South Asia, needs to be inclusive, not homogenizing, by developing a culture of diversity and a participatory-pluralistic[15] concept of society.

At the same time, the distinction often made between religious nationalism and religious fundamentalism is not tenable all the time; nor so the conflation of theology with fundamentalism. While theology is reasoning and discussion concerning the nature of God, fundamentalism is a strict if not blind adherence to religious orthodoxy, often as a reaction against modernism. Again, if religious fundamentalism is motivated solely by religious principles and beliefs rather than by "broad concerns about the nature of society" and governance, religious nationalism conceptualizes a social and political destiny within a frame of religious morality and rationale.[16] The latter may not reject secular politics, as we see in the plays from Bangladesh and Pakistan, even while dismissing secular ideas of a nation-state. It is this very fusion of "state" and "church" that leaves enough scope for the nation-state's eventual collusion with religious fundamentalism. Secular morality (with its customary private/public distinction) is naturally at odds with religious nationalism's defining moral basis for politics, which is statehood, after all, on grounds of religious uniformity and homogeneity. Fundamentalism's narrow dogmatism and "religious literalism" may thus make invisible inroads into religious nationalism's seemingly broader perspective.

This volume also explores, in this context, the relationship between a faith and the scripture that is believed to encapsulate it. The reading of scripture by the interpretive community will always be different from the individual's secular-liberal, or creative reading of it. The first kind of reading establishes a tradition and does not deviate, even in its accommodation of occasional contingencies, from its "sacred" aim to arrive at the "literal" meaning of the text. But literalism is always a difficult proposition. As Mark Knight notes, "interpretive communities for whom religion is a central thread are especially susceptible to bringing their own prejudices to the texts they read." The "qualities of religion per se" is not the issue here, but rather the "dynamics" of such communities' interpretation.[17] None of the plays in the anthology really attempt a "creative" reading or retelling of Islam in the way Salman Rushdie's *Satanic Verses* does. The charges against Rushdie's "blasphemous" novel that led up to its ban in several countries and occasioned the *fatwa* (sentence) against his life, as Ruvani Ranasinha has it, range from the retelling of "an old legend that some of the Qu'ran's original verses originated with Satan and were later deleted by Mohammed" to choosing the name "Mahound" for Muhammad ("Mahound" being "a medieval demonization" of the Prophet's name). Notwithstanding this argument, some of the plays here do "open up a space of discursive contestation," to borrow phrases from Homi K. Bhabha, that directly or indirectly places the Quran within "a perspective of historical and cultural relativism."[18] The anthology largely appreciates, by juxtaposing divergent views from the same religious community, the problem of believing in one Islam because the "Muslim nation" is heterogeneous—which further problematizes the "fundamentals" of Islam as of any other faith virtually. As Abu Khalil maintains, *one* interpretation of the Quran may not be possible especially because of the ambiguity inherent in the phraseology of the text itself.[19] More importantly, the interpretative community or spiritual leaders "ruling" the "congregation" may bring into their reading those "facts" of history that they wanted, raising a supposedly embarrassing question if religion in general can at all be separated from politics. The collection encourages a liberal reading of Islam by not subscribing to Islamic fundamentalism, and also disapproves of any other form of religious (or even secular) intolerance meant to counter Islamicism by distorting Islam deliberately.

No less important is it to realize that the attempted recuperation of historical meaning through the text about a mythic past is less a rediscovery of historical truth than a veritable article of faith. The imposition on a society of what is passed off as the inviolable historical-transcendental truth is not only an aberration in the post-Enlightenment world, but may prove coercive in social relationships and political praxis. When such fundamentalism passes from religious preaching to the intervention of clerical leaders in dynasties and governments, repressive state policies acquire legitimacy in the name of religion or may masquerade as theocratic exhortations that the faithful must respect. The secularization of the Islamic law thus reduces Islam to an identity marker that can be manipulated in the interest of awkward nation-state politics. This emerging interface of religious fundamentalism and religious nationalism anchors itself in the concept of "Islamic state" that, according to Ayesha Jalal, would be "dedicated to exclusive juridical application of Sharia [Islamic laws]." Even if such developments can be understood in terms of the fleeting nature of interpretation, "selective appropriations of the Islamic tradition" (Jalal)[20] and the self-conscious guile of the traders in religion (as in *We Shall Resist/Hum Rokaen Gae*) in the running of an Islamic state, or of a state that aspires to be one, have proved dangerous in these times.

The liberal thought with no transcendent foundations may not be enough to sustain humans, and the anthology does not reject religion or bear any hostility to an expression of religiosity. Even the plays that vehemently question religious superstitions, for example—*Life of Araj/Araj Charitamrita*, do not seek to banish "religion from the public sphere" by "seizing on the worst excesses" of belief. Yet, all the plays collected here in fact aim to "locate belief within a [...] humanistic framework" that articulates worries about both fundamentalist intolerance and "secular fundamentalism,"[21] encouraging a redefinition of the sacred that needs to be created in consonance with the progress of human history and protected from political abuse. In other words, the anthology does not propose purging the universe of divinity but envisions a sacred that will not discriminate between faiths and will also accommodate principles that may have nothing to do with (religious) faith at all. Tolerance is a precondition for it. But the volume moves past the principle of tolerance, which is described by Mark Knight as "an inadequate mechanism for sustaining a heterogeneous society," to the concept of hospitality to find areas of mutual agreement and acceptance, as encoded in the plural epistemology of Araj, and in the gestures of the well-wishers visiting the riot victims in Zahida Zaidi's *The Far-reaching Night/Bahut Dur Tak Raat Hogi*. Tolerance ends when the Self is directly affected by the activities of the Other, and fails to remain disinterested in them. But the principle of hospitality builds up an inclusive framework of truth and reality based on "imaginative sympathy," of multiple "interpretations of the world" moderating each other.[22] These truths and interpretations may be as much a confluence of the secular and the sacred as a combination of different religious views within a democracy that is deliberative rather than coercive,[23] persuasive rather than manipulative. This stance is therefore equally different from the self-righteousness of both religious and secular activists and can be augmented by respecting otherness. It postulates a dynamic world that transforms "negative connotations of our socio-religious existences into an intercultural conciliation that works on [dissent and] differences rather than morbid conformity."[24] It is such egalitarianism of thought that this anthology seeks to give space to, respecting in principle an absence of consensus about issues but discouraging any type of absolutism.

III
Islam and the Partition

We should be in a position now to initiate a discourse on the trajectory of (political) Islam in modern South Asia, which is reflected, in a variety of ways, through the plays in this volume. Although India was officially divided along religious lines in 1947, it was more politics than religion—or politics played around Islam, especially during the last two decades of the colonial era—that split up the subcontinent, a blood-bathed event, the memory of which still shapes the relations between India and Pakistan, and continues to be revisited on smaller scales *within* the two nations, as if to settle old uneven communal scores. There is hardly any modern political phenomenon that has as many versions as the story of the subcontinent's partition. Whether partition can be fully ascribed to the All-India Muslim League's "two-nation" theory that Indian Muslims were "a distinctive and separate community that had resisted assimilation" into a Congress- (and also "Hindu"-) led India, or whether it was the British "divide-and-rule" policy that culminated in the sundering during the so-called transfer of power, "[t]here is now overwhelming evidence to suggest that [...] the contradictions and structural peculiarities of Indian society and politics in late colonial India" ultimately shaped the "communitarian discourse" on the "Muslim" subject as a separate identity category, in which the British Raj, the League and Congress equally participated.[25] Such a reading dislodges both the theory of "primordial animosities" between Hindus and Muslims as the main cause for the political dissonance and communal violence in colonial India *and* its obverse, namely the notion of the two great religious communities held together by tradition that was split apart by the colonizer's axe, focusing instead on the specific sociopolitical contexts that led all three parties to *use* Islam as the last resort to achieve their ends, however exclusive mutually.

It was not practically until the British construction through the 1881 census of religious-ethnic identity in South Asia that an Indian Muslim identity as a religious minority *vis-à-vis* the Hindu majority took shape, providing occasion for the making of the South Asian Muslim subject as a political category and influencing its convoluted course of development for decades to come. Subsequently, it was the British policy of communitarian representation in 1937 provincial elections, safeguarded by several acts and reforms introduced in between, which "consolidated Muslim political constituency," and "the idea that people sharing a particular faith constituted an identifiable group with common interests."[26] Inspired by Muhammad Iqbal's vision of a Muslim state,[27] as articulated in a 1937 letter to Muhammad Ali Jinnah, which poet–politician Chaudhri Rahmat Ali named "Pakistan," the Muslim community resolved to define itself as a nation rather than remain a minority any longer despite all longstanding internal disagreements over electoral politics in majority and minority provinces. It is at this historical juncture that Jinnah became the most significant figure to the Muslims in South Asia, one who would draw up a blueprint of a new nation meant to be acceptable to all of them.

Jinnah might or might not have resorted to a "notional" rather than "real" Pakistan, as Jisha Menon argues after Jalal,[28] after his efforts to secure parity of Muslim representation with Congress at the center had failed. But the thin line at the theoretical level between notional and real collapsed as soon as the prospect of a separate nation he was harping on took the form of what Jung would call "a psychic epidemic" among the majority of Indian Muslims, impelling a desperate Jinnah to go for the Direct Action Day (August 16, 1946).[29] On the other hand, Congress also eventually preferred a stronger center with their majority over territorial integrity. The subcontinent witnessed an unprecedented bloodshed that both preceded and followed the midnight hour (August 14/15, 1947), creating a fertile ground for unending communal politics in postcolonial South Asia. The massacre occurred with an intent to cleanse one's home of the Other; or people hurriedly left the "enemy's" ground to find their real home across the "border." Those who did not relocate and stayed on were now relegated to a minority status in their old homelands – like Muslims in India and Hindus in Pakistan. Asghar Wajahat's *Jisne Lahore Nahi Dekhya Oh Janmya Nahi/Unborn in Lahore* (2000) and Naseer Shamshi's *Lal Qilay se Lalu Khet/From the Red Fort to Lalu Khet* (1952) are moving dramatic portrayals of this crisis. In fact, there is a wide spectrum of literary encounters with the lived experience around these enormous shifts of home, status and identity with deep political resonances—such as Khushwant Singh's novel *Train to Pakistan* (1956), describing migration amid killings and rapes; Sadat Hasan Manto's stories about the painful bartering of people according to religious affiliations; Bhisham Sahni's short story, *Mujhe Mere Ghar le Chalo/ Take Me Home* (1994), poignantly articulating an exhausted old man's feeble cry for home; and Badiuzzaman's story, *Antim Ichchha/Final Wish* (1991), drawing through one face "thousands [...] of faces, neither Hindu nor Muslim," looking homeward. The drama of the partition moment is possibly best captured, in all its strangeness and chaos, in Salman Rushdie's *Midnight's Children* (1981)—a "mythopoetic" account of the birth of an independent nation narrated through a protracted clash of personal (family) and cultural identity.

Kashmir is often perceived as the "unfinished business" of partition as it is still the proverbial bone of contention between India and Pakistan. Before the British left the subcontinent, the princely state was given the option to remain independent or accede to India *or* Pakistan. Maharaja Hari Singh, then Hindu ruler of the Muslim-majority Kashmir, could not decide instantly, which frustrated Pakistan as it had expected the state's ready accession on grounds of religious affiliation and cultural homogeneity. Attacked by tribal forces and regular troops from the North-West Frontier, the Maharaja felt constrained to sign the Instrument of Accession with India in October 1947 for military assistance from New Delhi. The first Kashmir war thus broke out, to be brought under control by the United Nations Security Council-managed ceasefire in 1949, which in turn put in place a military control line virtually dividing the erstwhile princely state into India-administered Kashmir ("India-occupied Kashmir" to Pakistan) and Pakistan-administered Kashmir ("Pakistan-occupied Kashmir" to India). In contrast to Pakistan's "rationale for Kashmir's incorporation" into it on the premise of territorial "contiguity" (a euphemism for "religious nationalism"),[30] India viewed Kashmir as its integral part by flaunting the Instrument of Accession and a secular nationalism that should demonstrate its spaciousness to accommodate people irrespective of caste and creed. However, a steady historical view has been that if Azad Jammu and Kashmir, apparently a self-governing region in Pakistan-administered Kashmir, is actually under Pakistan's heavy administrative and military control, or if Pakistan's legal cover of self-empowerment to the Gilgit-Baltistan region cannot hide its plan to eventually absorb this territory, non-fulfillment of the pledge of India's first Prime Minister Jawaharlal Nehru that the accession would be confirmed by "wishes of the Kashmiri people" makes many doubt India's regard for the basic rights of the Kashmiris, even as New Delhi contends that the atmosphere had never been conducive for the plebiscite to be held. From this perspective, the lack of will on either side to respect the people's wishes has resulted in a cul-de-sac situation in the Valley, letting the real issue being hijacked by Islamist outfits. Abhishek Majumdar's *Djinns of Eidgah* deftly addresses these complex realities that will be discussed in the following sections.

IV
Islam and Postcolonial South Asia

India

"The struggle to produce a sense of cultural unity against the British," Dipesh Chakraborty observes, "made mainstream Indian nationalism Hindu."[31] The anti-British stance predicated at one level on the superiority of the Hindu spiritual-cultural past,[32] later turned anti-Muslim as the Muslim community, in general, did not readily warm up to the notion of a free (but Hindu-dominated) India for historical reasons. The Nehruvian concept of post-independence India was apparently a Western secular liberal vision separating religion from state, but actually indigenizing secularism as toleration of, and neutrality toward, all religions. This model of secularism was founded on the idea of "peaceful pluralism [often claimed as] equivalent to the separation of politics and religion."[33] But the state's implied involvement in religious issues by way of its avowed equal *support* to all religions puts neutrality practically at the risk of being tilted toward the majority/dominant religious community.

This secularism has often been taken hostage by political parties, with predominant or latent Hindutva elements in them, for electoral gains, in two diametrically opposite ways—either by projecting India as a Hindu *rashtra* (nation), or by appeasing the Muslim minority. Here's yet another irony, and perhaps more blatant at that. All opposition to, or any meddling with, the secular fabric of the state was conceived in the West-influenced Nehruvian archeology of post-independence India as religious fundamentalism. But in practical and political terms, the pursuit (garbed or direct) of majoritarian (and therefore culturally and politically Hindu) nationalism has been accepted as normative: "Hindutva will reign supreme! *Jo Hindu ki baat karega woh Bharat per raj karega!*" (from Salman Kurshid's play, *Sons of Babur* [2008]). Vinayak Damodar Savarkar's idea of "Hindoodam" during the 1920s did not include Muslim converts of the same "fatherland"/"holyland" because their adopted religion came from elsewhere. Although he had expressed his belief in a 1909 address that assimilation of "all that is best in the Muslim, Parsi, Jewish and other civilizations" would make Hindustan "appear all the more beautiful,"[34] his definition in his 1923 book of "Hindutva" as ideology different in many respects from "Hinduism" as religion sowed the seed of radical Hindu nationalism. Significantly, the present Rashtriya Sayamsevak Sangh (RSS)[35] chief Mohan Bhagwat's assertion that the cultural identity of all Indians is Hindutva[36] demonstrates the right wing's continued effort to virtually homogenize "Indian" culture.

Postcolonial identity politics in India around caste and creed—historically, a colonial baggage—actually functions through a heteroglossia of secular democracy, a supposedly promising neoliberal economy, and political parties' mobilization of Hindu cultural resources for electoral triumphs. Even Congress, perceived as a most secular political party of the country, compromised its principles in this race for votes during the 1980s. The appeal of then Indian Prime Minister Indira Gandhi to Hindu sentiments against secessionism during the campaign for 1983 elections to the Jammu and Kashmir provincial assembly apparently swung most Hindu voters with sympathies for the Bharatiya Janata Party (BJP) to Congress, unwittingly enabling the Visva Hindu Parishad[37] (VHP)-BJP combine to add momentum to the Ramjanmabhoomi campaign in Ayodhya.[38] Rajiv Gandhi government's studied failure to appeal against a 1986 local court order to open the gate to the disputed Ram Temple site in Ayodhya has been significantly highlighted by veteran Congress leader-turned president of India, Pranab Mukherjee, in his recent book, *The Turbulent Years: 1980–96.*

The dubious role of the Congress regime in fomenting, and then rooting out the Punjab militancy, has gone down in history as another dirty ploy to remain in power by stagemanaging a crisis of "national unity'—a stratagem that nevertheless boomeranged on it. After the military assault, Operation Blue Star, on the Amritsar Golden Temple in 1984, which killed controversial Sikh preacher Jarnail Singh Bhindranwale, along with many of his followers and numerous visiting devotees, Indira Gandhi declared, as Rajni Kothari reports in his book, that "Hindu *dharma* [faith] was under attack" by the secessionist Sikhs who were being encouraged by Pakistan.[39] The anti-Sikh riot, which followed the gunning down of Mrs. Gandhi by two of her Sikh bodyguards barely five months after the army operation, continues to be a deep scar in the psyche of the nation, even though the Congress Party has tried to induce a collective amnesia about the hoary event ever since.

The broadcast of the Hindu epic *Ramayana* as a television serial in 1987–8 has also been criticized by many as a camouflaged electoral tool used by Congress to win Hindu votes, especially in northern India. The inaction of the Congress government at center, as well as in the state of Bihar, is again blamed for the exacerbation of the 1989 Bhagalpur riot which killed thousands of Muslims, among others, and for the subsequent denial of justice to the riot victims. This shift in Congress electoral tactics continued, contributing to the consolidation of a common Hindu identity that was eventually hijacked by the BJP (a lesser-known party till the 1984 general elections) to organize itself into a major national party a decade later.

Slamming Congress's brand of state-led nationalism as "pseudo-secularism," on the other hand, veteran BJP leader L K Advani set out on his phenomenal *Rath Yatra* in 1990 (his chariot journey in the run-up to the 10th parliamentary elections), whipping up a Hindutva fever across northern India that elevated him to the level of a god man. This also catalyzed the demolition of the centuries-old Babri Masjid two years later in broad daylight, to the utter failure of the central and state government machinery—facts ironically alluded to in Hussain-ul-Haque's short story in Urdu, *Neev ki Eent/The Foundation Stone* (1995). What the Sangh Parivar exploited to communalize electoral politics at that point in time is the belief that a Hindu temple once stood at the sacred site where Lord Rama was born, and that it was destroyed by Babar, the founder of the Mughal Empire in India, to construct a *masjid* (mosque) in its place. Replacement of the mosque with a new Ram temple was now expected by the Parivar to be a pious, corrective enterprise that all pure-hearted Hindus would support. The bloody partition of India thus hangs over the subcontinent as a specter, and any communal strife in post-independence India is somewhat a revisit of the partition in one way or another. Mahesh Dattani's *Final Solutions* (1992–3) aptly portrays this saddening reality by showing how a present riot frighteningly reminds an old woman of a similar one she had lived through as a young girl in 1947, suggesting a cycle of violence. The play had to be dropped from a theater festival in Bangalore, in 1992, for fear of a possible escalation of communal tension following the Babri Masjid's demolition, although it was performed the next year.

Dattani's play proves almost prophetic. The Masjid demolition was followed by the Mumbai (Bombay) serial blasts in 1993; the post-Godhra "riots" in 2002 followed the attack on the Parliament of India in 2001. Whether there are causal connections in this pattern of violence may be debatable, but the loss of lives and the trauma it entails have elicited strong public protests, and generated moving aesthetic representations. Zahida Zaidi's *Bahut Dur Tak Raat Hogi/The Far-reaching Night* is a dramatic rendition of the post-Godhra carnage which drowned large portions of Gujarat, especially Ahmedabad, in blood, and reduced properties to ashes. The play suggests that while historical "fact" and its theatrical/fictional delineation should *not* be taken as synonymous, a play's critical reception can be strongly impacted by the interrelationships and tensions between them. Fifty-nine passengers on board the Sabarmati Express died due to a fire in one of its coaches in February 2002. The conspiracy theory, largely upheld by both a special court in Ahmedabad and the Special Investigation Team (SIT) in 2002, claims that the fire in the coach was a preplanned attack by a group of Muslims on pious Hindus (*kar sevaks*) returning from pilgrimage.[40] The other theory, as corroborated by the Justice Bannerjee Commission, describes the Godhra train fire as a pure accident that had nothing to do with any retaliatory measures by a minority group.[41] The carnage that followed continued for weeks and even months after the fire and made the ground situation more horrific, and the truth more elusive.[42]

The Seagull Theatre Quarterly devoted a whole issue (32.33), titled "a cannibal time," to the archiving of this phase of free India's political history, even comparing it to the Nazi Germany's Third Reich. Alongside interviews, essays, and photographs, the issue includes a play, Sisir Kumar Das's *Bagh/The Tiger*, featuring two women who hide in an abandoned house in riot-ravaged Ahmedabad, and have their separate social and religious identities dissolve in moments of terror, portrayed deftly through a mixing of reality with fantasy. Equally significant in this context are Maya Rao's *A Deeper Fried Jam*, a solo cabaret premiered at the National School of Drama's Bharat Rang Mahotsav (2002), and Anuradha Kapur and Ein Lall's 2003 adaptation of Bertolt Brecht's *Antigone Project*, an innovative mixing of text and documentary video material. Both are critiques of violence against Indian Muslims in 2002 Gujarat.

The Kashmir conflict has largely shaped the anti-Muslim discourse in post-independence India. It has taken a grave turn since the popular uprising of Kashmiri Muslims against the Indian state in 1989, apparently lending credence to the propaganda that the majority of Indian Muslims are pro-Pakistan. This view necessitates a quick look back through the 1970s. The Simla Agreement between India and Pakistan in 1972 turned the 1949 cease-fire line with minor deviations into the Line of Control (LoC) between the two countries.[43] And the process of Kashmir's integration on the Indian side, with its first definitive seal in 1957, was completed in 1975 by an accord signed between then Prime Minister Indira Gandhi and Kashmir's National Conference founder Sheikh Abdullah,[44] superseding the Kashmiris' stubborn expectations, as many would argue, about the promised plebiscite. In short, it is this complex of events, together with the infamous 1987 elections, and erosion of democratic institutions in the region, which sets the stage for the insurgency in the Valley from 1989 onwards. The undivided Jammu Kashmir Liberation Front (JKLF) was the principal secessionist force in the political drama with its huge support base in the Muslim population until 1995, while other players in the arena—such as Hizbul-Mujahideen, Jamaat-i-Islami, and the Hurriyat organizations with their hardliners—are currently perceived as pro-Pakistan elements, or irredentist forces, seeking unification of Kashmir with Pakistan. The subsequent involvement of the "Islamic" terror outfits such as the Lashkar-e-Taiba (LeT) in the Kashmir conflict violently communalized the otherwise ethno-nationalist movement of 1989. In January 1990, many Kashmiri Pandits, the only surviving Brahmin Hindu natives of the Valley, were brutally killed by Muslim radicals, and even more went into exile in different parts of India. Irawati Karnik's *Gasha* (2013), directed by Abhishek Majumdar, drama-tizes this poignant reality through the story of a man who returns to his homeland after twenty long years, only to find that he no longer belongs there. It deserves mention here that under the current BJP dispensation, Kashmiri Pandits are fighting for their rights, especially for their rehabili-tation in the Valley, in a rather politically aggressive manner, describing themselves as a wounded "Hindu community."

The Amarnath Shrine controversy, following the Jammu and Kashmir government's decision in 2008 to transfer ninety-nine acres of land to the Hindu temple, further exacerbated political tension in Kashmir.[45] Ramu Ramanathan's *Kashmir Kashmir* (2009), which premiered in Mumbai in 2009, plays out in a style part realistic, part surrealistic, and part absurd the present-day Kashmir Valley, "irretrievably entangled in a web of politics and militancy."[46] The 1989 uprising had lost much of mass support over time due to its excesses of violence. But protests rocked the Valley again, mainly in the form of the pelting of stones at security forces (as seen in Majumdar's *The Djinns of Eidgah*), following the killing of three youths in an allegedly fake encounter staged by the Indian Army in 2010. This form of protest took on gigantic proportions six years later, in July-August, 2016, beginning with the killing of a commander of the Kashmir-based Hizbul Mujahideen and leading to the deaths of numerous protesters. Caught between the now defunct "homogenizing discourse of Kashmiriyat,"[47] the militancy of infiltrators from across the border,[48] Pakistan's aggressive claim to Kashmir as part of its territory, a gradual dilution of Article 370 in the Valley, and the Indian forces on ground authorized to kill arbitrarily under the Armed Forces (Special Powers) Act (AFSPA), civilians there live a life perpetually threatened by all sides in the bargain. A profound sense of loss pervades the whole of Kashmir, which is subtly captured by *The Djinns of Eidgah*, a play that delves deep into a crisis, generated by contrasting narratives of nationhood and claiming the lives of numerous youths who do not consider themselves Indian. *Rizwaan* (2010), another Majumdar play on Kashmir, also conveys a full sense of this suffering and devastation through the battered life and family of a young man, representative of a generation of people in Kashmir who carry their addresses in their pockets so that their bodies may be delivered home in any fateful eventuality. Viewed together, the last four plays referred to above (*The Djinns of Eidgah*, *Gasha*, *Rizwaan*, and *Kashmir Kashmir*) serve as a sharp reminder that in "a city of sieges/ None shall escape,"[49] underscoring the dire need for a sincere dialogue between the stakeholders. And the stakeholders need to remember that the separate histories of communal sufferings, of the *azadi* movement and state repression, and of nation-building on either side of the LoC must meet in mutual empathy to write an alternative story of twenty-first century Kashmir that could protect common interests and ensure cross-border peace.

Pakistan

The history of Pakistan begins with the story of the partition of India in 1947. Although the architect of the new nation-state, Muhammad Ali Jinnah, sought to keep religion and state apart, Pakistan declared itself an Islamic Republic in 1956 and tended over time to develop into an Islamic state with an authoritarian government, guided by a rigid, if not repressive, "Islamic" ideology. A cultural identity centered on such ideology[50] was also what the nation initially felt it needed for self-definition. As a result, most of what were considered as "Hindu" elements of Indian art and performance came to be rejected in the domain of culture. Besides, Islam, theologically, was perceived by the mullahs as disapproving of representational art because the human imitation of the God-created world and its creatures would be a "sin." This eventually resulted in treating theater, with several other performing art forms, as un-Islamic, although it was clear that the actual fear of the state lay in the subversive power of performance as such.

The idea of a nation apparently built on an exclusive religious identity started showing its inherent fault lines from the very beginning, and the state that was paradoxically expected to be secular in its dispensation failed to recover from an undemocratic power circuit practically. As the decolonization process began in the newly independent Pakistan, the issue of linguistic and ethnic diversity proved more challenging than expected in the nation-building process, problematizing the trope of an *imagined* community held together by a common culture or a shared vernacular that must be able to produce a national identity, however fictive. With the inevitable outbreak of "subnational and regional identity movements,"[51] Pakistan soon found itself transfixed in a bid to radically Islamize its very entity for its own sustenance, which was originally conceived by Jinnah as a space where "[y]ou may belong to any religion or caste or creed that has nothing to do with the business of the State."[52] Significantly, Anwer Jafri's *Hum Rokaen Gae/We Shall Resist* begins with this speech of Jinnah's, delivered to the New Constituent Assembly on August 11, 1947, to comment on its total loss of relevance in contemporary Pakistani politics, if not also on the contradictory impulses latent in it.

Ironically, Pakistan had to encounter the challenge of proving itself a unified nation by pronouncing the Muslimness of its majority population, even as this encouraged sectarianism among the Muslims themselves by imposing on them an imperative to prove which or whose version of Islam was most authentic and would find state support. On the linguistic front, the production of Urdu as the principal marker of South Asian Muslim national consciousness on the grounds that it embodies "the best that is in Islamic culture and Muslim traditions and is the nearest to the languages used in other Islamic countries,"[53] antagonized, in turn, other ethno-linguistic (Muslim) tribes—a vicious circle that continued to widen the gulf between what Partha Chatterjee would call the "nation and its fragments." The use of the military to guard against all possible invasion of any other language or culture from within, and, thus, reinforce the national/Islamic culture of Pakistan, has led to a nexus between the army and the mullah orthodoxy at the expense of political governance.

After General Zia-ul-Haque took over as the country's Chief Martial Law Administrator, and elevated himself to president in 1978, he implemented harsh Quranic punishments for any violation of Sharia (Islamic laws). The Islamization program gathered momentum following the Soviet invasion of Afghanistan in 1979, and the use of Afghan soil and Pakistani resources by the United States for breeding Islamic radicals who would launch the Taliban jihad against the *kaafir*[54] Communists. With Zia(-ul-Haq)'s patronization of the austere Deobandi tradition[55] in an attempt to establish an Islamic state, which clashed with other Islamic traditions prevalent there, the ground became fertile for sectarian conflicts rocking the whole country, and destabilizing whatever civic and political order was in place. The aim of each such tradition was to "gain control of the Islamist discourse," as S.V.R. Nasr maintains, and determine "the ideology and practice of Islamism" there. The dominant Sunni brand of Islam now set up a network of madrasas across Pakistan, producing a new type of religious education at a time when state-supported Islamism masquerading as authentic Islam "was poised to define public policy" and national consciousness.[56] The parallel theater of Pakistan rose to prominence in the early 1980s largely in reaction against Zia's Islamization program, and coincided with the Movement for the Restoration of Democracy. Conceived by urban intellectuals and drawing on Pakistan's protest theater of the 1950s, as well as on its folk performance traditions, most of this enterprise sought to sensitize the masses against the collusion between state and religious ideologies. Ajoka Theatre's debut play *Juloos*[57]/Procession (1984), an adaptation of Indian playwright Badal Sircar's *Michhil*/Procession (1972), is especially remarkable for challenging the coercive Martial Law and the gagging censorship of the time that is most succinctly delineated in Salman Rushdie's *Shame* (1983)—a story of political violence and retributive justice, shame and shamelessness, surveillance and sex told in a fairy-tale manner.

The plays collected from Pakistan demonstrate the debilitating effects of religious extremism that eventually constituted the blasphemy laws to elide the religious Other—be it a Hindu or a Christian, or even one belonging to the Shiite sect of Islam. The "Islamic-unIslamic" divide especially targeted the Ahamdiyyas (also known as Mirzais), who view themselves as propagating the pristine values of Islam after the teachings of their self-proclaimed messiah, Mirza Ghulam Ahmad. With their roots in the right-wing Islamic groups'[58] portrayal of the Ahmadiyyas as "heretics" in colonial South Asia, the anti-Ahmadiyya movements have broken out in post-partition Pakistan at different times, culminating in the 1974 official declaration of the community as non-Muslim. The rise and resurgence of Talibans and other radical Islamist organizations/outfits in the course of time has brought about further changes to the meaning of Islam and Islamic education, making exclusion a strategy of radicalizing Pakistani nationalism.

As seen in Shahid Nadeem's and Anwer Jafri's plays, the draconian blasphemy laws of the Pakistan Penal Code, which remain in place after all their amendments and modifications, are still evoked—not only against religious minorities but also against whoever is perceived to defile Islam in word or deed. Further, Hudood Ordinances,[59] referenced in *Hum Rokaen Gae*/*We Shall Resist*, merged Pakistan Penal Code offences with Hudud laws based on Hanafi jurisprudence to supposedly bring the legal system of the country "closer to the precepts of Islam."[60] This occasioned major changes to the existing laws, especially on sex-related crimes (*zina*) and theft (*sariqa*), which were widely perceived to be simply inhuman because they included such punishments as amputation of limbs, flogging and death by stoning. Protests followed, especially from women's organizations, since *zina* was totally discriminatory against females. This was also the time when the Women's Action Forum emerged, and Tehrik-e-Niswan, an activist theater group,[61] began its sojourn in 1981 with *Dard Kay Faasley* (*DKF*)/Distances of Pain, a commentary on the miserable condition of women in times of national chauvinism and religious bigotry. *DKF* was soon followed by several other plays on similar issues—Tehrik-e-Niswan's Urdu adaptation of Safdar Hashmi's *Aurat/ Woman* (1982) being the most significant. The various scenes of gender oppression in the play are woven together through songs and the narrator's commentary, revealing influences of local folk performance traditions.[62] Ajoka also produced plays that spoke for women and against the discriminatory state: *Barri/Acquittal* (1987), portraying rape and forced abortion under the shadows of Hudood Ordinances; *Kala Meda Bhes/Black is My Robe* (1996), exposing the exploitation of women by village pirs;[63] and *Dukhini/Woman of Sorrow* (1997), dramatizing the plight of females due to cross-border human trafficking.

The sectarian discourse almost absent from the "Pakistan" movement during the early twentieth century currently dominates Islamic radicalism that characterizes the whole nation. Many observe that following the short spells of democracy between 1990 and 1999, and the subsequent US pressure on Pakistan to curb terrorism, the madrasas[64] in Pakistan suffered a setback and, with it, the Islamization program, too. It was then that sectarianism spread its roots. The mullahs in lower rungs lost their power and were thus left frustrated to the point of waging a war against the political authority.[65] Personal vendetta and criminal activities thrived under the garb of Islamic purification, as shown in the two plays from Pakistan. The state, patron of such misadventures during Zia's time, was left nearly incapable of bringing the crisis under control. As Islamic parties and outfits increasingly used militant brands of Islam to increase their sway over state policy, the state eventually had no option other than to borrow their rhetoric and strategy to prove its allegiance to Islamic principles and, thus, keep a large section of an already Islamized electorate on its side. The result was an indirect state nod to the ongoing sectarianism that further polarized society. The other plays of Nadeem also attest to this: *Teesri Dastak/The Third Knock* (1991) and *Bulha* (2001) comment on the nexus between religious orthodoxy and material aggrandizement, and between politicians and clerics, respectively. Tehrik-e-Niswan has also staged several plays that critique "Islamic" excesses in their own ways: while *Roshni kay Dareechay/Portals of Light* (1997), an adaptation of G.E. Lessing's *Nathan der Weise*, is about religious tolerance in contexts of three Abrahamic religions,"[66] *Kaafir/Infidel* (2009) dramatizes the story of religious prejudices through an interfaith marriage.

Over the last thirty years or so, the face of jihad in South Asia has completely changed. "Jihad," which for poet Mirza Ghalib (1797–1869) was a "struggle to be human," with a strong mooring in ethical and spiritual principles, or " jihad" that later on meant "anticolonial nationalism,"[67] since the Zia regime has been a militant program largely harnessed for worldly power and glory. Recently, the meaning of jihad has further degenerated through a lethal mixing of worldly and spiritual glory for a class of people (especially the youth) who find all avenues to an otherwise decent living closed in these hard times.[68] No wonder, they rush to lay down their lives for the pride of place *on this earth as in heaven*. Pakistan bleeds as jihadists seek to capture state power and cleanse the state of the "infidels" within. *Hotel Mohenjodaro* (2008), an Ajoka stage adaptation of a 1967 Ghulam Abbas short story, aptly depicts a Pakistan fragmented and chaotic, while Tehrik-e-Niswan's *Insha ka Intezar* (2008), an adaptation of Samuel Beckett's *Waiting for Godot*, presents Pakistan in a somewhat absurd state of waiting.

The "original" apology for making Pakistan an "Islamic Republic" remains divested of Islamic principles. The crucial question today is whether competing Islamic truths can eventually have anything in common to the benefit of all without being a travesty of the basic human ideal. Another question is whether there will ever be an open debate on the contemporary scope and relevance of jihad. For, there are many in Pakistan who share a moderate view of Islam and disapprove of this militancy in the name of Allah. No permanent shift is perhaps possible from the "outer husk" to the "inner kernel" of Islam[69] once the essence (if there was ever any) has been mediated forever by a long, complex religious-political-historical process. Yet the morbid theatricality of the contemporary spectacle that is gaining its own kind of universality demands interruption and intervention from within. The plays from Pakistan are scathing theatrical commentaries on futile killings in the name of faith. There are several works outside of this anthology, which, like Ajoka's *Dara* (a historical play of immense contemporary relevance), advocate religious pluralism, a search for truth in all faiths essentially.

Bangladesh

The creation of Pakistan, as Bose and Jalal observe, was "a most decisive political abortion" of "the theory that there were two nations in India, Hindu and Muslim"—because the "Union of India," as Congress asserted, would "continue to exist without the Muslim-majority areas," but with a sizable Muslim population in it. Without parts of Punjab on its west and Bengal on its east, Pakistan appeared to Jinnah as a "mutilated and moth-eaten" state.[70] More important, the partition of Bengal looked ironic as West Pakistan came to dismiss Bengali Muslims as "impure" Muslims. The Bengali language and culture were perceived to be inimical to "Muslimness" which was largely sought to be defined in terms of the languages and cultures of the Middle East. Jinnah visited Bangladesh (then East Pakistan) in March 1948 and declared Urdu (written in the

Perso-Arabic script) to be the *lingua franca* of the whole of Pakistan, a language which—with no "scriptural role in Islam," and spoken by a minority in post-partition Pakistan—was given a hallowed status to bolster a coherent Pakistani Islamic identity.[71] Munier Chowdhury's *Kabar* (*The Grave*; performed by political prisoners inside an East Pakistan cell on February 21, 1953) first challenged, in a liminal space of life and theatre, the Pakistani state narrative of nationalism, produced through its language policy and politics.

The presumption of one Islam was inherently wrong because no religion can ultimately transcend mediations by elements of local language, culture, and ethnicity. No wonder, Islam in Bengal (including today's Bangladesh) has always been different from Islam in West Pakistan or in other Islamic countries. Nineteenth-century religious reform movements aimed to "restore" the authenticity of Islam among the Muslim population of Bengal, mainly through translations into Bengali of Islamic literature and the attempted Arabicization of the Bengali script—a trend that continued into the twentieth. Masum Reza's *Life of Araj/Araj Charitamrita* alludes to this phenomenon in its rather coercive form by showing how a young boy is forced to learn Arabic against his wishes, and schools that do not teach that language are pressured to shut down. Yet Bengali Muslims had embraced a distinct Bengali ethnic and linguistic identity without having to "officially" denounce their religious affiliation.[72] So the type of "Islamic" nationalism that was propagated by making Urdu the state language of Pakistan came to be contested by the secular nationalism of Bengali, now Bangladeshi, Muslims. In 1952, Bengali was declared the *lingua franca* of East Pakistan, and February 21, the new State Language Day. Thousands of people were killed or maimed that day by the state for beginning the Language Movement that culminated in the Liberation War of 1971. This day, popularly known as Ekushe (Twenty-first) in Bangladesh and now celebrated as International Mother Language Day, became the most powerful secular symbol on which the new nation of Bangladesh would be founded.[73]

The West Pakistan-led army, in collusion with anti-liberation Islamist elements in East Pakistan, killed millions of Bengalis, and raped hundreds of thousands of women during the months-long Liberation War—gory facts that later occasioned many plays including Syed Shamsul Haq's verse drama, *At the Sound of Marching Feet/Payer Awaj Pawa Jai* (1976). The enormous cost at which the secular, liberation-loving people of Bangladesh had earned their freedom has always made them vigilant against any resurfacing of anti-secular forces. Several amateur theater ensembles emerged across East Pakistan in response to the Language Movement, and there was an explosion of stage plays immediately post-liberation that strove to build up a collective consciousness and uphold the ideals of a liberated and liberal Bangladesh. In Haq's play, while the village head betrays his men and women by conniving with the Pakistani Army, his daughter kills herself to teach him the value of freedom. Ekushe has a song dedicated to Liberation sacrifices (Abdul Gaffar-authored *Amar bhaiyer rakte rangano*), while the Rabindranath Tagore-authored *Amar sonar Bangla* became the Bangladeshi national anthem later. In fact, the poems and plays of Tagore have always been a beacon of hope to the people of Bangladesh in times of crisis precipitated by any form of fanaticism: noteworthy are Nagorik Natya Sampraday's *Achalayatan/The Petrified Place*, on the stagnation of life due to blind beliefs and dogmatism; *Bisarjan/Sacrifice*, on the danger and futility of fundamentalist thinking; and *Raktakarobi/Red Oleanders*, on the need for sacrifice for truth and freedom.

Yet, what paradoxically threatened post-liberation Bangladesh was the rise of Islamist nationalism during Ziaur Rahman's rule (1977–81). Rahman led the Mukti Bahini[74] during the war and apparently reinforced his secular credentials by adding the principle of "economic and social justice" to the principle of socialism in the Mujib-instituted Constitution of Bangladesh, but he *also* deleted "secularism" and replaced it with "absolute trust and faith in Almighty Allah."[75] Religious nationalists argue, much like their former Pakistani rulers, that the Bengali *Muslims* of Bangladesh must be differentiated from the *Bengalis* of West Bengal on the lines of Islam and Islamic culture. While there are subtle differences between religious nationalism and political Islam, the former postulating Islam as the marker of their national identity and the latter actively participating in the political system of the nation-state, the connection between the two is no less prominent either. Religious nationalists have often sought to have their presence in national politics through political Islamist parties like the Jamaat-e-Islami that would directly prefer "an Islamic form of governance."[76]

The failure of the Mujib government,[77] on both political and economic fronts, indirectly led to the entry of Islamist parties into the national politics of Bangladesh. Though the Bangladesh National Party (BNP) initially maintained its difference from its ally, Jamaat-e-Islami, by adhering to the parliamentary form of government, the Islamization of the nation had already begun. Ziaur Rahman garnered support to his brand of Bengali nationalism from religious and conservative parties that used his regime to re-Islamize Bangladesh. Recitation of Quranic verses, for instance, was made mandatory to begin any BNP meetings. Rahman's chief of staff Hussain Muhammad Ershad, after he became president, toed the line by giving leverage to religious parties and finally amending the Constitution to proclaim Islam as state religion. Following Ershad's enforced step down in 1990, elections were held in Bangladesh and the premiership of the country passed for some time between Khaleda Zia and Sheikh Hasina, Rahman's widow heading the BNP and Mujib's daughter leading the Awami League (AL), respectively. While the latter supposedly upholds the narrative of secular nationalism, the former fights for religious nationalism, with support from Jamaat-e-Islami that ideologically is not conducive to parliamentary democracy.

In East Pakistan, Jamaat-e-Islami was the lone party to have opposed the Liberation War and collaborated with the Pakistani Army. The party was charged with war crimes in post-liberation Bangladesh and eventually banned, although it soon resurfaced as it found favor with subsequent presidencies and governments that rode on the wave of Islamism, thus opening the sluice gate to a surge of other religious political parties. This religious politics frustrates the "fusion of Bengali culture and humanist Islam" that the majority of Bangladeshis had once held to be their "own distinct national identity."[78] The ideology of universal Islam is sought to be revived through its repeated ritualistic performances to turn Bangladesh eventually into an Islamic state. Syed Jamil Ahmed points in an article to one such performance, called *waz mahfil*, describing it as a gathering of Muslim devotees where an Islamic scholar, seated on a platform at one end of a large ground, exhorts the congregation, with "his vocal modulation [...] characterized by a chant-like pattern" (73), to follow Islamic Sharia in every sphere of life.[79] Interestingly, plays have never been found wanting in the form of protest against such dangerous trends: Nasiruddin Yousuf's *Ghum Nei/Sleepless* (1994) and Mohammad Bari's adaptation of Zahir Raihan's popular short story *Samayer Prayojane/As Time Demands* (2005) merit special mention here as crucial reminders on stage of the stark realties of the 1971 war.

The BNP–Jamaat alliance "lost" to the Awami League in the 2014 elections, although the opposition did not participate in the polls and the results were, therefore, not considered legitimate by many within and outside of the country. The Islamization process continues even after the hanging of Jammat leaders Abdul Quader Mollah and Ali Ahsan Mohammad Mojaheed as "war criminals" in December 2013 and November 2015, respectively, while the Awami League functions undemocratically to keep the BNP–Jamaat alliance out of power by any means. Alongside original stage plays, like the two in this volume (*At the Sound of Marching Feet* and *Life of Araj*), Bangladesh can boast of an indigenous theater which has never shied away from asking tough questions on contentious issues and encouraged liberal thinking. In Madar Pirer Gan,[80] for example, the performers—Hindus or Muslims, or both together—challenge Islamic orthodoxy by dramatizing their strong belief in the inclusive Sufi cult of South Asia. Jari Gan is another such performance subgenre where two groups of performers, led by their respective lead narrators, "debate issues of contemporary relevance" in a makeshift auditorium with audiences sitting around them.[81] Countless street plays have also been produced since the 1980s to pitch for secular democracy.

Liberal texts and performances in Bangladesh have often encountered Islamist ire. Taslima Nasrin's 1993 novel *Lajja* (Shame) not only attracted wide attention for taking a stand on the pogrom against a minority of Hindus that followed the demolition of the Babri Masjid in India, but also forced the writer to leave her country in the wake of death threats from religious fanatics. The performance of *Katha Krishnakali*/The Krishnakali Tale (2002), aimed at rallying against cross-border trafficking of women, was attacked in Faridpur, and its director and author were accused of hurting Muslim sentiments. Such attacks in non-theatrical contexts, as Jamil Ahmed notes, have generated in turn theatrical representations like *Kainya* (2001), which critique "Islamism by arguing that the truth in life is not one [...] but manifold."[82] With the women's movement gaining momentum between 1977 and 1987 (when religion became a constitutional weapon of political control), women not only figured as prominent activists against the Islamization of Bangladesh society but also as remarkable characters/actors in productions such as *Kokilara*/The Kokilas (1989), *Binodini* (2005) and *Behular Bhasan*/Behula's Voyage (2010). The supposed universality of Islamic truth is also challenged, at a different level, in *Bishad Sindhu*/Ocean of Grief (1991), a stage adaptation of a nineteenth-century novel by Mir Mosharraf Hossain. It mocks religious bigotry by projecting the story of martyrdom at Karbala as "a result of the rivalry [...] over the succession to the Caliphate," and turning the production into a mosaic of cultures.[83]

The two plays from Bangladesh collected here, with a difference of two-and-a-half decades between them, showcase the continuity of liberal theater to ever slam all forms of fanaticism in the country and champion humanist concerns. The plays, which address different times, are also done in different performance styles: *At the Sound of Marching Feet*, a verse drama, is presented in a simplified-realistic style; *Life of Araj*, a prose drama for the most part, incorporates a number of folk songs rendered to the accompaniment of indigenous music. Yet they connect with each other in portraying the dangers of religious extremism as well as in their own moments of Bangladesh's liberation, already achieved or close at hand.

V
Plays in the Anthology[84]

The plays collected here are rich in their performance aspects; they, in fact, point to the flexibility of South Asian theater to combine verbal and non-verbal, textual and non-textual elements in such a way as to create a distinctive variety of theater with its own generic plurality. Further, the verbal may mix prose and verse, storytelling and song in a text that comes fully alive only when put to performance. But where the plays' representational, rather than merely presentational, status is concerned, their relationship with social/historical reality becomes most important. The rest of the introduction consists of nuanced notes to the individual plays anthologized here with a view to helping the reader or the theater practitioner locate them within their historical-cultural frames and understand them further in the light of their performance and reception histories.

From Bangladesh
At the Sound of Marching Feet/Payer Awaj Pawa Jai

First produced by Dhaka's Theatre, in 1976, under Abdullah Al Mamun's direction, and frequently revived since both at home and abroad, this verse drama revisits the brutal genocide and rampant rapes carried out by the Pakistani forces during Bangladesh's War of Liberation. The play begins in the courtyard of the Headman of a district, with villagers forming the Chorus, some of whom do not speak, but rather bring out the essence of the moment through choreography. The villagers report that the "partisans"[85] of "Bangladesh" are coming from the East, and the village women and children present here are seeking the protection of the Headman. The Headman has always rallied the villagers against the "partisans," calling them traitors, and has colluded with the Pakistan Army and religious parties on East Pakistan's soil that used Islam as a weapon to crush the ethno-linguistic movement instead. He tries to assuage the villagers' fear by stoking courage in them and by invoking the comforting thought that God Himself stands sentinel on this land. The Headman loses patience as the villagers refuse to depend solely on God who they think would rather want them now to use their own resources to forge their fate. The young men gathered there, challenge the Headman, and also react against the Priest's casual talk about divine justice when so many lives are at stake. As the Priest accuses the Headman of having in him more hysteria than history which might give the crowd a victory, the Headman attacks him indirectly by pointing to the collusion of clerics with politicians. The mood of the villagers gradually changes, and they corner the Headman by telling him that the army that he says is all over to protect their villages is not to be seen anywhere around while the "partisans" are making steady advances. The villagers start to suspect that the Headman is conniving with the enemy in order to sabotage the Liberation War.

The first play of Bangladesh to have been selected for the 1981 World Drama Festival in Seoul, and revived in times of crises of secularism—for example, by Dhaka's Theatre in 2014 during BNP and Jammat protests against the reopening of trials of "war criminals," *Payer Awaj* may be said to have started a new kind of theater that critiqued "the ignorance, super-stitions and misuse of religion'[86] prevalent in post-liberation Bangladesh society, even after the loss in 1971 of nearly three million lives, the rape of thousands of girls and women, and the migration of about ten million people to India. A (secular) cultural nationalist project, the play subverts "the argument of the religious nationalists" by proving the "fraudulence and deceitfulness'"[87] of the Headman who eventually attempts to wriggle out of the enemy's trap by sacrificing his own daughter to a Pakistani Army officer. But the daughter exposes the father: the Captain had her one night when her father could not turn him out of the house as his long betrayal of his "liberation" brothers tied him forever to their enemy. In a moving speech to the villagers, she regrets that it was her father who had once taught her the first Holy Word. She interrogates the roots of Pakistani nationalism, and critiques the way the idea of God is being appropriated to play "dirty games." As a mark of ultimate protest, the girl takes poison in full public view and falls dead.

Payer Awaj Pawa Jai ends with a big explosion, the killing of the Headman by his own bodyguard, and with the Mukti Bahini (Liberation Forces) flooding the stage and waving a huge flag of liberated Bangladesh. Ending on this note of victory, the play compensates in a way for the death of the Headman's daughter and, by extension, recognizes the sacrifice of all freedom fighters. Playwright Haq believes that the message of the play is even "more relevant today than it was when the play'[88] was first produced. The indulgence of a section of people and political parties in religious bigotry continues to dent the very secular foundation of the country. Incidentally, the "war crimes" came up for fresh hearing at the International Crimes Tribunal (Bangladesh) in 2009, followed by the award of death sentence to a number of "war criminals."[89] Questions nevertheless have been asked of late whether the Bengali nationalist rebellion was totally innocent of similar crimes against the common Urdu-speaking Biharis[90] during the war.

Life of Araj/Araj Charitamrita

Based on the life of Araj Ali Matubbar, a self-taught native philos-opher, Masum Reza's *Araj Charitamrita*—first produced by Dhaka-based theater group, Natyakendra, in January 2001, and directed by Tariq Anam Khan—rigorously questions Islamic radicalism. The play begins with the Sutradhar (Narrator) introducing Araj to the audience as one who, full of questions, always looks for reasons rather than comfort or consolation in the blind alleys of faith. The play begins with characters entering the stage with musical instruments and ancillary props, and the Compère asking them if they are ready to begin the performance. The Gayen (leader of a singing troupe, called "Bard" here) appears singing, dropping vital details of Araj's birth and life. Most of the villagers around him, with their absolute faith in the Shariat (also spelled "Sharia") and their incomprehension of Araj's questions about things big and small, do not often know how to respond to his musings.

The audience first encounters a young Araj looking up at the kites flying high in the sky and comparing the green one to his soaring dream of education that he cannot realize due to abject poverty. He becomes enamored of Munshi Abdul Karim, a village school teacher to whom teaching is a passion. The grown-up Araj is praised and helped by this teacher for his devotion to studies and his resolute will to understand logically things that have ever been accepted in the name of God. Araj understands that Allah metes out punishment to non-believers, but wonders why believers are also affected by it. Nor can he naively accept that the meaning of the Arabic language, a marker of "authentic" Islam, shall be comprehensible to Bengali Muslims only in their grave. Araj is unconvinced by the guardians of the *Shariat* that there can be no argument about the Mystery of Creation. He is deeply disturbed by the forced closure of Karim's school under the pretext that Karim was imparting un-Islamic education by not teaching Arabic.

All this not only makes Araj vulnerable to the machinations of the mullahs and the police, but also causes a rift with his relatives and neighbors who fail to appreciate his serious concerns. Araj leaves home and walks thirty miles to reach another rural school for education, and the Chorus sings praise for him, while reflecting on the humiliation he had to endure. Nothing goes right there either, and after years pass by, Araj is forced to come back home to begin life again as a farmer with no land to his name. Araj marries and has a family. He sings for a folk troupe that disintegrates, and does other odd jobs to subsist; yet Araj never gives up his pursuit of knowledge. Exposing the "contradictions within Islamic epistemology" in practice, as Jamil Ahmed notes, the play poses disquieting questions "in the theatrical context of a remote village at a time when Bangladesh was being swept away by the fury of Islamism and hardly anyone dared to ask them."[91]

Araj, thus, incurs the wrath of lesser Islamic scholars and also of the power brokers who exploit religion to serve their selfish ends. He is treated as an infidel, since he takes equal interest in the Hindu *sastras* (scripture), a blasphemous act to Muslim fundamentalists in South Asia. There are references in the play to the impending imposition of Urdu as the *lingua franca* of Pakistan, including its eastern wing, where Bengali is the mother language. Allegiance to West Pakistan is demanded as the police chief bluntly quizzes Araj on the books he has read, some of which were written by the established Hindu literati of undivided Bengal. Asked if he believes in the Quran, Araj says that he understands it only as much as he can follow it in Bengali. Araj is not against religion as faith, but rather against superstitions and hidden agendas masquerading as religious truth. He tirelessly wants to understand things in a way that does not necessarily drive a wedge between religion, philosophy and science—all of which rather raise different questions in his mind about the same thing. There are a few scenes, though, where his method of inquiry into the nature of truth distinguishes between the realms of science and religion ignoring their interconnections in the human mind and history.

Araj is forced to give an undertaking to the authority that he would not anyway spread the knowledge he has acquired from different sources. But before the end of the play an old Araj appears, resolved to breach the undertaking, and with him the Kazi articulating hopes about the liberation of Bangladesh in the near future. Araj's manuscript goes to press, but he is beaten up by a group of state-sponsored goons for his act of transgression. The deeper irony is that such fanatic acts keep recurring in post-liberation, contemporary Bangladesh: the current spate of killings of liberal-minded bloggers and publishers of literature critical of "Islamic fundamentalism" serves as an apt example. But the Araj Alis of this world are indomitable, and it is here that *Araj Charitamrita* addresses issues of intolerance and resistance across time and space. The last scene presents him as donating his body to a medical college in Barishal (another "un-Islamic" act, since the body of a Muslim must have a proper burial), and the Sutradhar reading aloud his will. Notwithstanding the seriousness of theme, the play abounds in scenes and speeches rich in wit and humor.

Natyakendra has performed the play in different theater festivals across the world—such as India's National School of Drama-organized Theatre Festival 2011 and Cairo International Theatre Festival for Experimental Theatre 2011. The play still runs as a regular Natyakendra production to packed houses in Bangladesh, often rocked as it is, by surges of fanaticism.

From India
The Djinns of Eidgah

The Djinns of Eidgah, which opened in Mumbai, as part of the 13th edition of the Writer's Bloc Festival, in 2012, and then received its UK premier at the Royal Court (London), in 2013, is set amid preparations for the festival of Eid, and uses the Kashmir conflict as an occasion to understand the issue of human plight in times of crisis, generated by contrasting and competing nationalist narratives. Instead of taking sides on the Kashmir issue, the play deals with its impact on the emotional, psychological, and social life of the people in the Valley, revealing how the conflict has turned "Paradise on Earth" into a zone of war waged between the *azadis* and Indian para/military forces, deployed by the state for preserving its "national integrity" and protecting the Kashmiris most of whom do not recognize themselves as Indians.

Dr. Baig is initially a detached observer of the ongoing political drama, who believes in the need for dialogue with the Indian side rather than in the *azadi* demonstrators' protest by stone pelting. A proud Kashmiri, he is against the use of violence on either side, but in favor of Kashmir's right to self-determination. Baig is worried about the strayed course of the *azadi* movement that is largely ruining the prospects of prosperity in the region. A grueling picture emerges of the atrocities inflicted by the Indian Army on the Kashmiris. Reports come in from characters of "unwarranted" shootings by "bastards in green helmets" at the funeral procession of a seven-year-old, resulting in the injuring of his twelve-year-old brother, of the soldiers' abuse of the Armed Forces (Special Powers) Act by harassing people without provocation, or killing them in made-up conflicts. Alongside this, questions also arise about how much one can afford to be a Hindu in this Muslim-populated state, and this is deftly dramatized in the form of a quarrel between two soldiers over whether it is proper to pray in a Hanuman temple when the Muslims are breaking their Ramazan fast at the end of a day. Still, Baig does not agree with his student-turned colleague Wani, injured from the previous day's encounter between the army and the stone pelters, that the movement can any longer be called a "fight for freedom" since the call for *azadi* has subsequently been hijacked by cross-border militancy. Baig does not consider it a jihad in its ethical sense, but rather a lethal game for "money, for guns."

Later on in the play, Baig, a child psychiatrist, is consumed by the case of a young Kashmiri girl whose mental impairment has supposedly been caused by the trauma of witnessing her father's violent death in an ambush which she now faintly remembers. This is followed by a most painful revelation of the doctor's own loss of his son to "militancy," for which he secretly holds his moral indifference toward the boy partly responsible. As the girl and the doctor play a game involving characters of Islamic origins (Amir Hamza, the Prophet's General in the fight with the enemies of true believers, for example), she remembers her "flying lamp [...] father's plate full of food [...] The last curfew [...] My father's bus," and the doctor is haunted by memories of his son's "last meal." Yet, while Baig upholds the Quran that forbids any act of violence, Khaled dies in an army shooting, and Bilal begins throwing stones (a significant act in the play as a regular demonstration of mass frustration in Kashmir, especially since 2010), in a fit of uncontrollable rage, at the windows of the mortuary. As Baig struggles with a soldier in identifying himself as a Kashmiri rather than an Indian, army bullets end more lives. The "martyrs" keep wandering about at the Eidgah as djinns, "made of fire, dust and smoke," living an in-between life—not unlike life in the Valley—waiting to be freed. The play draws upon Islamic legends and fables to lend a structure of life to the disordered world in Kashmir.

For the play, testimonies were taken from patients and staff at a psychiatric hospital in Srinagar, as well as from two Indian soldiers posted there at the time. A "potent mix of reality and fantasy," as observed in a 2013 *Guardian* review of the play in London, *Djinns* "seems equally skeptical of the fundamentalist faith of Muslim suicide bombers and of an [aggressive] Indian militarism,"[92] both of which together produce "a generation of radicalised kids" whose dreams are dissipated and who untimely die in a land "lost to conflict."[93] While the *Guardian* review describes the play as "politically enlightening and theatrically hypnotic," the *Mumbai Theatre Guide* lauded the earlier Writer's Bloc production of the play in a 2012 review "[f]or its beauty, for its overarching melancholia, for the astuteness of its rhetoric." The "strongly visual" character of the play, its set design and the "tone and texture"[94] of the sound contribute to the vividness of the scenes that breathe the spirit of the place. The play deserves more performances in India, especially in the Kashmir Valley itself, and in New Delhi, where it has a chance of connecting with the audience more directly, and touching the country's political nerve center more effectively.

The Far-reaching Night/Bahut Dur Tak Raat Hogi

The year 1947 marks a watershed in the history of South Asia, since it witnessed both political freedom and partition of the subcontinent along religious lines. The celebration of freedom was significantly dampened by the communal massacres and migrations that ensued. The wedge drawn between Muslims and Hindus due to the machinations of political leaders hungry for wealth and power, has assumed with time such immensity and intensity that India's social fabric has been torn asunder in countless incidents of communal conflagrations. What has exacerbated the situation further is the perceived participation of politicians and state machinery in the harassment of minorities at the time.

Zahida Zaidi's Urdu play, *Bahut Dur Tak Raat Hogi* (2006), brings out the complexities of the communalization of society, and the price that ordinary people have to pay for it. The play revolves round binaries to bring out the communal divide. The spatial binary of heaven and earth is offset by the religio–cultural binary of one community clad in green—representing Muslims—and the other clad in saffron—symbolizing the Hindutva brigade. *Bahut Dur Tak* begins with a dialogue between the Almighty and Satan regarding the state of affairs on earth, and it transpires that actors on the earthly stage are all set to mount a play of unprecedented cruelty and deviousness. With Satan leaving for the venue to watch the bloody drama unfold, the play-within-play proceeds to depict in the next nine scenes the condition of humans in inhuman circumstances. What emerges is a conspiracy that sees its fruition in an orgy of violence directed against the community attired in green. Targeted economically, socially, and administratively, this community reels under the onslaught, while the other exults in the success of their scheme to teach their enemies a lesson. The irony that the play brings to the fore is that the victims onstage are portrayed as perpetrators of crimes against country, society, and humanity, while the guardians of the law play a passive role or collaborate with the real criminals.

Zaidi's play presents a carnival of characters, most of whom are symbolic of political personages in post-1947 India, especially those that emerged in the bloody aftermath of the 2002 episode at Godhra railway station in Gujarat. They represent the ideology of India's Far Right and embody the consequences of what is shown as an unholy alliance between the state machinery and the party in power, an alliance that is however not limited in scope to any particular Indian region. The play reaches its climax in the heavens, toward its end, when the Almighty and Satan engage in another dialogue. This time round, Satan is replaced by a second Satan, recently born on earth, and about to be crowned as the epitome of evil. The playwright has dedicated her play to the memories of nameless victims of communal violence. Zaidi's play reminds one of an Indian prime minister's invocations of *Raj Dharma*, or unbiased governance, in the face of brutality following Godhra's train episode.[95]

The play has not been performed yet—for two possible reasons. Written in Urdu (now spoken by a minority of Indian Muslims), and published by Zaidi's family press (Abshar Publishers) a few years before her death, the play may have had very limited circulation as a text. And the contentious issues that it deals with may also have contributed to its invisibility on the stage.

From Pakistan

We Shall Resist/Hum Rokaen Gae

Anwer Jafri's play, *Hum Rokaen Gae*, exposes how Islam can be misused to ensure personal and political gains, to gratify the libido, and to convert non-Muslims by force. Opening in a traditional South Asian (*nautanki*) folk style of directly addressing the audience, and thus making the performance self-reflexive by nature, *Hum Rokaen Gae* has a narrator who relates the tale. The narrator announces that he will turn back time and take the audience to a distant past that is ushered in by a period song to the accompaniment of live music and dance. Directed by Sheema Kermani of Tehrik-e-Niswan, the play was first performed as part of the Shanakht Festival,[96] in Karachi, in 2009, and later revived many times at theater conferences and seminars, both on the stage and in the open.

The play initially goes back to the partition era by referring to Jinnah's August 11, 1947, address to the new nation that would receive the official seal three days later. The speech emphasizes the need to keep faith in private life separate from the public space. This is followed by another song that underscores the different facets of corruption that soon crept in to the offices and departments of the newborn state. As the song ends, the cast moves round in a circle in groups of two's and three's. Each group depicts a phase of Pakistan's political history. The narrator chips in a little later to regret the steady loss of values in post-partition Pakistan, and anxiously refers to the fledging violence in the name of religion, to sectarian conflicts, and to discrimination against religious minorities.

Meanwhile, the apparition of a Christian woman, supposedly an agricultural laborer during her lifetime, appears on the scene to narrate her life story, and how she was killed. Men and women enter dancing the Bhangra,[97] singing a folk song, and creating a rural scene working in the field. From this point on, the stage bears witness to a procession of negative images—of religious violence, lust for women, fraud, and deception. The woman needs money to save her dying child, but the landlord will not lend her any unless she does him sexual favors. The rich landowning people are seen to be aided by the maulvis in maintaining their network of power, and they, in turn, support the maulvis materialistically. The Choudhary and the Maulvi[98] curse the woman as well as the others who protest against their sexual misconduct, and denounce all as non-Muslims. In a spate of violence, the Christian "infidels" (poor farmers who have worked in these fields for long) are killed and their properties destroyed.

The play tells three other stories. In the second, a man seems hysterical and goes running around, asking the Maulvi if he knows who killed him.

Then unfurls the story of a father who visits a friend to invite him to his daughter's wedding and also to ask him to refund the money he had once lent him. Unwilling to repay the loan, the friend denounces the man as an Ahmadi, bringing charges of blasphemy against him for printing the word "Bismillah'[99] on top of the wedding card, and gets him killed without being called a murderer as the elimination of an "infidel" is valorized in such circumstances. In the third, an old woman discovers a newborn left by the wayside, and is ordered by the men around to leave the child there as the case comes under Hudood Ordinances. The baby is a proof of the mother's sin which she wanted to erase by dumping it there. But the audience learns through the three episodes narrated subsequently through speech and mime that it is the child of the old woman's granddaughter who was raped by the local Choudhary, and then by the Pir[100] who supposedly performed wonders on her so as to cleanse her of the lump in her womb. In the fourth and final story, a group of goons tease a Hindu girl, while a Muslim man who protests gets arrested as the policeman is deluded into believing that the good man is the culprit. Finally, the gang takes away the girl for their enjoyment, and also to convert her to their version of Islam. Toward the end of the play, the whole cast appears on the stage, and looks for people in the audience to join them in ending all this foul play in the name of religion and nation.

With its mix of black humor, farcical songs, and dances, *Hum Rokaen Gae* has been supported by pro-democracy activists and theater lovers from all classes, making it clear that the space for progressive and liberal thinking in Pakistan "is not shrinking; it's just that people are trying not to claim it for fear of the unknown."[101] The signature campaign in April 2012 against the persecution of minorities as a run-up to a street performance of the play indicates that people today are not so laid back as before.

Watch the Show and Move on/Dekh Tamasha Chalta Ban

Premiering at Alhamra Hall, Lahore, in November 1992, the year in which the death penalty was made mandatory for blasphemy in Pakistan, *Dekh Tamasha Chalta Ban* has since been performed widely in Pakistan, and also in India. Its revival on January 18, 2011, was a fitting reply to a rally organized the day before by Tahaffuz Namoos-i-Risalat Mahaz, a conglomerate of eight Sunni Barelvi parties, to praise Mumtaz Qadri, the self-confessed murderer of Punjab Governor Salmaan Taseer. The more-than-fifty shows the play has already enjoyed have recorded phenomenal audience reaction against all forms of religious fanaticism.

Shahid Nadeem's play is also a commentary, replete with black humor, on the abuse of the blasphemy laws in Pakistan to settle personal and political scores. Pakistan's state law must be in conformity with the principles of Islam (disputed though they are *within* the Muslim community), even after all state experiments with democracy. The blasphemy laws might have been originally conceived against any possible desecration of Islam, but in practice they target social workers, teachers, rights activists for voicing concerns over false charges leveled against the minorities—ethnic, religious, or political—and, thus, aim at eliminating any difference of opinion or opposition. Initially, the blasphemy laws were not so widely abused as in recent times, as evidenced by the 2011 assassinations of Salman Taseer and former Minorities Minister Shahbaz Bhatti, both of whom demanded reforms to the laws to stop their abuse. Thus, the play proves quite prophetic, the playwright observes. That theater, as exemplified by *Dekh Tamasha,* matters is borne out by the recent ruling of Pakistan's constitutionally mandated Council of Islamic Ideology that "anyone who wrongly accuses a person of blasphemy against Islam must be executed,"[102] although this is still far from the ideal an Ajoka play like Nadeem's would advocate. It is no less significant that in October 2011, the anti-terrorism court of Rawalpindi found Mumtaz Qadri guilty of murdering Taseer and sentenced him to death. The Pakistan Supreme Court upheld the verdict, and Qadri was finally hanged in February 2016.

In the play, the narrator (also a character in it) takes pains to clarify that what he is going to show in action has no connection with reality— an obvious attempt in actual life to circumvent censorship. White-clad men supposedly stand for good and black-clad men for evil, but virtually leaving no distinction between the two sides when it comes to bigotry and the trial or killing of the innocent. The real-life parallels, when the play was being written, were the cases of Dr. Akhtar Hameed Khan and a Faisalabad teacher. A former employee with Khan's Orangi Pilot Project for the urban poor complained in 1989, following his dismissal for alleged misappropriation of funds, that Khan had defiled the Prophet in an interview given the previous year. Subsequently, a Jamaat-i-Islami leader filed cases against Khan, citing charges of blasphemy against him. Similar charges against Khan were filed on other flimsy grounds as well, and it took him nearly five years to clear himself of all the charges. The other parallel was from the 1990s: Tahir Iqbal, a Christian convert from Islam, was accused of teaching his students anti-Islamic lessons and consequently charged with blasphemy that kept him behind bars till his death in 1992. In the play, the zealots are ever ready, with the noose in full view, to hang those who have sinned against Allah by not submitting to Him or have disobeyed the Holy Prophet by not adhering to the tenets of Islam as interpreted by "the vicegerents of God." Weak and hapless people are caught one after another and done in "for the sake of" of religion, justice, truth, community, discipline, and peace. Women are stalked, people questioning the "holy" way of life are threatened, teachers, who want little children to flourish away from sectarian hatred and violence, are killed. The killings become so rampant that human flesh is sold in the open market, and potential buyers inspect the displayed bodies meticulously for preferred portions from them. A poet trying to spread the message of love is not heeded at all. When the moral guardians and executioners run out of victims and the narrator cannot extend the script to include more executions without waiting for the playwright to add on, they get hold of the narrator, ignoring his pleading that he is not part of the play, and hang him. The implication is that indifference toward the goings-on in society does not guarantee anyone immunity against injustice and sectarian violence.

The employment of the narrator figure, the use of verses for the poet and the hawker producing two different kinds of results (emotional and ironical, respectively), of Bulleh Shah's[103] lines to begin the play, black-and-white costumes to distinguish between the two groups of men, the play-within-a-play device through an appropriation of the *tamasha* theater style[104]—all make *Dekh Tamasha* an absorbing performance piece and an ironical commentary on the abuse of religion and the travesty of justice in contemporary Pakistan.

Not a Conclusion

Dramatizing in different styles several types of bigotry, the plays collected in this volume eventually articulate similar concerns and urgencies around the "Muslim" subject in South Asia. The anthology takes nearly the whole of the subcontinent into consideration because the subcontinent is historically "a continuum, a network of interactive parts."[105] Unlike Pakistan and Bangladesh, India as a nation-state has never had an official religion. And yet, the perceived threat to minority faiths and cultures in recent times is slowly eroding the country's plural fabric. This volume subtly exposes the unacknowledged and unconscious bonding between religious extremists of the subcontinent who have "mistrusted the liberals within their respective folds,"[106] misrepresented the rich shared past and emulated each other's narrow-minded interpretations of religion and culture to whip up the mutual mistrust required for their morbid brand of religious politics that fears the ideals of love, plurality and hospitality. The concept of total separation of religion from the public spheres of a modern state may speak of a contradiction inherent or latent in the Westphalian model of religion and state (with its own national ideology), as each of the two elements has historically used the other to enforce or legitimate itself. But religious movements aiming to control the functioning of states is a dangerous trend due to its basic exclusionary if not eliminatory strategies. Interfaith relations with respect for mutual difference, a decline in the dominance of one religion, together with an increase in religious plurality within a state beyond mere "toleration," the transnational movement of structured religions, and an improvement in the quality of secular life[107] may broaden the meaning of religion in contemporary contexts, as well as reduce the chances of religious conflicts in the South Asian region inhabited as it is by several religious (and ethnic) communities. This may also encourage an imagining of a union of the secular and the sacred in that as "worship can prevent secularization from becoming meaningless [...] [so] secularization can save worship from being meaningless."[108] This volume is an effort to begin work in that direction, using theater as a tool for peace and amity, and also for rehearsing what Jill Dolan would call "new social arrangements," however tentative.

Notes

1   See the sixth paragraph of "India" in section IV of the introduction.
2   The brutal killings of Muslims in parts of Gujarat following a train fire that charred to death many Hindu pilgrims who were returning from a religious ceremony at a disputed site in Ayodhya. For details, see the seventh paragraph under "India" here.
3   Thousands of Sikhs were massacred by Congress Party workers and sympathizers following the gunning down of Indira Gandhi, then Prime Minister of India, by her Sikh bodyguards.
4   Former British Prime Minister Tony Blair's late apology, in a television interview with CNN in October 2015, for the wrongful decision to go to the Iraq war in 2003, and his admission that there are "elements of truth" in the theory that the invasion catalyzed the emergence of ISIS, are points of interest in this context. The weapons of mass destruction, the presumed presence of which in Iraq provoked the war, simply did not exist. Blair, however, found it hard to apologize for the decision to oust Saddam Hussein. See: http://edition.cnn.com/2015/10/25/europe/tony-blair-iraq-war/ (accessed 28 October 2015).
5   See Frank Ankersmit, "Historical Representation," *History and Theory* 27.3 (1988): 210, 212, 205–28.
6   Robert Weimann, "History and the Issue of Authority in Representation: The Elizabethan Theater and the Reformation," *New Literary History* 17.3 (1986): 450, 449–76.
7   Freedom. For details, see the last paragraph of "Islam and the Partition" in section III here.
8   Mark Juergensmeyer, *Religious Nationalism Confronts the Secular State* (Delhi: Oxford University Press, 1993), 23.

9   Arun Kumar Banerji, "Germs of Intolerance: Religion, Politics and the Rise
     of Radical Islam," *The Statesman*, December 27–8, 2015, 6.

10   It is interesting to note here that the ancient blasphemy laws of the United
     Kingdom, however different they might have been from those of a third-
     world country, were only lifted as late as 2008. Such laws, in some form
     or other, are still prevalent in several other European countries, such
     as Denmark. All this, in addition, ironically proves the continuation or
     possibility of dominance of one religious tradition in an otherwise secular
     nation-state of the West.

11   Benedict Anderson, *Imagined Communities: Reflections on the Origin and
     Spread of Nationalism* (London: Verso, 1994), 17.

12   M. Walzer, *On Toleration* (Noida: Frank Bros. & Co., 2004), 83.

13   Benedict Anderson, 7.

14   For details, see Tabish Khair, "The Truth about Secularism," in Ranjan
     Ghosh, ed., *Making Sense of the Secular: Critical Perspectives from
     Europe to Asia* (London: Routledge, 2013), 107, 101–10. Also see the first
     paragraph of "India" in section IV here.

15   This type of society would accommodate people of varied ethnicities and
     faiths, and respect differences.

16   Juergensmeyer, 5–6.

17   Mark Knight, *An Introduction to Religion and Literature* (London:
     Continuum, 2009), 73.

18   Ruvani Ranasinha and Homi K. Bhabha, quoted in Knight, 78, 81,
     respectively.

19   As'ad AbuKhalil, "The Incoherence of Islamic Fundamentalism: Arab
     Islamic Thought at the End of the 20th Century," *Middle East Journal* 48.4
     (1994): 699, 677–94. "Sharia" means Islamic laws governing a Muslim's
     private, public and spiritual life.

20   Ayesha Jalal, *Partisans of Allah: Jihad in South Asia* (Ranikhet: Permanent
     Black, 2009; by exclusive arrangement with Harvard University Press,
     2008), 240.

21   Knight, 79, 80, 75, 83.

22   The concepts of tolerance and hospitality here draw on Knight, 83–4.

23   This observation partly feeds on John Dryzek, quoted in Ranjan Ghosh, ed.,
     Introduction, *Making Sense of the Secular*, 20.

24   Ranjan Ghosh, ed., Introduction, 20.

25   Sugata Bose and Ayesha Jalal, *Modern South Asia: History, Culture,
     Political Economy* (New Delhi: Oxford University Press, 2006), 135.

26   Jisha Menon, *The Performance of Nationalism: India, Pakistan, and
     the Memory of Partition* (New Delhi: Cambridge University Press, 2013),
     10.

27   Iqbal's vision should be read in the context of Saiyid Ahmad Khan's
     demand that the British government treat the Indian Muslim community
     as a separate political category. Khan (1817–98) and Iqbal (1877–1938)
     were two influential Muslim thinkers who sought to combine Islamic and

modernist thought to meet the challenges confronting Muslims in late colonial India.

28   Jisha Menon, 26.

29   The day might have been originally intended to hold meetings and rallies countrywide to explain to the public the Muslim League's final resolution to achieve Pakistan, but in Calcutta (now Kolkata) the League's action far exceeded all limits and culminated in large-scale killings across the two communities. The day is often referred to as the Great Calcutta Killings.

30   Jisha Menon, 167.

31   Dipesh Chakraborty, "Modernity and Ethnicity in India: A History for the Present," *Economic and Political Weekly* 30.52 (1995): 3378, 3373–80.

32   The following excerpt from Peter Van Der Veer's "Hindus: a superior race" is instructive in this context: The Hindu Nationalists evoked memories of a "Golden Age" in which the Aryans were a specific nation in a specific territory, called *Aryavartya*. Perfect knowledge had been given to the Aryans in the Veda[s]. At times this Aryan ideology sounds very familiar to the "chosen people" rhetoric in European nationalism." In *Nations and Nationalism* 5.3 (1999): 4–30.

33   S. N. Balagangadhara and Jakob de Roover, "The Dark Hour of Secularism: Hindu Fundamentalism and Colonial Liberalism in India," in Ranjan Ghosh, ed., 123, 111–30.

34   Quoted in Prabhu Bapu, *Hindu Mahasabha in Colonial North India, 1915–30: Constructing Nation and History* (New York: Routledge, 2013), 110.

35   A Hindu nationalist organization, founded in 1925, which holds considerable sway over the ruling BJP in India.

36   http://www.ndtv.com/india-news/citizens-of-hindustan-hindus-rss-chief-mohan-bhagwats-comment-sparks-outrage-647688 (accessed 12 August 2014).

37   A right-wing Hindu nationalist council, founded in 1964.

38   For details, see Sumantra Bose, "'Hindu Nationalism' and the Crisis of the Indian State: A Theoretical Perspective," in Bose and Jalal, eds, *Nationalism, Democracy, and Development*, 121, 127, 104–64. Also see the next paragraph of this introduction.

39   Quoted in Sumantra Bose, 123.

40   http://www.ndtv.com/article/india/godhra-verdict-31-convicted-63-acquitted-86991 (accessed 2 March 2011).

41   http://www.rediff.com/news/report/godhra-verdict-justice-bannerjee-stands-by-verdict/20110223.htm (accessed 25 February 2011).

42   Truth continues to be elusive even as verdicts have poured in ever since. While the 'mastermind' of the attack on the Sabarmati Express was acquitted in 2011 due to lack of evidence, fourteen years after the incident a man who allegedly played a key role in executing the plan has been arrested. On the other hand, a designated special court sentences to life imprisonment eleven of the people who were directly involved in the

Gulberg Society killings of 2002, a verdict that will, in all probability, be challenged for sparing the convicts the capital punishment.

43   This agreement between the two countries followed the creation of Bangladesh the year before, and signifies for India the lapse of the 1949 mandate of the United Nations Military Observer Group in India and Pakistan. By this agreement the two countries resolved to settle their differences by peaceful means and through bilateral relations.

44   In 1938, Abdullah led a protest against the autocratic rule of Maharaja Hari Singh and sought to replace it with self-governance. He acted as head of government in post-1947 Kashmir more than once, but also served several terms of imprisonment between 1953 and 1964, and even thereafter, for his refusal to pledge "loyalty" to India. For details of the Kashmir dispute, see Reeta Chowdhari Tremblay, "Kashmir's Secessionist Movement Resurfaces: Ethnic Identity, Community Competition, and the State," *Asian Survey* 49.6 (2009): 928–34, 924–50.

45   The Amarnath Shrine is a famous Hindu temple, dedicated to Lord Shiva, in the Kashmir Valley, attracting thousands of devotees every year. The objective of the land transfer was to set up temporary facilities for pilgrims during the *yatra* (pilgrimage) season. This was vehemently opposed by different separatist factions of the Hurriyat through large-scale demonstrations and unprecedented rallies. The Amarnath Yatra, which was never a point of dispute in the Kashmir struggle, has since become a site of contest for politically motivated reasons.

46   Deepa Punjani, review of *Kashmir Kashmir*; see http://www. mumbaitheatreguide.com/dramas/reviews/02-english-play-review-kashmir-kashmir.asp (accessed 27 August 2016).

47   Jisha Menon, 157. I would like to add that the term "Kashmiriyat" was revived in the mid-1970s to signify if not imagine a centuries-old secular fabric of Kashmiri society, upholding unity in cultural diversity.

48   This militancy goes beyond the Valley. The attack on Indian Parliament in December 2001 and India's 26/11 (namely, the Mumbai attacks in November 2008) are two most horrific instances in recent times that have eventually turned the anti-Muslim campaign in India more virulent.

49   Bilqis Zafirul Hassan, "City of Sieges," in Tarun Saint, ed., *Bruised Memories: Communal Violence and the* Writer (Calcutta: Seagull Books, 2002), 108.

50   Fawzia Afzal-Khan, *A Critical Stage: The Role of Secular Alternative Theatre in Pakistan* (Calcutta: Seagull Books), 1.

51   Alyssa Ayres, *Speaking Like a State: Language and Nationalism in Pakistan* (New Delhi: Cambridge University Press, 2009), 7, 5. [Such movements involved the Bengalis on Pakistan's eastern side and the Punjabis on its western, and also the Baluchis, Sindhis, Pakhtuns, and Pathans.]

52   http://www.bbc.com/news/world-asia-24034873 (accessed 27 August 2016).

53   Muhammad Ali Jinnah, quoted in Sufia M. Uddin, *Constructing*

Bangladesh: Religion, Ethnicity, and Language in an Islamic Nation (New Delhi: Vistaar Publications, 2006; by arrangement with the University of North Carolina Press, 2006), 3.

54   Disbelievers in Islam, or infidels.

55   Originating from orthodox Sunni Islam, the Deobandi tradition considers itself as a purist Islamic school of thought that believes in a Muslim's duty to protect his religion at any cost.

56   S. V. R. Nasr, "The Rise of Sunni Militancy in Pakistan: The Changing Role of Islamism and the Ulama in Society and Politics," *Modern Asian Studies* 34.1 (2000): 140, 149, 139–80.

57   "Juloos" in Hindi/Urdu means "michhil" in Bengali, and both meaning "procession" in English.

58   Most remarkably, Majlis-i-Arhar-i-Islam.

59   The Hudood Ordinances were promulgated by Zia-ul-Haq in 1979 to enforce punishments as stipulated by the Sharia for theft and fornication.

60   Charles H. Kennedy, "Islamization in Pakistan: Implementation of the Hudood Ordinances," *Asian Survey* 28.3 (1988): 307, 307–16. [The Hanafi School, built upon the teachings of Abu Hanifa, is "one of the four major schools of Sunni Islamic legal reasoning." For details, see http://www.oxfordbibliographies.com/view/document/obo-9780195390155/obo-9780195390155-0082.xml (accessed 26 August 2016).]

61   Founded by Sheema Kermani, in 1979, Tehrik-e-Niswan (literally, The Women's Movement) is a cultural action group with a mission to create greater awareness about women's rights and to promote art and culture.

62   See Asma Mundrawala's "Theatre Chronicles: Framing Theatre Narratives in Pakistan's Sociopolitical Context," in Ashis Sengupta, ed., *Mapping South Asia through Contemporary Theatre* (Houndmills: Palgrave Macmillan, 2014), 103–34.

63   This term is generally used for a highly religious person.

64   An Arabic word for an educational institution. Nowadays it refers more to a type of school that follows an orthodox Islamic curriculum.

65   Nasr, 151.

66   http://www.tehrik-e-niswan.org.pk/default2.asp?active_page_id=95 (accessed 24 May 2015).

67   Ayesha Jalal, *Partisans of Allah,* 302, 176.

68   Ibid., 287.

69   Ibid., 286, 306.

70   In Sugata Bose and Ayesha Jalal, *Modern South Asia*, 155.

71   Alyssa Ayres, 13.

72   Sufia M. Uddin, *Constructing Bangladesh*, xvi, xv–xxi.

73   For details, see Sufia M. Uddin, 124–36.

74   Liberation Forces (in English).

75   In Sufia M. Uddin, 137.

76   Ibid., 163.

77 The government led by Bangladesh's first Prime Minister, Sheikh Mujibur Rahman.

78 Naila Kabeer, "The Quest for National Identity: Women, Islam and the State in Bangladesh," *Feminist Review* 37 (1991): 55, 38–58.

79 Syed Jamil Ahmed, "Hegemony, Resistance, and Subaltern Silence: Lessons from Indigenous Performances of Bangladesh," *TDR* 50.2 (2006): 73, 70–86.

80 The lays of Madar Pir, a local Muslim saint.

81 Syed Jamil Ahmed, "Hegemony, Resistance, and Subaltern Silence," 76, 80.

82 Syed Jamil Ahmed, "Designs of Living in the Contemporary Theatre of Bangladesh," in Ashis Sengupta, ed., *Mapping South Asia through Contemporary Theatre*, 142, 135–76.

83 Mohammad Abdul Awwal, quoted in ibid., 143.

84 In the previous section, the countries are arranged in historical-chronological order chiefly to capture the political trajectory of Islam in the subcontinent pre- and post-1947. In the listing and description of plays, however, alphabetical order is maintained for the countries in question.

85 Freedom fighters.

86 http://www.theindependentbd.com/index. php?option=com_content&view=article&id=228959: payer-awaj-pawa-jay-staged-at-ongoing-ganga-jamuna-theatre-fest&catid=182:city-life& Itemid=220 (accessed 6 September 2014).

87 Syed Jamil Ahmed, "Designs of Living," 139.

88 http://archive.thedailystar.net/newDesign/print_news.php?nid=214942 (accessed 24 December 2011).

89 Those people in East Pakistan (now Bangladesh) who worked against the Liberation War are today considered by the Awami League and the majority of Bangladeshis as "war criminals."

90 Urdu-speaking Bihari Muslims are generally considered "stranded Pakistanis" in Bangladesh who "harbor" pro-Pakistan sentiments. This attitude persists even after the Supreme Court ruled in 2008 that children born to the people of that ethnic minority after 1971 would be granted Bangladeshi citizenship.

91 Syed Jamil Ahmed, "Designs of Living," 143.

92 Michael Billington, review of *The Djinns of Eidgah*, http://www. theguardian.com/stage/2013/oct/22/djinns-of-eidgah-review (accessed 24 October 2013).

93 http://www.oberonbooks.com/djinns-of-eidgah.html (accessed 27 August 2016).

94 Vikram Phukan, http://www.mumbaitheatreguide.com/dramas/reviews/20-the-djinns-of-edigah-english-play-review.asp (accessed 6 December 2012).

95 I am thankful to Ameena Kazi Ansari for her direct help with the play's summary.

96 An annual cultural event organized by the Citizens Archive of Pakistan.

97 A Punjabi folk dance.

98   "Choudhary" is a title for a *zamindar* (landlord) in colonial times. "Maulvi," originally, is an honorific title bestowed on an Islamic religious scholar.

99   "In the name of Allah."

100   Originally, a holy man.

101   http://citizensfordemocracy.wordpress.com/2012/06/11/live-and-let-live-stop-violence-in-the-name-of-religion-2/ (accessed 27 August 2016).

102   Richard S. Ehrlich, "Pakistan's blasphemy laws to require death sentence for false accusers," http://www.religionnews.com/2013/09/24/pakistans-blasphemy-laws-require-death-sentence-false-accusers/ (accessed 15 October 2013).

103   A Punjabi Sufi poet.

104   See endnote 1 in Nadeem's play.

105   Ketaki K. Dyson, "Democracy, Secularism and Religious Fanaticism," in Tarun Saint, ed., *Bruised Memories* 141, 123–41.

106   Jawed Naqvi, "Why Emperor Akbar haunts Hindutva," *The Statesman*, October 16, 2014, 7.

107   For a detailed discussion of such factors, see Peter Beyer, *Religion in the Context of Globalization* (London: Routledge, 2013), 13.

108   Raimon Panikkar, quoted in Ranjan Ghosh, ed., *Making Sense of the Secular*, 1.

Plays from Bangladesh

At the Sound of Marching Feet

A verse play by
Syed Shamsul Haq

Translated from Bengali by the author

For Halima, my mother

The original Bengali version was first published by Sandhani Prokashoni, Dhaka, in 1976.

Characters

Headman *of a cluster of villages*
His young **Daughter**
Priest
Villagers, *old and young, male and female*
Headman's bodyguard

Time: On the eve of the liberation of Bangladesh in 1971, indeed, of any third-world country fighting an army of occupation.

Place: Courtyard of the Headman.

Setting: A big tree, or its suggestion; a chair; a couple of ordinary benches; and logs of different sizes and shapes for people to sit or lean on.

Note: Villagers form the Chorus of this play. The director is expected to distribute the lines creatively among the actors. There are many non-speaking members of the Chorus who will bring out the essence of a given moment through choreography.

(*The* **Headman**'s *outer courtyard. Two men waiting for others to come. Dawn breaks in. The villagers come in twos and threes.*)

Villagers
People are coming from East and North.
People are coming from West and South.
Like a surging flood on the Great River's face,
Like a storm of dust on the Great Desert's face,
Men are coming by canoes, rafts, and boats.
Men are coming with their wives, kids, and goats.
Flowers refusing to burst from the bud,
Fruit trees stand barren and black,
Dawn is scarce over, when darkness is back.
We have nothing to give any kids to suck,
but dried-out pap.

The **Priest**, *in a white robe, enters, holding the Quran in one hand and a staff in the other.*

Priest
There is no God but God. And He knows best.
There is no God but God. And He knows best.
Well, out with it now!
What is it you want?
Don't just stand there like stuffed dummies,
or cattle if you please.
Come on now.
What is it you want?

Villagers
The Headman.
We want to see the Headman.

Yes, the Headman.
That's whom we want to see.
Where is he?
Where is he?
Wherever can he be?
He knows it's him we want to see.
He knows, we're coming.
He's been told, we're on our way.
He knows, we're coming.
Well, then, where is he?
Where is he?
Wherever can he be?
He knows, it's him we want to see.
So if it pleases your Lordship
if you should happen to know,
would you be so kind, your Lordship
as to let his Honor know.
We're now all here in session.
Yes, Milord,
Please do, Milord,
Please let his Honor know, Milord.
We know how good and kind you are.
Yes, kindness itself.
When fever strikes our kids, Milord,
why, who but yourself, Milord,
do we bring them to, Milord?
And when Death itself, Milord,
draws near our beds, Milord,
who but yourself, Milord,
would we want water from, Milord?
So if it pleases your Lordship,
if you should happen to know,
would you be so kind, your Lordship,
as to let his Honor know,
we're now all here in session.

Priest
He'll be here. He'll be here.
You can rest assured of that.
A storm's coming is known first
by a country's tallest tree.
A flood's coming is known first

by a country's biggest-fanged fish.
A drought's coming is known first
by a country's most vicious, old vulture.
A winter's coming is known first
by a country's most cold-blooded snake.
So he'll be here. He'll be here.
You can rest assured of that.

Villagers
Please, Milord. We beg of you.
Do tell him to come. Do tell him to.

Youths *enter.*

Youths
Hey, why all this bowing and scraping?
Why all this beating about the bush?
If the skunk's unwilling to come of his own accord,
then, to blazes with pleading and simpering,
grab hold of him and give him one mighty push!

Priest
Growl and grumble, as you will,
the honorable of needs must still
be treated with due respect.
If you axe down this great banyan tree,
tell me, you fool, in scorching summer where,
where will you turn for shed and shelter?
Tell me.

Youths
Still,
we want to see him.
See?

Priest
He's nowhere said,
he won't see you.
He's nowhere said,
he's beating it,
or going to ground
like some jackal or whipped hound.

Youths
"Jackal?" How extraordinary, you should choose
a word so apt? A word so rich in innuendo?
Almost as if you know
what we suspect, and the very words we'd use
he's bolted, hasn't he? The craven cur.

The **Bodyguard** *enters, with a lathi in hand.*

Bodyguard
Get back.
Stand aside.
Make way.
The Headman's coming.
Stop crowding in like goats, I tell you.
I want no more'n a couple of you,
as close as that. The rest of you,
get back.
Stand aside.
Make way.
The Headman's coming.

The **Headman** *enters, sits in a chair.*

Villagers
Our humble greetings and salutations,
your Honor.
If it pleases you, your Honor,
we would acquaint your Honor
with our "difficulties," your Honor.
We are deeply disturbed, your Honor.
We cannot sleep, your Honor.
A scorching wind blows to us, your Honor,
carrying from across the field's grave tidings,
your Honor.
Rumors rather, your Honor.
Yes, rumour, your Honor ...

Headman
Yes, yes. Oh, do get on!

Villagers
Yes, your Honor,
People are saying, your Honor, ...
the Partisans are coming from the East ...

The Partisans will, so they say,
be crossing the Great River, your Honor,
by tonight, or tomorrow morning at the latest.
And a strange beast, your Honor,
Blind and mad with rage
grips, squeezes, and tears at our vitals,
your Honor!
So men, women, children, all of us marched here,
wanting to know what to do, your Honor.
You've always been a father to us, your Honor.
If you remember,
it was always you who told us, your Honor,
not to have any truck with the Partisans,
your Honor,
saying they were enemy agents,
and all they wanted to do, your Honor,
was to hand our country over to our enemies.
But what can we do now?
They'll be here
by tonight, or tomorrow morning, your Honor!

Priest
There is no God but God. And He knows best.
There is no God but God. And He knows best.

Villagers
Some people add, all
district towns, all
markets and river ports, are all
falling into Partisan control, and all
buildings are now flying the Partisan flag.
All this, of course, we've not seen with our own yes.
All this, of course, is rumor, you understand, all
springing up like forest fires, all around us.

Headman
So you've seen none of this. To me,
that's obvious enough.
We always do hear further than we see.
Yet I wonder
you haven't heard the crackle of those
timbers going up in flame,
and haven't seen

the hot glow emanating from those self-same
timbers, burning to burnish on the skies
a deep-branded answer to Partisan lies.

Villagers
We have been keeping our ears open,
your Honor.
When a grown man is reduced to cringing like a kid,
when whether you live or die
sways hither and thither
like a tight-rope walker
up against the sky,
when all your physical strength drains down the grid,
what else is there
but to keep your ears on stalks?
Yet we heard nothing. Nothing that walks and talks.
Nothing did we hear. Nothing.
Nothing but the wind.
Once it seemed
as if the world
were like a woman lying in labor
with nothing but pitch-blackness for her neighbor.
And our chests churned
and palpitated
as hers did, again and again.
On your instructions,
whenever any kid came to any of these villages
from those Partisans,
off we've always sent them packing,
as, stick in hand,
our wives and daughters band
together, and soon
send packing
any cawing crow
as starts his row
near our house at noon.
On your instructions,
we've kept our eyes skinned everywhere
and whenever we've spotted anyone suspicious anywhere
we've tailed them
and handed them
on to you.

By now, there must have been quite a few.
But afterward,
my God, the blood-curdling cries!
Yet still nothing have we said.
We've just clung to the rope of God
and off we've gone to bed,
just to lie, corpse-like,
since now living and being dead
and waking and sleeping are all alike,
as now, too, to us
are tender spinach
and greens poisonous.

Youths
Now here's something new, for sure.
Hey Headman, what's the matter?
We've never seen you short on words before.
Why, from your throat words would come leaping
like fishes from a stream,
such lovely words, thick clustering,
like strawberries and cream,
or like jewelry all aglitter
setting wedding guests atwitter
when smothering the fetching bride of a fat old man.
So what's up, Headman?

Headman
Such impudence!
Rude to my very face in my own front yard!
My God, I swear I'll hit you hard!
How dare you?
I'll flay you!
I'll tear out your tongue
and feed it to the dog!

Youths
Just you dare try!

Headman
And so I shall, say I!
Here grab hold of him. Bring him here.
What's this? Don't you hear?
You all stand like statues!
Bring him!

Bind him!
Is there now not a man among you?
When an enraged ox lowers his horns, and then
charges, you check him, unaided. You're not afraid then.
And when the
Great River[1]
with tears and sobs is swollen,
like some hysterical maid,
then you're not afraid.
You grab hold of her stormy tresses without aid,
and still back home you wade!
Yet now, is there not a man among you?

Priest
There is no God but God. And He knows best.
There is no God but God. And He knows best.

Headman (*aside*)
It's as if a face I'd known almost like my own
had suddenly transfigured itself
into something totally strange and totally unknown.
As if a pouncing cat or swooping bird
had snatched away a hanging before my eyes
and zoomed with it into the skies.
As if an edifice of golden worth
had crumbled down
showering me in mud and earth.

Bodyguard
Just you give the word
and I'll get the Army.

Headman
Come, come, man.
They'll not keep a dog, man,
and bark just for a treat.
Looks like muscleman's getting cold feet.
Not even steel plating
can keep fear from infiltrating.

Villagers
Please, excuse the lad, your Honor.
You may feel angry, or
whatever you may feel,

this much is surely real;
he's just an ignorant kid;
and we're sure deep down he's sorry for what he did.
Anger, your Honor,
is like dust on a mirror.
The mirror's shine is hidden
till of dust it's ridden.
So please, your Honor,
we beg of you, your Honor.
We are feeling just like a poor old cow
butchered y'know how—
by a cagey-handed priestly mob
as didn't rightly know their job.

Headman
All these excuses are, I contend,
most surprising.
Why, I dare say,
only the other day
you'd have thought the entire world at an end
if anything so insulting
had so much as was hinted at that day.

Priest
From planted mangoes you get mangoes.
From planted plantains you get plantains.
Since barefeet won't float
men generally cross by boat,
but if inner truth you seek
then I dare say, so to speak,
a barefoot or two
have occasionally seen men through.
Yet being prepared is best
sins come home to rest.

Headman
Those words of yours ... the ones you uttered just now ...
I didn't quite see ... how ...
Were they perhaps meant for me?

Priest
Words? Words of mine?
Now how does one divine
the ownership of words? I ask you.

Words, once uttered, belong not just to the few.
Not just to me or you,
but, surely, to all?
A telling remark tells all
without distinction, surely?
And anyway,
if that's the game you want to play,
then let him the cap fits wear it, is all I have to say.

Headman
"Cap," You say!
You're talking through your hat,
if you ask me. So kindly desist.
I'm afraid, I must insist
you restrict your remarks to your own sphere,
and leave mine to me, exclusively.
These people have come most urgently
on worldly business.
Now, have you gotten that, conclusively?

Villagers
Your Honor, what's the good of all this idle prattle,
when we've real problems to tackle?
Coals refuse to kindle and rice pots to boil.
And from all around comes the steady clink of graveyard toil.
Thudding spades till up the ground
with deafening artillery sound
and suddenly
strange, silent men, tall as tall,
and silent as the graves themselves
stand at our door
casting over
heaven and earth their dark, pitch-like cloaks
till even hearts of oak
crack
and the wings of the bird of life within our breasts begin to
smack
as if at any moment it might take flight and soar.

Headman
I see. I see. There's no need to say more.
You know, my friends.
The mind of man with all its little twists and turns

hasn't changed one jot
since creation itself was a tremulous dot,
eager to glide from God's pen.
I ask you, since when
has one man's experience so much differed from another
as to be totally unique?
Let only he among you who believes these speak.

Oh, come on now, brothers,
take heart.
Why, I do remember when only the other day I did depart
on business.

You were with me. And you. And you. And you three there.
It was moonless.
And our way lay across moors desolate and bare,
and round by the burial ground
where never a sound
did the dark night air disturb.
And there it was I had your fears to curb.
Don't you remember, chaps,
how you kept saying
"We are being followed?"
And I kept saying,
"It's nothing."
"No, no, we'll be collared," you wailed.

"We're being tailed,"
I tell you.
"Don't you
see that mountainous man without a stitch
swinging that skull, there, by that ditch?"
You were all petrified,
paralyzed,
and so pale with funk
you looked like puking adolescents ruing what you'd drunk.
I was the only one left on his feet.
Don't you remember, chaps?
Now tell me honestly, now,
are these not facts,
the more tired you get, the more the mind reacts?
The lower your spirits get,
the more you are beset

with ghosts, and goblins, and fears and apparitions
that, I bet,
when vigorous, you'd dismiss as sheer superstitions.
Fear is like a drum,
the more you beat, the more the apparitions come.
Why, fears are the most fortunate things you know!
The only ones that need no rice to sow,
for they're self-feeding
and, damn it all, even self-breeding,
for they're not troubled by wives and kids,
as we poor perished are.
So set aside your fears, like weeds from your fields.
and tell me truly, what your real worries are.

Villagers
What we want to know is ...
What we want to know is ...
What we want to know is ...
What we want to know is ...

Headman
Yes, go on ...

Villagers
What we'd like to hear is ...
What we'd like to hear is ...
What we'd like to hear is ...
What we'd like to hear is ...

Headman
Well, go on.

Villagers
What we want to know is:
are the rumors true or false?
What we'd like to hear is:
are the dangers they speak of true or false?

Priest
There is no God but God. And He knows best.
There is no God but God. And He knows best.

Headman
Ah. Then let me answer your question with a question
Is there any act of any worth that is totally danger-free?

Don't you see?
From manger to cross
the life of man is nothing if not danger and inevitable loss?
But of all the tasks it befalls man,
to do the protection of his native soil
out-dangers them all, in sweat and toil.
This is no plowing of the clod.
This is no catching of the cod.
This is the laying of one's total shadow on a water sheet
without one ripple raising,
let alone a ripple's multiple repeats.
Arduous, as it already is,
this task becomes, I lay,
a thousand times the more so,
when the country's decay
from within is,
when the country's enemy within is,
When the pillar's cracking from within is,
as with us it is unfortunately so.
Then indeed is it the day of the thunderbolt!
Then, indeed, one's first impulse is to bolt.
But, I tell you, we must abandon all thought of self
and stand our ground firmly, as if rooted to it like that
great banyan tree itself.

Priest
Some men their lives shall give
that others might live.
Others their lives shall forfeit
for self-seeking in surfeit.
Yet those who shall bemoan not gaining selfish ends
shall find on Judgment Day
God's grace never descends
on self-seekers such as they.

Headman
Ah, what pithy truth you say!

Priest
Pithiness truth's edge whets
yet that sharpened edge sets no "ifs" or "buts,"
but only does steady cuts.
Thus all too often we do become but
the butts of our own sharpest cuts.

Headman
You don't say.
Ah, well. Be that as it may.
Brothers! Let me finally say,
when God protects us,
who can harm?
Why, when Moses faced a hiding
the seas themselves began dividing with no fuss
at all.
And at God's call,
across
Moses marched,
dry foot, all the way.
He didn't need a boat,
Or on barefeet to float—
So why be at a loss
when God Himself stands sentinel upon our nation?
Rest assured. All these rumors are false.
If we can but keep faith bright,
dawn shall break the darkest night.
And danger itself shall flee
and a jackal in the jungle be.

Villagers
Hear you talk, Headman,
you'd think men were but sheep,
whose responsibility lay solely in God's keep.
But God gave man
a brain,
and told man plain,
"It's not your fate
to forge my writ,
but to use your wit
to forge your fate."

Headman
You sods!
How dare you?
How dare you
doubt His Glory?

Villagers
Headman, as you well know,
that isn't what we meant.

You keep twisting what we say
and making poor God a prey
to your argument.
We can't speak for this whole nation,
but only for these
seventeen villages
and for these
twenty-thousand souls as dwell therein.
But wherein,
though we be workers
on land
and sea
and on these rivers,
still, we be true believers,
right God-fearing souls,
bound by the bond
of kinship to these seventeen villages.
And, thus, at times of prayer we stand
wherever we may be
on land and sea
and on these rivers,
and we do sincerely pray
even though
our doing so
might, like as not, in such circumstances,
hasten our final day.
And when we see
the sick, the orphaned, and the blind,
we forget not to be kind
to them, whose place,
but for God's grace,
we might be sharing.
So we give till the pinch of giving
reduces us to nibbling
like mice
on dry spinach and rice.[2]
And when in sudden storms the House of God crumbles,
even though our own roof tumbles,
we burst our ribs to set His House right,
with never a thought for our family's plight
and how they'll get through the night
with torrents streaming through the thatch

to make our bedding on the floor a match
for any steamy swamp or bog.

And anyway when our ribs crack
and God's Home's aright
we float asleep on our sopping beds that night
just like a log
thinking the worst is over
and we're virtually in clover.
And anyway the sun
soon dries us out
when we're out
sowing rice sweltering in the sun.
But famine walks the land
doffed cap in hand
for scooping up corpses from our little band,
we leave our fields
and enter the tiger's lair
in search of jungle roots
and fruits.
And when we grandly dine on this mangy fare,
we don't forget a thanksgiving prayer
to that tireless Shepherd in bed up there
Who regards us as sheep
safely asleep
in His keep.

Priest
There is no God but God. And He knows best.
There is no God but God. And He knows best.

Youths
Yes, all that business
about Glory and Righteousness!
And Divine Justice!
When most of us are left to root about like lice.
And to us God, being nice,
gives only faith.
Yet to the chosen few like you
He gives the obligation to live it up like you,
plus the right to measure
whether our faith's the right sort or not.

Headman (*aside*)
Yet that's just the pity
about ordinary folk.
They see none of life's beauty.
They're too busy
to see it.
And when once anger starts
burning them,
even ancient, carved oak
isn't safe from their flames.
When once what little sense they have
starts smoldering,
they leap about the banks
in their wild destructive pranks
without the least glimmering
of what on earth it's like to be
in charge of this leaky barge
they call their seventeen villages.

Bodyguard (*whispers to the* **Headman**)
Some of them youngsters out there
are getting pretty het up.
I don't like this set-up
one bit.
Who knows what could come of it?
Heated feelings are infectious.
Anything could occur!
You just give me the wording
an' I'll have the Army birdying
here so fast
they'll think it's Judgment Day, at last.

Headman
Oh, all right,
if you insist.
Yet!
Hang on a bit.
Let's think about it
first
a bit.
There are many ins and outs
to it
that need thinking first.

When your back starts itching
your first impulse is to start scratching
with whatever thing
comes first to hand,
and
sometimes
it's a cobra's tail
whose sting
makes you somewhat bewail
your failure to think about it, first.
So the first thing's
to think about
whether there's
some other way out.

Suddenly his ears prick up.

Listen!
Oh, do be quiet and listen instead of talking!
I can hear the distant thunder of water
cascading into the Great River!

Yes!
Just listen!
Can't you hear it?
Don't you hear it?
What's that you say?
It's scraping
with the great claws of its current,
scraping
and scooping,
and clawing at the banks.

Villagers
Why, at this time of year
the River's no more than fluffy cotton wool
giving to a steady pull
and slowly trailing away
far, far away
to where some weaver's wife
sits in the sunshine, twisting it into thread.
Why, there's virtually naught in that River's bed
at this time of year.
As far as the eye can see, two huge,

enormous, cliff-like banks stand
with way below 'em
just glittering sand
and way above 'em
a circling kite or two,
and no way, nowhere, not a single sound
except perhaps a whimpering sound or two
from the dry, old wind,
rustling hotly about on our baking, old land.

Headman
Oh, do be quiet, can't you?
Can't you
hear that?
That sound of hooves, thud, thud,
thudding over the fields and villages,
and over the market tops,
that characterizes a cavalry horse,
dot, dot, dotting
toward us like strange Morse?
Surely you can hear it, can't you?

Villagers
No, we can't!

Headman
"Can't?" you say!
But, good God, men,
it's as plain as day.
There! There! There it goes again!
Oh, to blazes with you men.
I say, Priest!
Don't you hear the beast,
just faintly now, from far, far away,
as it careers
cantering this way?
Oh God, am I the only man with ears?

Priest
No.

Headman
No?

Priest
Why, no, I, too, have ears.

Headman
Yes, yes. But did you hear with them exactly
what I heard?

Priest
Well, no, not "exactly."
That wouldn't be the right word.
But I do see your dilemma, exactly.
For you
time is of the essence, for
darkness is brewing. So brevity is called for
in answering you.
What is real
is
what we feel.
But what we feel we feel
is seldom real.
The mind of man is like a hall of mirrors,
reflecting and reflecting, constantly reflecting,
and always causing errors.
So if you
seek control,
control first your mind,
otherwise, you'll find
your mind
controlling you.
Will that do?

Well, then, let's put it this way.
you say
you heard
cascading waters or cavalcading hooves.
They say
they heard
no cascading waters or
cavalcading hooves.
The difference is simply one of "no" difference.
There was but one event
with two eventualities
not two realities.

In short, you heard the same
but you didn't hear the same.
It all depends on where you stand.

Headman
"It all depends on where you stand?"
You know, I don't quite see, what you're getting at
or where all this is getting us.
I stand
where we all stand.
Right here,
in these seventeen villages,
bound by the same bonds
of kinship
and friendship
as everybody here.
Don't you see that?
But tell me honestly.
What possible reason can there be for us
hearing differently?

Priest
You know, Headman, this clan,
this tribe,
this race,
this nation,
call it by any appellation
you wish or can,
is to a man haunted
by memories! Tribal,
racial memories,
deep, deep
in the recess of national consciousness.

And of all these memories,
the most time-old
and the most
compelling is that
of the coming of the Horse,
the Apocryphal Horse
of Vengeance.

Put your ear to a shell
and what does it tell,

but the whispering-whisper of its hooves?
Put your finger to a vein
and what do you gain,
but the pulsating-pulse of its hooves?
Put your ear to a rock,
and what is that knock,
but the rocketing-rock of its hooves?
In this whole world around
you'll not find a sound
from the beating
in hour veins
to the thundering
of the rains,
from the shell upon the shore
to the rocks above that soar
that doesn't indicate
or inculcate
the coming of the Horse,
the Apocryphal Horse
of Vengeance!
Sayth the Lord
whenever oppression and tyranny draw nigh,
"For Vengeance!
    Vengeance!
    Vengeance! I cry!"

Villagers
A farmer grew his grain,
yet was it grain or a life of pain
he garnered in regret?
A boatman trawled for fish,
yet was it fish, or a life cod-ish
he gathered in his net?
A man wove a design,
yet was it a design or a life maligned
he saw with eyes all wet?
A mother raised a daughter,
yet was it a daughter, or a life to slaughter,
the oppressor's bed did get?

Priest
In short, Headman, their suffering
rocks the Throne

and heralds the Horse. All who cause pain,
for whatever gain,
strike at the very fabric of heaven
and herald the Horse.
The anguished soul cries out
"Where's the Horse,
the Apocryphal Horse
of Vengeance?"
The hot winds sigh out
"Where's the Horse,
the Apocryphal Horse
of Vengeance?"
The Great River gushes out
"Where's the Horse,
the Apocryphal Horse
of Vengeance?"
That's what you heard, Headman!
Not cascading waters!
Not cavalcading horses!
But the Horse!
The Apocryphal Horse
of Vengeance!

Headman (*the* **Headman**'s *ears prick up on hearing a sudden sound.
Then after a pause, during which he tries to figure out the source of the
sound, he resumes*)
Where is it? It's not there!
Ha! That sound's not there!
Everything's where
it was before,
And Priest! Whatever you say, I challenge
you!
Who but school kids
care for conning books?
To grown men, they're but a bore!
For who writes books
but poetry, priestly kid-scribblers?
That mangy band
of long-haired, rhyme-mongering drifters,
full of childish fantasies from cloud-cuckoo-land,
whose brand
that Horse of yours doubtless bore!

Why, we've heard enough from books
about that flaming Horse
to make us want to hail a flaming hearse
and fling our flaming selves inside!
Who can abide
such drifters?
When that sun up there
starts pumping its bellows into the furnaces of the sky,
those poets in Mummy's bed do lie,
then is the time for grown
men's hands
with iron-tipped plows these lands to reap
where their likes have sown
their grape-shot shooting seeds.
Listen, brothers.
Ignore this poetry, priestly weeds.
Listen, brothers.
Listen, I tell you.
Listen, all of you
form these seventeen villages.
Who but an idiot pillages
his own pockets?
Who but an idiot spits upon
his won pay-dockets?
Who but an idiot kills the cow
his morning milk rests upon?
Who but an idiot breaks the bough
his own arse sits upon?
Don't you see?
All we have to fear are fantasies of our own making!
Peace of mind is ours, just for the taking!
None but Partisan lackeys
seek like jockeys
to whip us to a losing
of their own damned choosing!
Since we still keep candles
for our dear departed
we should not faint-hearted be,
but instead ourselves should be bright candles
of courage constant.
This alone shall keep our boat constantly afloat,
and thus, alone, I'm sure,

bear us safely to the shore!

Priest
There is no God but God. And He knows best.
There is no God but God. And He knows best.

Headman
Listen, brothers.
Listen to me.
Let me put it plain
as plain.
In war such as this
the only possible outcome is
either utter defeat or total victory.
But when peasants pit mere brawn
against a trained army, totally equipped, and utterly sworn
to defend to death the ground it stands
what else but black armbands
can those peasants' friends and relations expect?
I ask you, brothers.

Priest
If your leader had less hysteria and more history,
he'd have the answer.

Headman
I see!
Back on your hobby horse again, are you?
just slinging at me again, I see.
I do have your meaning right this time?
That is what you mean, isn't it?

Priest
I mean what I see.

Headman
And what do you see?

Priest
Precisely the same as you.

Headman
How do you mean?

Priest
Close your eyes. Yes, go on. Do.
Then you'll see.

Headman (*closes his eyes*)
All I'll see then is darkness. Is that what you mean?

Priest
Yes.

Headman
Whom for?

Priest
For him, it seems,
for whom else?

Headman
I understand everyone else,
but not you.
It's sometimes impossible to see
what you hint at when you talk to me.
There was a time
our thoughts did rhyme
in perfect harmony.
Yet now our thoughts clatter
one against another,
as if each were but a sword,
destined and determined to create discord.

Priest
It all depends on where you stand.

Headman (*with a wry smile*)
Yes. So you have said!
Why, your family and mine stand
together, now as always,
as they've always stood and always shall stand,
as long as they both shall live.
Your family and mine can
no more live
separated
than that banyan can,
separated
from its sustaining roots.
Don't you see,
you and I are but a pair of boots,
meant for marching side by side, together,
as we always shall be?

We stand or fall, only together,
sheltering your head and mine,
beneath the same umbrella, now and always, Sir.

Youths
Let us see what the Priest says to this.
A bloody, fat lot of good
that moth-eaten, old umbrella's
going to do you two, moth-eaten, old fellahs,
when bullets and shells piss
down on you, good
and proper.
What a cropper
you'll come then!
Those Partisans are real men,
not self-made fantasies,
as that stupid clot claimed!

The **Priest** *slowly lowers his head and rests it on the butt of his staff.*

Villagers
Forgive them, Your Reverence. "They know not what they do."
Their abuse wasn't aimed at you.
You mustn't mind 'em. They're distraught,
as, indeed, we all are. They're just worried stiff.
And worry has a way,
so we've heard doctors say,
of making nerves all frayed,
stiff, and tense,
till youngsters lose all sense
of what they do or say.
But believe you me,
it's much more worrying to see
their effect on you.
You look as people do,
so to speak,
as though they're right up the creek.
We're just ordinary folk.
Ordinarily, we'd have no right to speak
as this to a man like you.
We just plow and sow.
Plain words alone register in our brains,
let alone the lot

of subtle, devious hinting
we've been hearing here today. So can't you just explain
as large and plain,
as you can,
all the ins and outs of it, just man to man?

Headman (*approaching the* **Priest**)
Explain to them
We'll win.
Tell them there's not a word of truth in all these rumors.
Just as there is no rabbit in the magician's bag.
It's just a gag
to excite weird, fantastic humors!
Just a great net of illusion
spread deliberately
to snap and ensnare us !
Yet all it needs is the intrusion
of sharp-edged truth amongst these
intermeshing threads
entangling about us,
and we'll be free,
free to go off peacefully,
to our beds.
So just explain to them.
The Partisans hold nothing! Absolutely nothing!
And there's nothing!
Absolutely nothing to detain us here,
but self-engendered fear.

The **Priest** *still stands unmoved. The* **Headman** *continues ...*

Brothers, when at the close of day heavy-eyed with sleep,
you go up to bed, leaving me a vigil to keep
on all your cares,
and on all the things you own,
on your wives and children,
and on your fruit trees and oxen,
please, never for one moment forget,
I'm not alone.
You may not know this yet,
but behind me
stands the country's Head.[3]
Ultimately,

on his head alone rests all
the burden of all
our people and sixty-four thousand villages in this land.[4]
When we're abed,
like a rock he stands, bearing the burden of all our cares
on his head.
There's not a thing he doesn't know
in which fields which crops grow
best; what thieves are likely
to get up to; where, how and when best to grab them;
and then, how best to make it hot
for that nasty, little lot
who've gotten you all so very much on edge,
those flaming Partisans.
Believe you me.

Head of the country, he's laid his plans
for them. They can't budge
without his knowing take it from me.
He's got the edge
on them. Every port, market, town and village in all
this land
is armed to the teeth and filled to the brim with all
his alert battalions.
There's not a single place even in the densest, darkest jungles
he's not gotten his eyes fixed firmly on.
Even the very skies
are his dominions,
and should his Air Force come and bomb,
the Partisan's be crushed like lice.
And then there's
that intermeshing net of marvelous contraptions
whereby, if need be, messages can be wired worldwide without cables.
That will turn the tables
on his enemies, I'm telling you.
In a trice our friends will come
marching over the mountains and sailing over the seas.
These seventeen villages aren't alone. Behind them stand
all the other villages in this country.
And behind this country stand
other friendly countries.
But the Partisans have no refuges anywhere

in this whole wide world,
In politics, they're clueless, and fondly imagine
the country will fall
to them, simply if they let off a magazine or two.
But let me tell you
they worry me no more than gnats
buzzing round the dung
where they belong.
I don't give a hoot
how many magazines they shoot
or how many offices they burn
or how many of us they manage to turn into stiffs.
There will be no ifs
about the eventual outcome.
The Army will come
at them like hissing snakes with rage-inflated hood.
Gnats may cause a few stings,
but when things
get pounded
by a blacksmith, for all eternity, they stay pounded.

Villagers
Then our worries are over, yes, Headman?
Then our worries are over, yes, Headman?
Then our worries are over, yes, Headman?
Then our worries are over, yes, Headman?

Headman
But, of course, man.
The Army's absolutely on the ball.
You can all
go home with tranquil minds.

Bodyguard
Okay, that's it.

The **Headman** *is about to leave.*

Villagers
I say!
Headman!
Sorry, to trouble you again,
but there was just one other matter on our minds …
On our way here, we did talk to all kinds of people and …

Headman
And?

Villagers
Well,
to put it in a nutshell,
for the past seven days or so
no one's seen
hide or hair of that Army ...

Headman
What's his name, and where
is that tattler who told you this?

Villagers
His name is ...
Why, absolutely everybody.
So where's the point in naming
only one? After the war started,
and Headmen here and there started
waving flags and joining the Partisans.
It was rumored that the country's Head
found his funds nose-diving like lead
and tax-collectors skidding,
and people just not paying a penny
of what revenues they owed.
Soon there wouldn't have been any funds at all.
So the country's Head was forced to call in the troops
to stand sentinel on all of us in all these villages.
Then things began to ...

Headman
Yes, yes. Tell
what you have to.
Briefly please, would you?

Villagers
Yes, your Honor.
Suddenly, overnight,
machine-gunfire sprouted all along the reservoirs.
Suddenly, overnight,
soldiers were digging foxholes
all along the river's edge.
Suddenly, overnight,

you couldn't move in your own front yard.
Indeed, it was hard
to tell any more
whether the yard was yours
or the Army's.
Suddenly, overnight,
wherever you turned to,
their bell tents were ringing all around you.
Suddenly, overnight,
the landscape had become, not made of greens of all kinds,
but made of all kinds
of khakis.
Suddenly, overnight,
All we could see
were strange faces,
all over the place, and fiendish, death-dealing machinery.
Our vegetable gardens were ruined.
And our fields laid waste.
At each counting of our poultry, cattle, and sheep
we would keep
counting less.
Yet according to you, all this mess
was solely for our safety's sake,
and the safety of all we had.
But now they've hopped it,
with all their guns and tents.
"'Cause, they've had it,"
people say.
"They have retreated."

Headman
That's a lie.
A downright lie.
They still are here, I tell you.
In new positions.
With new
strategies and formations.

Villagers
So you say.
But everyone else says otherwise.
Otherwise,
how come absolutely no one has seen hide

or hair of them?

Headman
Haven't they?

Villagers
No, not for more than seven days.
Not a soul has seen them.

Headman
Haven't they? "Not a soul," you say?

Villagers
That's what everyone says.

Headman
And if I say, otherwise?

Villagers
We'd just ask you
Where could we see it with our own eyes?

Headman
The troops still lie here.

Villagers
We don't see them.

Headman
They're here, guarding us as before.

Villagers
We don't see them.

Headman
Why, only last night the Captain called round here.

Villagers
That's not true.
We don't believe you any more.
Tell us the truth.
Tell us the truth.
Tell us the truth.
Tell us the truth.

Headman
I AM TELLING YOU THE TRUTH.

Villagers
No, you're not. You're telling lies.
It's all lies.
It's all lies.
It's all lies.
It's all lies.
You're lying.
You're lying.
You're lying.
You're lying.

The **Headman's daughter** *rushes in. The* **Villagers** *look nonplussed as she hardly steps out of her house, usually.*

Daughter
Stop that! Stop that! I beg of you.

Headman
Daughter, dear? Is that really you?

Daughter
Yes, it's me here.
And I tell everyone present here,
please, believe him.
My father is right.
The Captain did call round here last night.
You needn't doubt it.
There are signs to prove it.
There are signs,
as those left on a branch by a frost's passing.
There are signs,
as those left on a bank by a flood's passing.
There are signs,
as those left on the ground by a man's passing.
There are signs,
as those left on a body by a pox's passing.
It's absolutely true.
The Captain did come. You
ask Father. You
just ask him, why he came last night.

Headman
Daughter!

Daughter
Daughter?
Who calls me daughter? You ask him. Just you
ask him, why he came last night?

Headman
Stop that! Stop that!
Get indoors at once, I say!
You shameless, brazen slut!
By what right do you parade yourself
before these strangers?
Get indoors. At once, I say!

Actually, men ... you'd never have guessed ...
I've not told you this before, but ...
she's not herself ...
She has been possessed ...
by evil ... for some time now ...
So, please, men, ... now ...
my honor is involved, ... you understand, ...
I can't let her stand ...
before you all ... like this ...
This ...
isn't right ...
Or, ...
rather, ...
it tends to besmirch my honor, ...
as a father ...

As father, ...
you yourselves must surely see that? ...
When one's honor is gone,
surely all is gone ...

The **Headman** *looks pale.*

Daughter
See, Father?
Not a man turns away his head,
even though custom decrees it.
Do you know why?
Do you know the reason for it?
Do you want to know why?
Just you look at your face? Look at it!

Headman
PLEASE!
You're my daughter!
Now just you go indoors. Come on now.
Please! Later, in private, you can tell me
all you have to tell
at any length you please. Do as I say now.
You're my daughter! Come on now.

Daughter
Yes, I've heard that one before.
"Come on now. You're my daughter.
If in a crisis I can't expect my own daughter
to help me,
then tell me, whom can I expect to?"
You do remember, don't you?
After all, it was—believe it or not—
not more than
a mere handful of hours ago.
Only last night! ... I'd just brought the ducks in
from the pond, and was getting them
all safely settled for the night
where the jackals couldn't get at them,
when Mother, standing in the yard,
after having said her prayers, called,
"Do fetch the vegetables in.
Night is coming on.
And if we don't get the supper on
it'll be midnight before we finish eating."
So there I was alone in the kitchen preparing the supper,
when suddenly the crescent moon appeared,
like a slivered marrow that slipped out of hand
and I don't know why, but suddenly I felt frightened,
almost as if someone was standing at the kitchen door.
Then I saw— it was you,
standing still as still.
"What is it, Father?"
I nearly told you,
how you'd nearly make me jump.
Then I wanted to laugh, but only a lump
comes in my throat. "Is there something you want?"
I asked. You looked so strange,

"Why, no. Where's Mother?" you said.
Then you went on in.
And from the kitchen I heard you saying,
"The Captain wants our daughter.
But it is all right. I have persuaded him to marry her.
I'll perform the service myself. It doesn't matter
that he's an outsider.
Why, heaven's above, that's not everything.
Just you wait, when this war's finished,
this house will be furnished
all in gold. By him."

Villagers
Headman, this wouldn't happen to be true,
now would it?
All this your daughter's told us.
It wouldn't, would it now?
And anyway
what became of her fiancé?
You know,
that schoolmaster fellow?

Headman
Don't mention him to me!
You know very well where he went, didn't he?
With those Partisans.
You don't honestly expect me, do you,
to honor plans
to hand my daughter to a scoundrel like that!
My hat!
He's our enemy!

Villagers
Enemy of what?
Of this country of ours?
Or of the prolongation of *your* power?

Headman
Of the prolongation of this country's honor,
And of your families and of the well-being
of all this land of ours!
That's all I want and all I mean to get!

Daughter
I see. That's all you want, is it?
And what about the well-being of your daughter?
Just when do you mean to get that?
Go on, just you ask him, what became
of that fancy son-in-law of his after
only one night with me?
Go on, just you ask him, how it came to be
that fancy son-in-law of his
slunk off like a jackal at midnight leaving me
like a duck he'd had his fill of? Just you ask him that!

Headman
Quiet!
Oh, do be quiet, you fool!
What hopes I had were like a hapless ox
spinning in a whirlpool
amidst relentless rocks.
Oh, do be quiet, can't you?
It was as if
a crest were being pushed up, higher and higher,
ominously,
just to come crashing down on me.
As if what wits I had were like a cut-stringed kite
whooshed higher and higher on the blustering might
of April winds howling across the moor.
There just wasn't anything more
I could do!

Villagers
Headman, now we're asking you to tell us plain.
'Cause this discovery
is just too fantastic to be true.
You stand there claiming to reassure us
against all fear, do you,
when you can't even protect your own daughter?
This is just too much!
It's very worrying when the calamity confronting us
is such
that it's utterly beyond our powers to cope
and our only hope
lies in turning to you, our district Head.
But it's utterly devastating

suddenly to discover the Head
all our hopes rest upon
can't even be depended on
by his own flesh and blood.
Yet there's at least one consolation sad.
We may not get fair shares of good
fortune, but, at least, we shall of bad.
So tell us plain, when did all this happen?
Come on, when
did it? And when was your honor destroyed
and this marriage performed?
And who performed it? Come on now, tell us.

The **Priest** *now raises his head, without looking at anyone.*

Priest
Now there's no point in looking at me like that.
I didn't perform it.
I have no knowledge of it.

Villagers
Then who did?
Then who did?

Headman (*after a brief hesitation*)
I did.
I gave him my daughter in God's holy name.
I know that on Judgment Day itself
God Himself
will acknowledge the same
as a marriage truly solemnized.
I know that once cleansed in His holy name
water from the dirtiest ditch becomes the same
as that from the holiest shrine.
I know that once saints and sinners,
madmen and sufferers,
the blind, the halting, and the lame,
have taken His holy name,
its worth
can't be invalidated by any power on earth.

Villagers
Are you trying to teach grandma to suck eggs?
As you and we all know,

every man, with or without legs
or any other faculties,
has an equal right to take His holy name.
Are you trying to deny that this is so?

Headman
It's you who deny it.
You fix your eyes on me as if
I was Cain
with nowhere in this world to go.

1st Youth
Cane?
Who is he,
when he's at home?

2nd Youth
The younger brother of Bamboo!
That's who he is.

Priest
Don't you ignoramuses
ever read Scripture?
Cain and Abel were
two brothers. Yet Cain
took Abel's life in this world's first murder.
And, thereafter,
he roamed this world carrying Abel's corpse,
constantly seeking to hide his sin.
Yet nowhere was there a place for him to hide it in.

Villagers
Ah! How very apt!
We could never have capped
that, Headman.
Right from dawn this day we've been suspecting
that nothing
in your conduct remains any more concealed.
Absolutely nothing.
All now stands revealed
out on the moor
in the heat
of day
like a naked corpse,

whose winding sheet
has blown away
in our sighs of desperation.

Daughter
The corpse of my future.

Villagers
The corpse of our whole generation.

Headman
Brothers!

Villagers
The corpse of all our future generations.
The corpse of our entire nation's hopes and dreams.

Headman
Listen, brothers!

Villagers
The corpses of sixty-four thousand villages.
The corpses of sixty-four million dreams.
Who murdered them?
Who murdered them?
Who murdered them?
Who murdered them?

Bodyguard (*he tries to hide his stave*)
I should be careful.
Someone may get an eyeful
of the sword concealed in this.

Villagers
Who is the murderer?
Who is the murderer?
Who is the murderer?
Who is the murderer?

Daughter
Ask him. He has the answer.
Just you ask him.

Headman
Oh, my darling, my precious darling,
what else was there to do?
Can't you try to see it from my point of view?

Just what alternative was there? Can't you just try?
There was I in the lane
yesterday,
when after being away
for quite some time
the Captain's jeep pulled in.
My heart was in my mouth the moment I saw it,
charging towards me again,
head down, as always,
with that strange toothiness,
blind in one eye,
camouflage-coated,
and with a single, horn-like protuberance,
pointing straight at me.
It halted in the yard, and out of it
leaped the Captain alone, I saw. What was it
this time? I wondered. Were all the rumors
true? Were these villages of ours
surrounded by Partisans?
As soon as I got him into the sitting-room,
he said, "Just how trustworthy, I wonder,
is a chap who's been betraying his own people to us
all this time?" Suddenly, I started quivering
all over, I couldn't understand anything
of what he was saying.
"Well, before we go … ," he added.
How can I explain how I felt upon hearing
these words? There just isn't the time!
"Captain," I pleaded. "I have never disappointed you.
Nor, if you remember, have I ever opposed you.
Surely you recall, how I always did my utmost for you,
how I always regarded your interests as mine?
When you didn't know your way about,
I was the one who led you.
When your rations all ran out,
I was the one who fed you.
When you yourself were unable to,
I was the one who caught traitors for you.
So now I beg of you, Captain, please!
Please, spare me, at least, my honor!
Her marriage's all arranged! So please,
I'll do anything else you please!

Please, spare me, at least, my honor!"
I don't remember now
how I even managed to stay standing,
or how many different arguments I tried in pleading
with him. All I do remember
was his saying
quite categorically,
"You either give me her willingly, or I just take her—
and your lives, as well, afterward!"
One thing I did see,
It was virtually no good trying to reason with him.
He was determined to have her.
The only question to be settled now was simply how.
So finally I said,
"Look, you and I are of the same
faith. We worship the same
God. We revere the same
shrines. So out of this common fellowship,
couldn't you consent to marry her?"
"Marry her? Consent to marry her?
You think I'm mad? Marry her!"
He burst into a mad uproarious laughter.
"Marry her? What a joke! Me, marry her?"
"Yes," I said, as calmly as I could. "Marry her.
No one need know
you've done so.
The ceremony will be a private matter
between you, me, God and her.
Then I'll give her
to you with my full consent."
The idea did appeal to him though,
he thought it an enormous joke and even said so
to my face.
But in my place
what would any father have done?
I had never taken much
notice of wedding ceremonies.
I had not much
idea of how they were done.
I don't remember much of this one, either.
All I do remember
was placing her hand beneath his

and three times taking
God's name, and saying—
No, I don't remember
what I said,
or what I did. I don't remember anything,
except a golden doll, in the river, slowly drowning.

The **Headman** *hangs his head and sobs.*

Priest
There is no God but God. And He knows best.

The **Headman's Daughter** *now goes up to the* **Priest.**

Daughter
It was at your knee, I remember, that I first heard
God's name, and the holy verses, and the Holy Word.
Twice a day, morn and noon,
when I was young, I remember.
I'd set aside my games with dolly,
and all else that then seemed jolly.
And twice a day, morn and noon,
you'd cross the fields, I remember,
and I'd sit waiting with clean hands and face
and the end of my robe placed
across the top of my head,
like women when they wed,
and with the Holy Book resting before me,
there I'd sit facing God, actually His House before me.
And I remember, if ever I erred
in reciting the Word
your stick would cut
right across my back,
for being too slack,
your reverence, you do remember?
I remember the mango blossoms hadn't burst yet.
And the dry dust in the ditches used to get
to circling up in playful winds,
and from the blacksmith's quarters, though so distant,
there would come
the captivating beat of a drum.
Oh, so distinctly, I do remember.
"Keep your mind on your lessons, girl!
Those who waste time on worldly

things aren't forgiven on Judgment Day.
All the best authorities do say
this. Don't waste time. God won't forgive you, girl!"
God? What was He
like? I wondered.
Whatever could He possibly be like? I wondered.
Then I remembered
seeing a white man on a horse charging through the village.
And his face
had been so fair,
I'd not seen any such anywhere before. And oh! his hair!
It was like a golden ball
burning brightly all
over his head. So brightly,
I didn't even see he had a body
really,
let alone a horse.
I saw him once, I never saw him again,
but whenever I'd think of God, again
I'd see the white man riding bodiless
through the village
on an invisible horse.

Priest
Careful, girl! Careful!
Have a care!
God has no form.
God is formless, everywhere.

Daughter
Certainly, your reverence, certainly.
The times you've told me, God is formless.
Sometimes it seems what you did to me
was like leading someone eyeless
through a market, leaving him totally clueless
about what there was to see,
whether there were tin soldiers or not,
whether the fish were fresh or not,
whether there were chalks and bangles,
and sweets and lollies on sale or not.
And just like him you led me eyeless and clueless,
through the psalms and all the verses
and all the stations of the cross.

Completely at a loss
all I could hear was the weeping and the wailing
but I never did know what was wrong.
But certainly, your reverence, certainly,
God is certainly formless.
But He might as well be quite tongueless, too.
For all I got
out of it
was what a lot
of distance lay
between what I say
and how God Himself would doubtless put it.

Priest
Careful, girl! careful! Have a care! You listen to me.
God's words are illumined by faith, not philology.

Daughter
I see,
your reverence.
If that's true,
then I'm to take it,
my lack of understanding is due
to my deficiency of faith, is that it?
If God is so merciful and omnipotent,
that the mere calling of his name
calls down upon us His mercy and His protection
from all evil,
then just you tell me, will
you, where was He?
Where was He last night when that snake bit me?
Where was He?
Just where does that all merciful,
omnipotent, protection-racketeer hang out,
when we bellow our lungs out
calling on Him for His mercy and protection?
Formless? Yes. He was certainly formless
last night, your reverence.
And he was most definitely earless!

Priest
Careful, girl! Careful! Have a care!
Man has no right to question Him!

Villagers
Why not?
Why has man no right to question him?
Who knows whether it's all false or not?
It isn't known.
It isn't known.
It isn't known.
It isn't known.
Let her have her say,
your reverence.
Yes, your reverence,
let her have her say.

Priest
Careful, ignoramuses! Careful! Have a care!

Daughter
Man hasn't the right to question Him.
No! Only the right to take His name
and while taking it to get up to
any dirty, filthy game
he pleases!
Like the one my father got up to last night
while taking it.
With God as your witness
you can fling sin
into any dustbin
you please.
As far as God in His wisdom divine knows or cares,
this "marriage" of mine was solemnized
with all the usual airs associated with His name!
It's just a name. Don't you see?
It's just a name. Don't you see?
It's nothing substantial like you or me.
But my! What power it possesses!
Say the Name and iron's as soft as butter.
Say the Name and sin is sanctified
and a den of thieves is glorified
into a shrine!

Priest
Careful, girl! Careful! Have a care!
That young fiancé of yours

has been putting you up
to all this, has he?
That schoolmaster chap!

Daughter
Oh, no, your reverence.
All the learning I ever did
I did not at his knee, but yours.
Yours are the teachings by which we live,
tongue silenced,
fettered-footed,
and blinded by the dubious knowledge
that virtuous lives here below are rewarded there above,
in the infinite mercy of His love!

Priest
So that teacher that lover of yours
casts doubt on this, does he?
So setting aside his books and pens,
he's taken up machine-guns and Brens,[5]
has he, slaying his elders
and not caring a hoot how many buildings he blasts
and sends under,
so long as all that outlasts his bombing and blasting
become all his, as he pleases, to loot and to plunder?

Villagers
Why you have to keep dragging
him into it all the time?
Justice! Justice! Justice!
Where is the rhyme
or reason in such pointless arguing?
Justice! Justice! Justice!
When did blaming others for everything
ever save anyone?
Justice! Justice! Justice!
What we want is justice! Justice is what we want!
Justice! Justice! Justice!

Priest (*aside*)
Suddenly I see a change in everyone.
Suddenly I see a furious blaze in all eyes.
Suddenly I hear a storm's screeching,
screaming frenzy rending the skies.

Villagers
Why this delay, your reverence?
Why don't you speak?

Bodyguard (*aside*)
Things are beginning to look very bleak.
I must say, I'm beginning to feel pretty silly,
standing here lumbered with this sword,
when at any minute
prying eyes might spot it.
Just supposing they first take it out on me!

Villagers
Why this delay, your reverence?
Why don't you speak?

Priest (*aside*)
Suddenly I feel
my very soul shuddering within.
Suddenly I feel
the prickly presence of my every sin.
Suddenly a furnace glow
freezes me.
Suddenly an anguish slow seizes me.

*A creeping barrage of whistling, thudding shells is heard and begins
drawing nearer.*

Villagers
Justice!
That's what we're demanding.
Justice!
Now!
While there's still time to save us, don't you see?
We're sick to death of empty wordspinning,
we want to see
something is done. Now! Listen everyone.
Time is running out.
Soon they'll be here. Don't you see?
Don't you hear?
Can't you hear
that barrage creeping closer
and closer?
By now,

the Partisans must be
on the outskirts of the village.
At any moment, they'll be here.
So why this delay?
Justice!
That's what we're demanding. Justice!
Now!

Daughter
Yes, you demand justice.
Because for you
there's still more living to do,
still more crops to get in,
still more festivities,
and more fireworks to see!
You'll have your sorrows, too, you'll see.
Days of suffering and torment,
floods, droughts, diseases,
snake-bites, and calamities.
Yes, you've a tomorrow.
And that means more days of joy and sorrows
mingled still lie in store for all of you.
But for me?
For me, joy and sorrow ended, once and for all,
in one savage milking.

All capacity for feeling
was all sucked right out of me.
There's no more feeling in my body
than you'll find in the skin of a leprous cow.
And pain? Why, I'm beyond pain even now.

Headman
Oh, my poor, poor darling!

Daughter
When truth's bright flames leap,
why, this globe and I
are suddenly seen as a unity
like a timid, little pigeon with its wings all free to fly.
And when in truth's bright flames I leap,
why, earth and sky are suddenly seen in entirety.
And freedom is there for all eternity,
and all it needs is a beat of my wings and in I leap.

Villagers
Oh, my God! Heavens above!

*The **Daughter** takes poison right before their eyes, and falls dead. The
village women scream, and wail hysterically.*

Headman
Oh, my darling!
Oh, my daughter! Listen!
Listen to me!
Don't die! Don't! Not like that!
Oh, my precious one,
in another time I would have saved you.
Couldn't you see that?
Oh, my dearest daughter,
whatever did you do that for?

Bodyguard
Who wants a whore like her at home?
Who wants to blacken the good name of his village,
by keeping the like of her around?
Having a whore like that roams around
blackens the good name of all the good women here.
So stop your caterwauling, can't you?
And unplug your lugholes, can't you?
'Cause I'm telling you
letting the dog lick your dinner
is better than having a sinner
like her around.

Headman
What was that you said?
My God! Because of me, people honor you.
What was that you dared to utter?
You were starving, and in the gutter,
and I gave you a home and a sword
to ward off all evil from me.
But now you want to bring evil on me,
do you?
Well, go ahead!
Now you want to kill me, with that sword,
do you?
Well, go ahead.
Go on, run me through.
I dare you!

Bodyguard
Who says I have a sword?

The village women take away the **Daughter**'s *corpse.*

Headman
No! Please! Don't take her away.

Priest
Oh, come on, please.
You can't stop the inevitable, Headman!
No matter what you say,
you can't stop that.
None
of us can.
She's gone.
I could see this coming, days ago.
No sword can ward off evil.
The only thing that can
and will is faith.
You had none.
And that's the bitter truth.

Villagers
Yes! That is the truth!
He didn't have a scrap of faith.
It's as clear as day.
Every one of us can see that now.
Brothers,
this creature standing here before us
now,
aping man draping himself in man's attire,
this monstrous liar
here,
is worse than any wild beast you'll ever corner
in the bush.
He's prepared to make a feast
of anything you, me, his wife,
his daughter,
—in fact, of just about anyone's life
by any kind of slaughter—
as long as his own lush
skin stays intact.
I tell you, brothers,

as long as this vile creature lives,
we are as good as dead.

Priest (*raising his staff above his head and holding it there*)
When an oppressor appears,
the true believer raises his sword.

Villagers
Death to the Headman!
Death! Death! Death!
Death to the Headman!
Death! Death! Death!

All are silent for a while.

Headman
You do know what you're saying?
Don't let yourselves be carried away by hard instinct now!
You do know what you've said, don't you?
I am one of you.
You are my people.
We are made up of the same dust.
We grew up on the same crust of land.
You do know what you're saying!
This is my blood you're demanding.

Villagers
How else can we be saved?

Headman
Will killing me save you?
I've lost everything.
My life is all I have.
Even now I can hear the shelling and the shooting drawing nearer.
I can hear the thuds, thud, thud of the marching feet.
There should be thousands coming by the sound of it.
All right then,
let's say, for the sake of argument,
I was an oppressor.
Tell me, just put your hands on your hearts and tell me,
will there never again be an oppressor
in any land
or country
ever
again,

once you've killed me?
Then where is the gain in killing me?

Villagers
Headman, we came here not for the sake of argument,
but of necessity for the sake of a judgment
in a matter urgent.
No matter how bad we call you
—and whether you are or not is now beside the point—
the point is we allowed you to be what you are.
We all did.
And that's why your death is needed.
Can't you see?
Unless your blood wets this road, we'll never walk it
with our heads held high again.

Priest
There is no God but God.
There is no God but God.

Headman
Then my last request is that you bury me with all due ceremony.

Villagers
Request denied.
Request denied.
Request denied.
Request denied.

Headman
Then, Priest, I ask you this simply for old time's sake.
Let my body be laid to rest if not in hallowed ground
then at least on it.

Villagers
Request denied.
Even if he did allow it,
We'd remove you from it.

The **Headman** *touches the chain of office round his neck. Slowly he
gazes up toward the heavens.*

Headman
You know, when I was a child,
I must have pestered my father half to death
asking him time and time again,

the same, obstinate question
"Father, why don't you take that chain off?"
And in answer to my question,
Father always used to give me the same mild
smile and the same mild joke
"It just won't come off, child. Not as long as I draw breath.
Nor would it come off my father, nor off his, either."
"Of course, it would, Father," I would continue to pester.
"Daddy, why don't you take that chain off?"
How father would have laughed!
It's taken his dumb child a whole lifetime
just to see a simple joke!

Suddenly there is a big explosion. For a moment all is dark. Then as the light comes back we see the **Headman**'s *body, and by it the* **Bodyguard**, *wiping blood from his long sword blade, and crying to the* **Partisans**, *who now flood the stage with guns and a huge national flag.*

Bodyguard
That puts paid to the big one,
But there are many little ones still around.
We'd better catch 'em, before they go to ground.
Come on, my lads, I'll show you 'em.
An' while I'm about it, I'll show you where
they buried those opposed to this oppressor.
Hundreds and hundreds of us died at his hands,
when all these lands were in his power.
This way. This way. Come on. Let's go.
Let me show you the Army camp. This way, please.
This scoundrel here had betrayed many of our lads
to his army dads!
They are still there. Quickly. Quickly. You must surround
the whole area before they go to ground.

Priest
Aye, that's right.
Wheel them in.
Wheel them in.
This is what is left
when sin
is left
to have its way.

So wheel them in.
Wheel them in,
I say.
And thank your lucky stars this day,
you ignoramuses, that you're not among them.

The lights fade out. Three remain. One on the **Headman**'*s corpse, another on the* **Priest**'*s face. And a third on the flag.*

The end

Acknowledgment

I thank John Boulton for his help with the translation of the play from Bengali into English.

Notes

1   The Yamuna River.
2   A dish often eaten by the poor.
3   The person in charge of the country.
4   An estimated number of villages in East Pakistan at the time, used as a way of describing the size of the population and of the land.
5   A series of light machine guns produced by the British in the 1930s and used until the 1990s.

Life of Araj

by
Masum Reza

Translated from Bengali by **Bina Biswas** and **Sayantan Gupta**

The original Bengali version was published by Yukta, Dhaka, in 2012.

Characters (in order of appearance)

Compère	Surjamani
Chorus	Jahan
Araj (*pronounced "Aroj"*)	Mridha
Gayen (Bard)	Kazem
Rajab	An Old Man
Nakai	Fazlu
Karim	A Person
Shariyat	2nd Officer
Taleb(ul)	Constable
Labejan	Superintendent of Police (S.P.)
Mohabbat	Kazi
Chintapati	Jabbar
Hamed	1st Person
Rahim	2nd Person
Noor Jahan	Kadir
Lalmone (Lalmonnessa)	Shamsul Haque

All characters in the play enter the stage carrying musical instruments and other ancillary props. They put these articles down. The **Compère** *asks them, "Are you all ready?"/"Yes," they say together and take their respective positions on the stage.*

Compère Dear learned folks, we present today the life story of a person whose habit was to question, and whose mind was full of queries. He strove to find truth through his questions—truth that would be objective and socially beneficial, truth grounded in science. There he was in our midst. But how many of us had seen him? Oh you learned ones, I pray to you, please look inside yourselves. Do you see any light? Do you?

Chorus Search, search, sea–rch
Is there anyone, is there he?
Search, search, sea–rch;
Next to me, near me,
I haven't looked for, have I?
No, no.
We say, no, no, no, and burn with remorse;
No, no, no, we haven't searched,
So search, sea–rch.
Bedazzled by the shine of faraway lands,
Here, in the lap of our very own soil,
How many of us have searched for him?
Not in the lands far off,
Here in your very own,
Look for him; the treasure is here.
Search, search, sea–rch.

Scene One

Araj I am of modern times.[1] I respect anything based on reason. Blind beliefs, conjectures, superstitions—all this is against my principles. If what was true yesterday is proved wrong today due to advancements in science, thus giving rise to another truth, I shall then salute the new truth. There are things on earth, about which philosophy, religion, and science do not agree. You have differences of opinion in the realm of religion itself. Dear learned ones, when two views cannot be simultaneously true about one particular thing, then how can the hundreds of views held by hundreds of faiths on the same subject be true at once?

Compère This seeker of truth is a son of Bengal, a common farmer whose name is Araj Ali Matubbor. Rather than looking for the proverbial black cat in a dark room, all his life he has admired the clarity of knowledge and reason. But do we know where he was born?

Gayen Yes, I know. Listen, all of you …
About seven miles off the town of Barisal,
Northeast we go to the village of Lamchari.
Copses stand there merrily charmed,
The Kittankhola encircles a patch of land,
On the west bank of this river's Lamchari,
Enveloped on all sides in golden corn.
It was 1307, by the Bengali calendar,
1900 it was, by the Gregorian,
It was the third of *Poush*,[2] early morning,
In the house of Mother Lobejan and father Entaj,
Araj Ali saw the light of the world.

The front part of the stage is lit up. A bundle of dry twigs is kept there. Young **Araj** *is looking at the sky, intently watching something. His friend,* **Rajab**, *enters.*

Rajab I knew I'd find you here. (**Araj** *seems to have heard nothing. His eyes are still fixed on something in the sky.*) Araj! Hey Araj! Come, Auntie is calling for you.

Araj Wait, wait! This is the last skirmish. The red is fighting the yellow. I'll go just after I see which one goes down.

Rajab Does anyone know when this fracas will end? Autie's hearth will be lit after you take these twigs home. Only then will the rice be cooked.

Araj (*laughs as he still looks upwards*) Only then will the rice be cooked. How will the rice be cooked? One needs grains of rice to cook rice, dear Rajab—one needs the rice. After the hearth is lit, eight green bananas will be boiled. A concoction from the shoot of the wild *Kochu* root[3] shall be prepared then …

Rajab Whatever it might be, unless the twigs are taken home, nothing can be done.

Araj Do one thing, Rajab. You take that bundle along. I won't go before I've seen the last skirmish.

Rajab Never have I seen you flying kites! But you spend days on end just watching the kite fights in the sky.

Araj They are not kites, dear Rajab. They are not kites.

Rajab Then what are they?

Araj They are my dreams and nightmares.

Rajab What?

Araj Each of the dreams has its own color. See there, the fighter green kite; that is my dream of learning.

Rajab I can't make the head or tail of what you say, Araj.

Araj The green kite makes my mind soar high. Then I float in the vast the sky. There a school building with a thousand doors suddenly rises up before me. Its fence has the color of moonlight, and its roof, the color of gold. All over there, the perfume of *shiuli* flowers.[4] Just as all the doors of the school open in unison to the tune of Farazi Uncle's *dotara*,[5] the red kite from the cluster plays a trick and cuts through the string of the green. Then my long-cherished dream vanishes to, I don't know, where. Then nothing but darkness envelopes me. (*Lifting the bundle of twigs on his head.*) It is then time for me to enter the six-cubit long and five-cubit broad shanty. Rajab—

Rajab What?

Araj Have you ever visited my house?

Rajab No, but I have seen it from the outside.

Araj *This* small. See, it is this small. Inside things lie scattered—utensil, oven, blankets, and oil-bedaubed pillows. Amongst all these are three persons—my Kulsum Auntie, my Mother, and myself. You know sometimes one of us stumbles over a pot full of water, and it rolls over. Our blankets and pillows get wet. Then all three of us have to spend the night just sitting up.

Rajab Our condition is no different, Araj.

Araj If, just by blowing hard, I could make the room as big as a playground, my heart would leap up on seeing broad smiles on the faces of Mother and Kulsum Auntie. Kulsum Auntie says that when Mother will laugh, the whole Lamchari village and the Kittankhola river will also laugh. Taking Allah's name, several times I have blown hard. But … (*Meanwhile, a physically challenged man, named* **Nakai Chandal***, has come in. Both his hands and legs are crooked. Somehow he manages to walk with a tremulous gait. While talking,* **Araj** *turns and sees him.*) Hey, Nakai Chandal Uncle! How are you?

Nakai Everyone in the village, young or old, calls me simply "Nakai." How come you call me Uncle? Rajab Ali, how are you?

Rajab I'm fine.

Araj Nakai Chandal Uncle, shall I ask you one thing?

Rajab This is your problem. Whenever you see anyone, you start asking questions.

Nakai Oh no! That's nothing. Go ahead. Ask.

Araj Why is your body like this?

Nakai All this had happened due to the *Bau* wind. While carrying me, my Mother had once gone out in the evening to throw the hearth ash. At that moment the *Bau* wind must have touched her. That evil wind caused this mishap.

Araj What is this *Bau* wind, Uncle?

Nakai That I don't know myself. I also keep asking the same question over. (*Looks upwards.*) Oh, dear God, what is *Bau* wind? (*Exits, repeating the question.*)

Scene Two

Enter the **Chorus** *in masks.* **Shariyat Maulana** *and* **Talebul Mokam** *enter from one side of the stage and* **Munshi Abdul Karim** *from the other side.*

Karim Assalamwalaikum, Huzoor.[6]

Shariyat Walaikum Assalam.[7]

Taleb Walaikum Assalam.

Shariyat (*whispers into* **Taleb***'s ear*) You haven't learnt any manners yet. Are you worthy enough to receive Munshi Abdul Karim's salaam that you are reciprocating his?[8] So, how's everything, Munshi Abdul Karim? You seem very much under stress!

Karim Right, Sir. Going from door to door has stressed me out.

Shariyat If you don't mind, what does that mean?

Karim I am planning to open a small school, Sir.

Shariyat Subhan Allah![9] Opening a school is a wonderful idea! But where is it going to be?

Karim In this village itself. In Dakshinpara. In the drawing room of my father-in-law, Abdul Karim Saheb.

Taleb Mashallah![10] I see the father-in-law and son-in-law have the same name, Abdul Karim? But, of course, it is not forbidden according to the Shariyat laws.

Karim So I have to go from door to door, looking for students for my school.

Shariyat That is great. But last year, in 1319,[11] Kazem Ali Sardar opened a school and started teaching Bengali and English, and no Urdu! The result was evident soon. The teacher of that school … what was his name? (*To* **Taleb**.) He became your friend, what was his name?

Taleb Munshi Abu Taher.

Shariyat Yes, Munshi Abu Taher. Taking leave for a couple of days, he went back to his own village, Muladi, but never came back. Vomited blood and died!

Karim Who said he had vomited blood? He had died of cholera.

Shariyat Huh! Let your cholera be! Why should a man die all of a sudden, unless he had committed a grave sin? In your *maktab* you must teach Arabic with great reverence. Or else, you will die without a grave and the last pardon. After death, all Bengali and English will become Arabic.

Karim But Sir, my school is an ordinary school, not a *maktab*. Only Bengali and English will be taught there as languages.

Shariyat What's the difference between a *maktab* and a school? Rosted rice is puffed rice, one and the same thing![12] "Maktab" is "school" in the Arabic language.

Karim But Sir, "maktab" is no Arabic word. It comes from Persian.

Shariyat It's all the same. Do you know Arabic and Persian are very closely related? Both are sacred tongues in the court of the Almighty Allah. A thousand thanks to Him that He had given me the fortune of mastering both these languages!

Karim (*with a wry smile*) That's true, Sir, and that's why "*maktab*" is an Arabic word! Come on, let's go.

Scene Three

*One side of the stage is lit up. From behind the screen, the chanting
of young students learning their lessons by rote is heard.* **Karim** *is
teaching them.* **Araj** *enters hurriedly and sits on the platform. He joins
the chant—*

*"One one's are one ... two one's are two ... three one's are three ... four
one's are four ... "*

Karim *ends the class. Yelling of children is heard.* **Araj** *is still reciting
the tables.* **Karim** *enters. After searching here and there, he finds Araj
in a corner and comes towards him.*

Karim Who's it? Aren't you the son of Entaj Matubbor?

Araj Yes, Munshi Uncle. My name is Araj Ali Matubbar.

Karim You were reciting the tables all alone, like mad! Where did you
learn all this?

Araj In your school the kids repeat the tables, spellings, and grammar
loudly with you. Hearing them, I have learnt, too.

Karim You still have a passion for studies I see!

Araj I would have started early if I had the chance. Last year, when
Kazem Uncle started his school, how old was I? I studied there for quite
some time. I learnt the Bengali alphabet there itself.

Karim (*with surprise*) If you are so much interested in studies, then
why don't you get yourself admitted to school?

Araj Sir? But I can't afford the tuition fees!

Karim (*with a sigh*) Araj, come tomorrow and join my school. Sit
inside to study.

Araj The fees?

Karim You needn't pay any fees. (*Exits.* **Araj** *stares at* **Karim**'s
*exit, spellbound. Then he runs into the school, again comes out. He is
excited. Suddenly, he says ...*)

Araj The reel of the green kite is now in my hand. (*Saying this, he
runs out.*)

Scene Four

The front corner of the platform is lit up. **Araj** *enters with a sheaf of banana leaves and a bamboo twig in hand. Laying the banana leaves down on the ground, he gleefully begins to write on a leaf using the twig. Then, he calls his* **Mother**.

Araj Maa, hey Maa, please come here, will you? (*He writes once again.*) Aaa[13]-Maw[14] ... Aam, mango! (*His* **Mother** *enters.*) Mother, look at my writing. See, this is mango. Want to have one?

Labejan How can that be a mango? Does a mango look like that?

Araj (*laughs aloud*) Mother, you are real illiterate! You don't know anything about reading and writing. This is the written form of mango. Aaa—Maw Aam, mango. I don't have a slate or books. Even then, I write so well. See ...

Labejan I have no time for all this. Tell me, why did you call?

From outside, **Araj**'s *distant uncle,* **Mohabbat Ali Matubbar***, calls out to* **Hamed Ali**.

Mohabbat Hamed Ali, are you there?

Labejan Who is it?

Mohabbat Bhabisaab,[15] don't you recognize the voice of your dear brother-in-law? I am Mohabbat Ali Matubbar. (*To* **Araj**.) Hey, where's Hamed?

Araj He's not come.

Mohabbat I went to his house, but he wasn't there. So I thought ... maybe he has come this way.

Labejan Today he has gone to Charberiya market to sell talismans. But why do you look for Hamed Ali?

Mohabbat He asked me to bring some news from town, about that land of yours that had been auctioned.

Labejan Yes, I had asked him to enquire. Did you get any news?

Mohabbat I met the Nayeb[16] of Lakutiya. Mr. Kailash Ranjan, in town. I have learnt that there's some hope of getting back the plot of land.

Labejan Really?

Mohabbat Yes. You'll get it back by paying off the dues in installments.

But when the land will be free depends upon how much you can repay per installment. Discuss this matter with Molla Hamed and decide. You should have made all these arrangements much earlier ...

Labejan In a house hard put to light a hearth, would all this have made any sense?

Mohabbat (*to* **Araj**) What are you scribbling, Araj?

Araj I'm writing.

Mohabbat Let's see what you are writing? (*Takes a look at the banana leaf on which* **Araj** *is writing.*) This is great! You have written so well! Where did you learn writing?

Araj I am a student in Karim Uncle's school.

Mohabbat Oh! But I don't see any books around? (**Mother** *hangs her head in shame at Mohabbat's question.*)

Araj I have no books, Uncle. I use the kids' books in school, and learn things by heart from them. Back home, I write on banana leaves what I learnt there.

Mohabbat Bhabi, can't you buy him a book? His handwriting is so clear, so good!

Labejan I can't, Deora.[17] Even though I wish to ...

Mohabbat (*with a suppressed sigh*) Okay. I go now.

Mohabbat *goes away. All lights are dimmed.* **Karim** *walks in with papers, files etc., under his arm.* **Araj** *is standing at one end of the stage.*

Karim A lot of money is being spent on land litigations I see. Here nobody utters a single word about paying the school fees. If it goes on like this, then the school has to be shut down, Araj.

Araj But Ustadji,[18] what will happen to the kids?

Karim With just that thought in mind, I am still running the school against all odds.

Araj While sitting in the class, many questions came to my mind. Shall I ask you a few, Sir?

Karim What questions, Araj?

Araj Sir, what is *Bau* wind?

Karim *Bau* wind is a type of bad wind. Evil wind. If it touches anyone, that person is going to suffer.

Araj How can the wind be evil?

Karim How can the wind be evil? Uh … that only Allah sitting up there can say, Araj.

Araj But Sir, it was Nakai Chandal Uncle's Mother who had gone outside and been touched by the *Bau* wind. But nothing happened to her. Why was it Nakai Uncle who was born disabled?

Karim Such questions you ask! People take me for a wise man. But even I had never given such questions a thought. (*Exit.*)

Araj If *you* don't know then whom shall I go to for answers? I have so many questions in my mind, Sir …

Chorus Araj, Araj, just look, just look.

Araj *Adarshalipi?*[19] Whose copy is this?

Chorus It's for you. Your Mohabbat Ali Matubbor Uncle has sent it for you.

Araj (*overjoyed*) This is my book? My book? My book? Sir, you have to keep the school running whatever way you can. I have got a book now! (*Exit* **Araj**, *saying repeatedly, "See, all of you, I own a copy of* Adarshalipi!*"*)

Scene Five

Two bards are debating over the Mystery of Creation. All characters from the previous scene except **Mohabbat** *are present on stage.* **Maulana Shariyat Ullah** *and* **Taleb** *are also there. At one stage of the debate, certain things are uttered that supposedly violate the Shariyat Laws.* **Maulana Shariyat** *cries out …*

Shariyat Stop! There can't be any debate on the Mystery of Creation. I failed to anticipate that while debating you'd ever reach this point. You have transgressed the Shariyat Laws; especially you, the great poet from Raypasha, Abdul Gani Saheb.

Taleb If I knew before that your debate would mean this, I would have never allowed it to take place! Apart from the Creator, who knows the Mystery of Creation?

Karim Ah! Will you stop please, Junior Maulana?[20] Maulana Saheb, what fault do you find with the debate? Neither you, nor I, no one knows anything about this Mystery. Two bards are fighting it out between themselves, partly according to their own views, and partly on the basis of their religious education. Why do you think the Shariyat has been transgressed?

Shariyat If you understood that, then the task of upholding the Shariyat would have fallen upon you, and not upon this Shariyat Ullah. The Mystery of Creation can be thought about, discussed, but not fought over. All of you present, please go back home. Bards, please go.

Some leave, some do not.

Karim Was the act proper, Maulana Saheb?

Shariyat Let your "proper" rest. Listen, you, Munshi Abdul Karim, get the devil out of your mind.

Karim Sorry?

Shariyat You have started a school where Arabic is not on the syllabus. Today you are commenting on the Mystery of Creation. Drive the devil out of your mind. Otherwise, the consequences will be bad for you. Your school will be under lock and key. Come, Sardar Saheb.

Exeunt all except **Karim** *and* **Araj**. **Karim** *stands, looking sad.* **Araj** *comes up.*

Araj Sir, (**Karim** *looks at him, but does not respond.*) the Mystery of Creation can be thought about, discussed, but cannot be debated. Why so, Sir?

Karim Never ask me any questions again. My answers to your questions do not satisfy you. Only the Creator knows the right answers.

Exeunt both. Lights go off.

Scene Six

Night—a full moon in the sky brightens up the atmosphere. From afar the Dafadar[21] cries out.

Chintapati Only Chintapati stays up—

All go to sleep in peace, Chintapati is wide awake …

Crying thus, he enters. He is a bit tipsy. He holds a lantern in one hand, and the staff of a Dafadar in the other. He tries to make out who is out there on the road and raises the lantern, saying.

Chintapati Who comes there?

Hamed (*from offstage*) It's me.

Chintapati Who's "me"?

Hamed Oh! It's me. Why do you need to know every detail? (*Enter* **Hamed**.) If anyone bravely walks in ignoring the warnings of Chintapati Dafadar, he does not have to be necessarily a thief or a robber!

Chintapati Ah! Brother Hamed! Isn't it you? But why are you here so late at night?

Hamed I'm out looking for my brother-in-law. That idiot hasn't been seen the whole day. It's midnight …   he hasn't come back yet. Mother-in-law hasn't taken any food. Just imagine! This worthless creature has taken away my night's sleep, too!

Hamed *goes close to* **Chintapati**. *Sniffs and continues.*

Ah! I see! You are drunk! That's why words keep tumbling out of your mouth. It's too bad to do a *dafadar*'s duty in an inebriate state.

Chintapati I'm not at fault, brother Hamed. All the fault lies with the full moon!

Hamed How?

Chintapati If you turn over a pitcher full of water, the water keeps flowing down. Similarly, from within the full moon, stuck to the sky, moonbeams keep pouring down. The fragrance of the moonlight pervades everything around.

Hamed Fragrance of moonlight? What is that?

Chintapati It's there, you know. Moonbeams have their own fragrance. It's like the fragrance of liquor, numbing all your senses. Further, when the milky white homemade booze from the house of the Chakis pitches in its lot, who can keep Chintapati Dafadar from it? Chintapati drinks and bids his sorrows adieu, saying "Goodbye all pains, goodbye."

Hamed What's your trouble today, Chintapati?

Chintapati It's too bad, brother Hamed. I bade it farewell so many times, but it does not go away.

Hamed Then let it be. I'll hear it all later.

Chintapati Hold on, dear brother, before you go. If I tell you, maybe it will go away. The other day I went to town. There I heard that a war was going to begin, a great war! The crown prince of some country had gone to another country. There he was killed by some unknown assassin. The result is, a war has broken out in the lands across the seas. One crown prince is dead, and for that countless innocent soldiers are dying elsewhere.

Hamed What about this makes you sad, Chintapati?

Chintapati You don't find anything in it to make me sad? Kings fight kings. It has always been that way. Always the kings fight one another and always the innocent subjects and salaried soldiers lose their lives. I am a paid sepoy[22] of the zamindar of Lakutiya. If any soldier dies abroad, he is my kin then. He is my foreign brother. Don't you understand the sorrow of a brother at the death of another brother, brother Hamed?

Hamed No, I don't understand what you say. Anyway, you stay steady. I'll be pushing off.

Hamed *goes out. Through the other side of the stage* **Chintapati** *also goes out crying, "Chintapati is awake alone ..."*

Scene Seven

Lights on in **Araj**'s *house. Enter* **Talebul.**

Taleb Auntie, hey Auntie!

Labejan (*enters from the other end*) Who's there? Oh, Junior Maulana!

Taleb I come to you under great stress.

Labejan Why? What's up?

Taleb I took up the charge of your son's education with high expectations. But all's gone wrong.

Labejan What! Has Araj Ali misbehaved with you?

Taleb No, he hasn't. (*Enter* **Hamed.**)

Hamed Hello, it is Junior Maulana! What's the matter?

Taleb Nothing much. I came to your Mother-in-law to discuss something about Araj Ali.

Hamed (*in a somber tone*) Why? What has he done?

Taleb Nothing much. But over the last five days or so, he hasn't come to me for training in religious studies.

Hamed Where is he gone again? Ammajan,[23] where's the devil?

Labejan Oh Hamed, please don't get so worked up. You're just back from the market. Go in, have a wash, and eat something first.

Hamed Mother, please don't spoil Araj any further. You don't ever put him to task. He does whatever he likes.

Taleb Brother Hamed, I came to tell you something. Will you please stop all this and listen?

Hamed Okay, go on.

Taleb Auntie, your son does not care for Arabic studies. Ah ... This is pure obduracy. If anyone shows such disrespect for Arabic, it causes real worries.

Hamed Now I see what brings you here, Junior Maulana.

Labejan But why?

Taleb He says, I don't want to read anything whose meaning I don't understand.

Hamed Why don't you give him the meaning then?

Taleb You people are no less stubborn, I see. What do you mean by meaning? Arabic has no meaning. The meaning of Arabic can be understood only after death, when the angels, Mankeer and Nakeer, come to the grave and ask you questions in Arabic.[24]

Labejan You hadn't told him this?

Taleb I did. A thousand times ... But he is not the one to accept. He bothers me instead with a thousand other questions. He wants to know the meaning of every Arabic word. The other day, your son asked me in public the meaning of a word. I gave him the meaning. Yet he went to Senior Maulana to crosscheck it. And Senior Maulana is such a terrible man that in spite of coming here from another village, he always wants to discredit me! He gave him a different meaning! Two

Maulanas giving two different meanings for the same word was very awkward. At this, your son clearly said that he didn't want to study under me. When he is studying under me, why should he doubt my scholarship? I felt very offended. And today I'll have a showdown with Senior Maulana. (*He makes a move to leave, but then stops.*) When a child turns wayward, then the elders have to take the responsibility of getting him back on track. (*He is about to leave again, when* **Araj** *enters with kite-making material. On seeing Araj, he says:*) Curb him. (*Exit* **Taleb**.)

Labejan What's wrong with you and the junior teacher? For six days you haven't attended his classes!

Araj Did he come to tell you this?

Labejan Why did you have to offend him?

Araj I did not offend him. If, while studying Arabic, I ever want to know any word's meaning, he invariably avoids it under the pretext of Mankeer and Nakeer. He says that when they finally come and ask you questions, then all the Arabic meanings will be instantly clear.

Labejan Yes, my son. That's what is written in the Scripture.

Araj But, Mother, if I don't understand something while I am alive, what shall I do with its meaning after my death?

Hamed Listen, Mother. Just mark what your son is saying. He is questioning the givens of Islam!

Labejan You, please go inside. I'll try to make him understand.

Araj What will you make me understand, Mother? I also posed the same question to Senior Maulana. He put a hand over my mouth and said, "My goodness, these questions should never be asked." Do you know what I feel like, Mother? Perhaps Senior Maulana doesn't know the answer either.

Hamed (*very angry*) *You* know it all, right? You know everything! Please go inside, Mother. First let me finish my part of the punishment. (*To* **Araj**.) How many times have I forbidden you to make kites? (**Araj** *is silent.*) Why don't you answer? Tell me, how many times? Answer me! (*Slaps* **Araj** *hard across his face.*)

Labejan (*to* **Hamed**) Let it be, son. Beating is not necessary. He won't make kites any more. Go inside, please.

Hamed This, only this is your fault. Even if I want to bring him to task for a good cause, you won't allow me to. Go on; if you want to spoil the brat, you are welcome. (*Goes inside.*)

Labejan (*stroking* **Araj**'s *cheek*) Does it hurt, my son? Why don't you listen to what he says? He is the one who is holding this family together. Had he not done so, we would be nowhere now. Whatever he says is for your own good. Why do you disobey him?

Araj (*moving away from his* **Mother**) I am going now, Ma.

Labejan Where to?

Araj To become a real human being. (**Araj** *runs away.* **Mother** *cries for Hamed.*)

Labejan Hamed, my son, stop the boy. Bring him back. Don't know where he will go. Go, son, bring him back, please! (**Labejan** *leaves, crying "Araj" ...* **The Choir** *begins singing.*)

> Araj has been slapped; he had done no wrong.
> To be a man he fled home, now free with a song.
> Araj has been slapped; he had done no wrong.
> To be a man he fled home, now free with a song.
> Looking for a school; oh dear, every place he tapped.
> He has been slapped; oh dear, he has been slapped.
>
> Life with no knowledge! wondered Araj in his mind,
> Walking and walking, Sharupkathi Thana[25] did he find.
> Araj has been slapped; oh dear, Araj has been slapped.
> At Sharupkathi did he find a madrasa school,
> To its teacher went Araj, intrepid and cool.
> (**Gayen** *enters.*)[26]

Gayen
> Despite all efforts nothing went right.
> Three days of exile, yet no respite.
> In this manner years go rolling by.
> Keep watching, all of you, without a sigh.

Scene Eight

On one side of the stage **Araj** *stands upon two boulders, staring at the sky. His hands are positioned in such a way that he seems to be holding something.* **Rajab** *enters. He is surprised to find* **Araj** *in that peculiar* *pose. He inspects* **Araj** *circling him, and then suddenly runs to the other side of the stage.*

Labejan (*enters*) What are you doing, my son? Hey, Rajab, what's he doing? My son, what are you doing?

Araj Please don't get scared, Mother, I am practicing.

Rajab What are you practicing?

Araj Guess ... Plowing. You thought I have gone mad—eh? Wait, wait, let me show you this. (*Takes a deed out from inside his vest and hands it over to his* **Mother**.)

Labejan (*turns the document over*) What is this? This paper looks like a land deed! Take a look, Rajab.

Araj *stands in a corner, looking sad.* **Rajab** *looks at the document and says:*

Rajab Yes, Auntie, this indeed is a land deed!

Labejan Araj dear, whose land deed is it?

Araj Ours! After your son-in-law got his job in the Police department, he cleared the dues; and now he sends us the deed of possession.

Labejan Really? Oh, that's great! Show me, Rajab, show me the deed. (*Looks at the deed.*) Ah! Such a lovely piece of paper! Its whole body is covered with black letters, with a green cap on top. Such a small bit of paper, but imagine its power! Whoever has it, will possess the five *bighas*[27] of land in Dakshin Chawk! The crops grown on that land will also be his. It's a long time since I'd smelt the fragrance of fresh paddy, my son. The intoxicating fragrance of fresh paddy from one's own land ... (*Moves close to* **Araj**.) But, what's this, my son? We have got our land back, yet your face is as dark as the monsoon cloud?

Araj The green kite has lost ... I am now reduced to a mere peasant behind a pair of bullocks, holding firmly the handle of the plow; Araj is plowing lands. In Dakshin Chawk, there will be series of furrows from the plow. Araj is now an ordinary peasant, Mother.

Labejan What more do you need? Tell me. The land is there, so is the kitchen filled with the aroma of boiled rice. You should really learn plowing now. You shouldn't go crazy about studying. (*Pause.*) Don't you care for my happiness, son? Our family will no longer starve. I'll bring a bride into this house, as pretty as the moon and as soft as water. I believe I have already made a choice. But considering the poor condition of our family, I couldn't bring myself to speak to the girl's parents. But now there's nothing to hold me back. Now my son owns five *bighas* of land!

Araj *goes inside with the deed.*

Rajab Auntie, whom have you chosen as Araj's bride?

Labejan Huh! I tell you and then you will tease her. You'll know only when it happens.

Rajab But please don't hurry through, Auntie. You have got your land back; let Araj start the cultivation. Repair your house first.

Rajab *and* **Labejan** *roam about.* **Rajab** *sees a girl and says:*

That girl is really beautiful.

Scene Nine

The **Chorus** *chants a tune from some ancient text.*

Lights are on and **Abdul Rahim Farazi** *is seen tending to his musical instrument. A tune is heard. He calls for his daughter.*

Rahim Noor Jahan, dear, there's a bunch of strings on the shelf. Bring them to me, will you?

Noor Jahan *comes in.*

Noor Jahan Here, Bajan,[28] here are your strings. This instrument is really naughty. The strings break every now and then.

Rahim Yes, dear?

Noor Jahan Will you sing some old folk song for my friend?

Rahim Which friend are you talking about?

Noor Jahan There's only one friend close to my heart, Lalmonnessa.

Rahim But, darling, I don't have time now. After repairing this instrument, I've got to go to market.

Noor Jahan Why would you have time for me? If it were brother Araj coming in right now, touching your feet, and saying "Guruji, I've come for training," you'd leave everything else to entertain him. Then time wouldn't matter. You have to sing for me as much as you can while tending to that instrument. Lali, hey Lali, come in here. Listen to my father singing. (**Lalmonnessa** *comes in.*) Sit down.

Rahim Lalmonnessa Bibi,[29] your father is also an admirer of my songs.

Lalmonnessa *sits down to pick lice from* **Noor Jahan**'*s hair, and* **Rahim** *begins to hum a tune.* **Araj** *calls him from outside in the middle of his "song."*

Araj (*from outside*) Guruji, are you home?

Noor Jahan Your favourite chela is already here. Now train him to your heart's content. I'm gone.

She and **Lamonnessa** *are about to leave the stage when Araj enters with three other men. Seeing them,* **Noor Jahan** *and* **Lalmonessa** *stop awhile and then exit.* **Araj** *salutes* **Rahim** *by touching his feet.*

Araj I have come for your blessings, Guruji.

Rahim My blessings are always with you, Araj.

Araj No, Guruji. I need special blessings today. Next Thursday, for the first time, I am going to sing outside the village, at Jawakati Union School grounds. Old folk songs … I have chosen Jahan Ali, Hossain Malik, and your namesake, Abdur Rahim Khan, as members of the Chorus. Please bless us all so we can uphold your name.

Rahim What will you sing there? First let me hear that. The blessings can then follow, right?

Araj Then listen. Hey, you folks, play the Chorus well. I have composed it in the spirit of Meser Ali Sikdar. Here we go …

The song begins. It has a Hindu theme. **Rahim** *stops him halfway through.*

Rahim Where did you get it?

Araj I got it from Chintapati brother. I bought him some liquor on a night with a full moon and said, "Brother Chintapati, please tell me something from your Scriptures." After a few gulps, he started to talk and then he went on without a *Pause.*

Rahim I hope you didn't take a few sips, too!

Araj Oh no! How can I take a drink, when at the very smell I feel like throwing up?

Rahim That's good. I have to go to the marketplace. (*To* **Araj** *'s Chorus.*) Folks, good luck!

Araj *stays back. The others leave.* **Rahim** *goes inside the house.* **Noor Jahan** *peeps in.*

Noor Jahan May I please speak to my father's darling disciple?

Araj Do you have anything to tell me? Please come in here. (**Noor Jahan** *comes in, along with Lalmonnessa.*)

Noor Jahan How do you sing so well?

Araj I have no answer to this question. What's your next question?

Noor Jahan Why don't you look around while singing?

Araj Why should I? What is here and there to look for?

Noor Jahan An elephant and a horse. (*Prepares to leave.*)

Araj Wait, wait. An ass is there between you two.

Noor Jahan What's that supposed to mean?

Araj Of the two of you, one is such a thing.

Noor Jahan And who might it be?

Araj Your friend, Lalmonnessa.

Noor Jahan Now, what can she have done to you?

Araj Had your friend known it, she would have never come in front of me.

Noor Jahan Known what?

Araj A marriage is being arranged between your friend and me.

The two run away, crying, "Oh my God!" **Rahim** *is coming out of his house with a shopping bag. They bump into him. Wedding tunes begin. A wedding scene.*

Scene Ten

Song
> Grind the turmeric, hurry up, hurry,
> Bring the *henna*, and don't you scurry.
> Araj Ali weds Lamonnessa
> Bring it all—turmeric and henna.[30]

There is light and shade in one corner of the stage. **Lalmonnessa** *is sitting there with her back toward the audience.* **Araj** *comes in. Both are wearing ceremonial wedding dress.*

Araj It's a special night. Why do you sit there with your face turned away, dear? Won't you show me your beautiful face? (*Lalmonessa is silent. Araj looks out of the window.*) Look there, dear. The moon is up, as round as the school bell. My Mother, the neighbors—all were saying that your face is as beautiful as the moon. Wait, let me compare and see whether they were right or not. (*He compares.*) No, it is not true at all. You are even fairer than the moon! All over the moon, there are a thousand scars. You have none!

Lalmone You needn't talk so much. I am fine. (*Yawns.*)

Araj I understand. Actually you are feeling sleepy. That's why you are not enjoying my talk.

Lalmone Sitting straight all day long has left me tired. (*Yawns again.*)

Araj If you splash water over your face, the drowsiness will go away. (**Lalmone** *yawns once again. Others start singing.*)

Song
>Sleep is here …
>So overcome by sleep are you,
>Betel leaf you didn't take to chew.[31]
>Two heads on the same pillow, but
>You have your eyes shut;
>Sleep is here … sleep is here … but …

The song is interrupted by the chant "Bolo Haribol"[32] which is heard from behind the screen. Lights dim; the scene changes. Some men enter carrying a corpse, chanting the name of Hari. They go away. **Chintapati** *is seen following the funeral procession.* **Araj** *comes forward. Lights brighten up.*

Araj Brother Chintapati, hey brother Chintapati. Who died?

Chintapati Nakai.

Araj Nakai Chandal Uncle is dead? Only a few days ago, I saw him sitting at the *ghat* of Namapara!

Chintapati Over the last few days, he spent all his time sitting there. Yesterday, he suddenly waded into the waters of the Kittankhola. While his head was above the water, he was heard asking, "What is Bau wind, God? What is Bau wind?" Before anyone could get hold of him, he floated away towards the midstream of the Ganga. His body was recovered today from the Dhopapara *ghat* at Gausa.

Exeunt all. The **Chorus** *comes in and a song begins.*

If I die by drowning,
It'll be a scandal ...

Scene Eleven

Lalmonnessa *and* **Labejan** *appear, the latter with a lantern in hand.*

Labejan Bouma,[33] it's already dark, but Araj and others are yet to come back from Kaliganj!

Lalmone He stayed up for two nights composing songs for the wedding party. They won't be coming back, I guess, before midnight, Mother.

Labejan Then you take your dinner and go to bed. It is not good staying up in this condition. Go. I'll take care.

Lalmone I can't sleep till your son is back. You had better go in and let me stay up. But, Mother, shall I ask you one thing?

Labejan Go on; ask.

Lalmone Your son sings so well; do tunes not play in your throat, too?

Labejan You want the singer's Mother to sing for you now—right? Wait, let me try.

(*Sings.*) The blind Gopal Gosain says ...

Araj *comes in as* **Labejan** *begins the song.*

Lalmone You are back? We thought you'd come back even later.

Labejan *watches* **Araj** *closely and says.*

Labejan What's wrong, my son? You don't look that well! Where's your instrument?

Araj (*in a sentimental tone*) I was going to throw it away into the Kewajangi pond. My companions didn't let me ...

Lalmone But why?

Araj Bibijan,[34] a brother slighted his brother.[35]

Labejan Did Abdur Rahim Mridha offend you?

Araj He had invited me there, but didn't introduce me to anyone. He was sitting in the drawing room, on a soft mattress, with pillows in glittering covers by his side, and made me sit with my companions out there, on the veranda.

Lalmone Did the others say anything?

Araj I don't know what the others thought, dear. But later, when it was time to sing, I sang wholeheartedly. I didn't tell anyone about the humiliation I had suffered. But I won't sing ever again, Mother; I won't sing ever again.

Lalmone Why?

Araj The song that has estranged me from a brother, I won't sing that song again. Dulabhai's[36] books are still there in the balcony, aren't they?

Labejan Why do you want those books now?

Araj It won't affect the farming—rest assured. Till now, I have worked through nights to compose songs. Henceforth, I'll stay up studying. Mathematics, History, Geography, Grammar—I'll study all of them.

Labejan But why?

Araj While singing there I made myself a promise. That Abdur Rahim Mridha, who had refused me a seat by his side, I will sit beside him one day. I will do that, you see.

Labejan Can you do that, my son? Can you? (*Slowly goes out.*)

Araj Bibijan, you are hurt, aren't you? How much I wished to win a gold medal for you from the Chanpasha contest! Please forgive me, dear. I'll now get you one from the goldsmith's.

Lalmone Of what avail is a gold medal from a goldsmith's? If you can give a fitting reply to Mridha Saheb one day, that will be my greatest reward.

Lights out.

Scene Twelve

Lights on. **Jahan Ali**, **Araj Ali**'s *singing partner, walks in, wearing a cap on his head.* **Surjamani** *comes in from the other side of the stage with a bag hanging from his shoulder.*

Surjamani (*sings*)

    A man with a horse, comes walking.
    After a while, he begins riding.
    Hordes of men fall dead, numbering lakhs;[37]
    Counting a few thousands, Surjamani packs up!

Jahan What's the matter, Uncle? On seeing me you have started singing?

Surjamani I feel enthused whenever I see you. Trousers in place of lungi; kurta[38] in place of vest; an additional appendage on the head, that cap. What's up?

Jahan Our troupe has disintegrated, but the stomach knows no rest. So I have begun my apprenticeship with Maulana Shariyat Ullah Huzoor.

Surjamani Can't you revive your troupe?

Jahan Uncle, if the head is gone, what can the body do?

Surjamani Who was the head? Araj Ali? I hear Araj Ali has started studying to become a Vidyasagar?[39]

Jahan He is a real man, Uncle. He can turn iron into gold.

Surjamani What do you mean?

Jahan The other day I saw him carrying books in both hands. When I asked him, he said he had the books of Class VII in one hand, and those of Class VIII in the other. He has already passed Class VI. Now he's preparing for Classes VII and VIII.

Surjamani But he never went to any school or madrasa! How does he claim to have passed Class VI sitting at home?

Jahan He had set questions for himself and answered them without consulting books. Later, he awarded himself marks and, on working out the total, found that he passed with flying   colors. But, Uncle, in English he scored a double zero.

Surjamani In that case I'll have to take him to Morris Saheb of the Christian Mission. He is a veritable dictionary of English. Um, taking Muslims to the Christian Mission ... I must have gone mad! (*Lights fade out on* **Surjamani** *and* **Jahan**.)

Lalmonnessa *comes in. From the other side* **Araj** *enters, his hands behind his back. Lights on them.*

Lalmone (*looking at* **Araj**'s *face*) Today your face looks lustrous!

Araj A thousand stars from a constellation seem to be lighting up this face.

Lalmone Again science—constellations, planets, stars, which planet is how far, which one is small, which one large.

Araj No, no, no such talks today. My dear, could you please tell me what this year is by the Bengali calendar?

Lalmone Why?

Araj Oh, do tell me please.

Lalmone 1339.

Araj Do you remember an incident that took place seven years ago ... in 1332?

Lalmone No, dear. You know that my memory is weak. But if someone shakes it a little, I can remember. Help me, please.

Araj That was the year that I quit singing. I had wanted to bring a gold medal from the Chanpasha contest and put it around your neck. I was sad I couldn't do that. I had promised myself that I would get a gold medal for you one day. (**Araj** *brings his hands to the front. He is holding a paper.*) Look, here is that gold medal. Look how it glitters!

Lalmone A gold medal? That's just a piece of paper!

Araj No, no, it's not a mere piece of paper. For a lowly farmer this is gold. If I give it to a skilled goldsmith, there will be enough jewelry from this gold to cover the whole body of Lalmonnessa. I have been elected a member of the Charberiya Union Board. That's what is written here. I have got a seat there on the strength of this paper. Where's Mother? Where are my daughters, Esharonnessa, Soleimannessa? Mother, your son is now a Board member. (*Suddenly he becomes sad.*) I keep forgetting that my old Mother can't even walk properly now. Can't it be that no one's Mother ever gets old? (**Labejan** *comes in, limping, and leaning on a stick.*)

Labejan What's up, my son?

Araj Mother, do you know what's on this paper? I'm now a Union Board member. Suppose, suppose this is the Board President's chair, and this is the chair of Abdur Rahim Mridha. *This* is my chair, just by his side. Today I sat in the chair next to his. Mother, didn't I once promise you both that one day I would sit next to Abdur Rahim Mridha? Today

I did, Mother. He didn't want it, though. But the others were so happy about it. He couldn't stop it … .

Labejan Will you take me to the Board Office someday, my son?

Araj What will you do in the Board Office, Mother?

Labejan I'll take a look at the chair. Rising from dusts on the roads of Lamchari, my Araj Ali Matubbar is now sitting in that chair. I'll take a look at it. There is as much ebb and flow in the life of a person as there is in the Kittankhola River … now it's full to its banks, now it runs dry.

Araj Why do you say this, Mother?

Labejan Suddenly things from the past are rushing back to my mind, son. When I came to this village as a bride, my life was like a river in full spate. Then, that river started drying … (*Breaks down in tears.*) Nothing remained, my son. Today you are sitting in that chair, and I feel that high tides are coming in from all sides making the river flood again.

Lalmone Let's go in, Mother. If you keep standing out in this courtyard, your body will ache again. (*To* **Araj**.) Oh, I haven't told you, Farazi Uncle has asked you to go to his place for supper.

Exuent all.

Scene Thirteen

Lightning across the sky, clouds roar. **Noor Jahan**, **Rahim's** *daughter, is sitting alone, lost in thought. She is humming a tune of Sakhina's Jari song.*[40] **Araj** *calls from outside.*

Araj Guruji, Guruji.

Noor Jahan Araj brother? Come in, please come in.

Araj (*enters*) You? When did you come? Has your husband come, too?

Noor Jahan I have come alone. It has been a couple of days now.

Araj How are you?

Noor Jahan I am fine.

Araj Where is my Guruji?

Noor Jahan He's gone to my uncle's place. The invitees have been asked to go there. He has asked you to go there, too.

Araj Okay. (*Goes to leave.*)

Noor Jahan I heard that my father's disciple had changed very much. That he had become a bigwig. But I see no change.

Araj What do you mean? (*A thunderclap is heard.*)

Noor Jahan The venue for the invitees has suddenly been shifted to Uncle's. You don't want to know why?! (**Araj** *is silent.*) So, my father's darling disciple, how are you?

Araj I'm fine. (*Pauses for a while.*) As I got in here I noticed a pall of sadness over your face.

Noor Jahan But not even once did you ask me the reason!

Araj What can be wrong with you?

Noor Jahan My nest is broken, Araj brother. Rather I broke it myself.

Araj Have you left the in-laws' house for good?

Noor Jahan Yes.

Araj Why?

Noor Jahan Araj brother, that house is Hell.

Araj But why?

Noor Jahan I gave birth to three daughters in a row. My in-laws always insulted me for this. Whenever I tried to say that the birth of a boy or a girl was in the hands of Allah, they started beating me. Their beatings have turned my back as hard as brick. My husband also beats me, saying that if I bear more girls then his family line will cease to exist. Many a time, I thought of leaving that house and coming back here, but I couldn't.

Araj Why?

Noor Jahan A wife's Heaven is at the feet of her husband. If I leave my husband that will be enough for me to land up in Hell!

Araj Then how could you come away now?

Noor Jahan He has married another woman in the hope of having a son. And I have suffered utter neglect and torture ever since. Araj brother, it's impossible to stay on in such Hell and hope for Paradise in the afterlife. (**Rajab** *comes in running.*)

Rajab Araj! Araj, go home now. Hurry!

Araj Anything wrong? (**Rajab** *is silent.*) What's happened to my Mother? (**Rajab** *keeps silent.*) Maa ... Maa ... Oh, Maa ...

Araj *breaks down in grief.* **Rajab** *takes* **Araj** *out.* **Noor Jahan** *looks on blankly.*

Scene Fourteen

The chanting of last rites from the Quran Sharif is heard. Inside the women are crying. Outside are seen **Abdur Rahim Mridha**, **Kazem Ali**, **Karim**, **Chintapati**, **Jahan**, **Rajab**, *and* **Rahim**.

Kazem Yes, she was a great soul!

Karim In order to feed her son and daughter, she had even washed the bodies of dead women.[41]

Mridha Today she has become a corpse herself.

Kazem In the midst of all this, she never forgot to say her namaz. Alas, such is the life of humans!

Karim Has the Maulana been informed?

Jahan Hamed brother has gone to fetch him.

Mridha The body shouldn't be kept in the house for long. That's bad for the deceased. The burial should be arranged fast.

Enter **Talebul**, *followed by* **Hamed**.

Talebul Ennaillaha, Ennalillaha! Has the body been washed up?

Rajab Yes Sir. (**Araj** *enters from inside, with a photographer.*)

Talebul Oh my God! You have brought this unholy equipment into the house of the dead? Why?

Araj I won't be able to see my Mother any more. So I'd have him (*Points to the photographer.*) take a few shots of her face.

Talebul Dear me! Dear me! What have you done, Araj? Don't you know that photography is un-Islamic? Further, the photo of a woman? And that, too, not of a living but of a dead woman? This is a grave violation of the Shariyat! I can't perform the last rites for the dead. I am leaving. Dear me! (*Goes away in haste.*)

Mridha Shame on you, Araj. Being a knowledgeable man, you don't know the difference between Shariyat and anti-Shariyat! Let's go, all of us. We shouldn't stay here any longer.

(**Araj** *pleads, but two of them walk out behind* **Mridha**, *saying, "Come along, come along."* **Kazem** *and* **Karim** *follow them helplessly. Only* **Jahan** *and* **Araj** *remain. The chanting from the Quran becomes louder. So, too, do the cries of women inside.*)

Araj Jahan Ali, Jahan Ali, then you please read out the last rites for my Mother.

Jahan How can that be, Araj brother? When the Maulavis and Muslis have passed the verdict that your Mother's last rites can't be performed, how can I do it, dear? I have to live in this society.

Araj Then, Jahan Ali, will there be no last rites for my Mother?

Jahan Even if there are no last rites, the body has to be buried. I am available for the burial.

Araj Even if you prayed a thousand times at the burial, it wouldn't be the same thing as the last rites. And if the last rites are not performed, what will a Maulana do at the burial? Go. Go away, all of you. I don't need anyone. I'll bury my Mother alone. I need no one . (*Saying this, he goes inside. Lights dim.*)

Gayen *begins a sad song.*

Gayen The blind Gopal Gosai says ...

Exuent all after the song is over.

Scene Fifteen

In dim light **Araj Ali** *is seen reading intently. A lantern burns before him. Enter* **Lalmone**.

Lalmone You are still up studying; how long will this go on? You have no concern for your own health. All day long you work so hard. Allah forbid, if a serious illness ... I'm worried for you.

Araj But, I can't afford to stop, Bibijan. The blind faith and superstitions going on for ages hurt me so much. My job is to root them out.

Lalmone Four years have passed since Mother left. You haven't got over that pain yet?

Araj That pain will keep on hurting me till my last breath. Tell me, what was Mother's fault? If taking a photo of the dead is against the tenets of faith, then I was responsible for the breach. Why punish my poor Mother?

Lalmone How many more people, how many more times, will you ask that same question?

Araj I can't forget it really. My Mother, who had never missed her namaz, who had never done anything against the laws of Shariyat … what did she get in return? Blind faith frustrates every good thing. (*He controls himself; continues after a pause.*) You go to bed. I have more things to read.

Lalmone (*taking* **Araj Ali**'s *hand in her own*) Can I tell you something?

Araj Yes, please do.

Lalmone You can study as much as you like. But please, don't get into arguments with the villagers over what you have learnt or believe.

Araj I never argue with anyone. I ask them the questions that bother me. When I get the answer, I might ask another question in reference to the previous.

Lalmone Please don't do that again. The Murids[42] of Pir Saheb[43] are saying so many things about you. I have heard it all.

Araj They don't want me to pursue the truth and light up the dark alleys of blind faith. Bibijan, this is but another instance of orthodoxy.

Lalmone But what if they harm you?

Araj If I don't harm anyone, then why should others harm me?

Lalmone Then you won't pay heed to my words?

Araj If you can convince me logically, then, of course, I'll accept your point. But if you ask me to stop just because of your ungrounded fear then I won't.

Lalmone Look, now you have two families to care for. You have five children at home. Mind you, if you …

Araj Honey, why do you try to pull me back from my search for truth?

Lalmone All other people of the village are of one type. Why should you alone be different? (**Lalmone**'s *eyes brim over with tears.* **Araj** *strokes her head. Lights dim.*)

Scene Sixteen

Lights on. The elders of the village arrive. **Araj** *is also there.* **Talebul** *starts to speak.*

Talebul Once upon a time, in a religious assembly, a Maulana stated that in the world of the Holy Allah each of His creations is flawless and has its own place. But there was one who did not believe him and began to look for flaws in His creations. The day rolled down into night, but the atheist could not find any flaw in any of Allah's creations. Dejected at his failure, the fool lay down for rest under a huge banyan tree. Suddenly he cried out, "Got it, got it. The banyan is such a huge tree, but then why is its fruit so small?" Right at that moment, by Allah's grace, one of the banyan fruits dropped to hit the fool on his nose. Instantly, all his boasts died down. He cried out loudly, "There's no flaw, no flaw in His creations. If the banyan fruit were of the size of a coconut, my face would have turned into a pulp by now." Hence, if an ignorant grump questions the Mystery of Creation, Allah brings him back to his senses in this way. All say, Allah is great!

All Allah is great!

Araj The words of Maulana Saheb make me very happy. He has spoken about "senses." I, too, have been busy in search of commonsense. Today I have been summoned here to face some sort of a trial. Carry on ... But can you all stop one's run of thought by putting him up for trial? I am inclined towards thinking, and my thoughts sometimes give rise to questions in my mind. When I get no answer myself, I ask others. It's always been so. I took a photo of my dead Mother's face, and she was denied her last rites. More questions now cross my mind. But one question should have one correct answer. What do you all say?

Mridha I agree. But will the common people be able to give you that inviolable truth? Isn't it wiser to consult those who are learned in the Hadish and are more conversant with the Shariyat?[44] Why should you go about asking everybody?

Araj I ask around because I am clueless. For example, what causes day and night? Will you please tell me?

All Tell him, Maulabi Saheb.

Talebul There's no call for questions on such a subject. Putting the sun in a golden boat, seventy thousand angels draw the boat across the sky from east to west. These angels then sit at the feet of Allah the whole night and worship Him.

Araj The Hindu Puran says that sired by Kashyap Muni, the sun was born out of the womb of his wife, Aditi. That's why he is called Aditya. He roams about in the sky in a chariot drawn by seven horses, with Arun as the charioteer. Thus the day and night occur. On the other hand, science says that the sun stands in its place while the earth, millions of miles away, spins on its axis around it. During this rotation, the side that faces the sun has day and the other side, night. Thus, regarding day and night, we have before us three views. Now, isn't it natural for us to wonder which one is true?

Talebul (*very angry*) There's only one truth. Whatever Islam says is true. There can be no other truth apart from Islam. Those who do not believe in the truth of Islam are denounced by Allah. And, if there need be, *they may be killed.*

Karim If you get so angry, what good will it yield? Has he ever said that he disobeys Islam? Keep your cool, Maulana. Otherwise, how will you conduct a fair trial? Carry on, Araj.

Araj I am also curious to know what the earth stands upon.

Talebul The earth stands upon the horns of a bull.

Araj And what does this bull stand upon?

Talebul Upon the forces of nature. You often hear of earthquakes occurring in different places. Do you know the reason? When this bull shifts the earth from one horn to another, then the earth shakes. That is what you people call an earthquake.

Araj In that case, Sir, why doesn't earthquake occur in all places at once?

Talebul That, too, is a game of the forces of nature.

Araj Scientists say that the earth is governed by the law of gravitation. Astronauts, travelling in spaceships, have gone all around the earth, but they haven't met any such bull. Now, the question that comes to my mind is whether the bull is true, or the force of gravity.

An Old Man I shouldn't be here in this assembly. Now I feel whatever Araj says merits consideration; now I feel his words also go grossly against the Shariyat. I have almost a foot in the grave. Hearing these things, or thinking about them, I don't want to lose this world as well as the next, my boys. Let me go.

Karim Oh, please sit down. There is no problem in simply hearing something. What you believe in is more important. Please take your seat.

Araj I am afraid I can't stay here longer. Got to attend a meeting in the Board office. If I go on asking all the questions that come to my mind, it will take about a week. Of the little I said, if anything is against the Shariyat, then please put me up for trial. But I would ask Maulana Sahib, who will judge what is right and what is wrong?

Talebul Only Khodatallah will judge it all on the Day of Judgment.

Araj Then why, right after someone is laid in the grave, do the angels, Mankeer and Nakeer, come down and ask questions? If they don't get satisfactory answers, then why do they mete out punishments right away?

Talebul That they do at the orders of the Holy Allah.

Araj If right and wrong get to be judged in the grave itself, then what's the need for the Day of Judgment?

Talebul (*after a brief silence*) So be it by the Will of Allah. Being a mere human being, how will you understand that? You have gone out of your mind, by going to the library of Christians, interacting with those atheist college teachers, and by reading a whole lot of books. You have become a non-believer, too. If you are not driven out of this village, then bad days await us all.

Rahim Come on, Maulana, whom will you drive out of the village? This Lamchari village was built by Araj Ali's grandfather. If you throw him out of this village, that itself will be the most sinful act ever.

Talebul Munshi Saheb, you are the eldest of this village. You give your verdict.

Karim Listen folks, there's nothing to judge in this matter.

Mridha What do you say! There's nothing to judge here? He has uttered so many things against Islam. He is provoking the villagers. Still you say there's nothing to judge? People of this village, what do you say?

Old Man We don't understand anything, friends. We shall abide by whatever you decide.

Karim Then pay heed, all residents of Lamchari village, all local Mussalmans. Araj Ali has never asked anyone to do or not to do this or that. He merely asks us questions. Asking questions has been his habit since childhood. The verdict is—let Araj Ali do whatever he likes with his own thoughts. You can always stay away from it if you like.

Talebul But what of his tormenting others with his array of questions?

Karim Ignore him, that's enough.

Mridha This is no verdict, I must say. He should not be allowed to say anything about religion to anyone.

Karim But how can you stop anyone from going to him to listen to what he says?

Talebul No one will go to him. None. All of you here, do bear one thing in mind. Don't invite trouble for yourselves by listening to this blasphemer. Always remember the Great Deluge.

Araj Maulana Saheb, don't you remember that in the flood meant for destroying evil, innocent animals also got drowned?

Talebul Just see for yourselves. He is now criticizing the holy flood of Nuh.[45]

Karim So what? Don't pay any heed to what he says!

Lights dim on them all.

In the midst of crashes of thunder, flashes of lightning, and wailing of the storm, **Araj** *is heard shouting, "Lalmonebibi, Salehabibi, hold them down! Hold them down! My books are all being blown away! Where are the children? Save my books. Grab them. Hold them tight to your bosom. Alas! Alas! My treasures of so many years are all getting blown away! Bibijans, save them! Save my books!" Bibijans and children scream; some of them run on-and-off stage in an effort to grab the torn pages. When lights come on, wet pages are seen strewn about on stage. Like a mad man,* **Araj** *enters picking up the pages and clutching them to his bosom. He breaks down in grief.*

Araj Alas, you Nor'wester! Thus have you swept away all my darlings!

Lights brighten. Enter **Talebul***.*

Talebul Can you all hear me? I was talking about Noah's flood, wasn't I? Last night's flood was like Noah's flood. In this way the Holy Allah cautions all infidels. Just see how the books, which turned you into a *kaafir,*[46] have all been blown away by a strong gale. Just see, how the pages of your books are rolling about in the street, waiting to be trampled underfoot. What more proof of Allah's power do you need to believe in Him? Throw away. Throw those pages away.

Araj Why do you belittle Allah, dear Sir? Allah is no fool!

Talebul What do you mean?

Araj Of all the books the cyclone has blown away, each has plenty of copies in the libraries across the country. So, what's your point now?

Talebul The storm was a sign, a divine sign.

Araj A madrasa building in Ulalbatina village has also crumbled down in the storm. What divine sign is that?

Talebul You have become a son of the devil. No one can make you turn around. But, before I go, I tell you this. You will have no one by your side in the false pursuit you've undertaken. All will oppose you. You won't succeed. All your work will be ruined by Allah. You'll become a living corpse, burning within.

Araj *and* **Taleb** *go off in opposite directions.*

Scene Seventeen

Jahan Ali *crosses over from one side of the stage in a gesture to leave, when* **Karim** *suddenly appears before him.*

Jahan Salamalekum, Huzoor.

Fazlu Walaikum assalam. Fazlul Karim, a magistrate. Are you Araj Ali?

Jahan No, Sir. I am Jahan Ali. I lead the prayer in a *masjid* at Lamchari.

Fazlu That means you are an Imam. Do you happen to know Araj Ali? I come here looking for him.

Jahan Oh yes, Sir! He is very close to me. Once upon a time I was part of the Chorus in his band of singers.

Fazlu Chorus in a musical band? Then you must be a singer besides being an Imam!

Jahan No, Sir. I became an Imam after quitting singing.

Fazlu I see. It is like the case of bandit Nizam. He became an ascetic after giving up robbery.

Jahan Yes Sir. So was it with Valmiki, the legendary author of the *Ramayana*.[47]

Fazlu How could an Imam utter the name of this inauspicious book? You have sullied your sanctity by taking that name. Go wash up again before you lead the prayer. I'll be waiting in my boat. If you find Araj Ali, do send him there. I've left the message at his home, too.

*Enter **Araj** from one side of the stage.*

Araj Assalamalekum, Huzoor.

Fazlu Walaikum assalam. I am Fazlul Karim, a magistrate.

Araj Yes Sir. We have heard so much about you. But we never had the opportunity to see you.

Fazlu I have also heard that name for quite some time. Araj Ali Matabbar. He walked seven miles to reach the town, and read books in different libraries there. Are you the one?

Araj Yes, Sir.

Fazlu Of which village are you the chief or Matabbar?

Araj That is my family name.

Fazlu "Matabbar" can never be a family name. It is a title conferred by the government.

Araj There has been some misunderstanding, Your Honor. It is not "Matabbar,"[48] but "Matubbor"; though there is no harm with "Matabbar" either. I have the necessary government approval to use the title, "Matabbar."

Fazlu Let it be. I don't like arguments. From today on, you won't use the name "Matubbor." That's it.

Araj I won't use my family name? What sort of a law is this, Sir?

Fazlu What do you understand of the law? Law is to be mastered by passing a number of exams. What do you understand of the law?

Araj You teach me, please.

Fazlu All I had heard about you is true, I see. You are an ignorant, arrogant anarchist. Do you think by merely rubbing shoulders with the likes of Mr. Morris of the Christian Mission and Professor Kazi Golam Kadir of the Brajmahan College, you have become a big shot?

Araj If I have broken any law, then I shall accept any punishment that you give me.

Fazlu What you have been doing in the name of Science is a nuisance ... but tell me first, are you a Mussalman?

Araj When my ancestors have been Mussalmans, how can I say that I am not one, Sir?

Fazlu Do you believe in the Quran?

Araj Yes Sir, I believe in it. But only as much as I understand it in Bengali. I don't understand Arabic. How can I follow something that I don't understand?

Fazlu Then perhaps within a few days you'll refuse to follow anything! Have you heard what Quaed-e-Azam Muhammad Ali Jinnah said? Urdu and Urdu shall be the state language of Pakistan. Within a few days all will be in Urdu. All rules, all laws, everything will be in Urdu. Then won't you follow the Urdu laws?

Araj I wish to understand the established ideas and notions of our society in the light of truth. I'm not against religion. But it is also true that when I look at religion, philosophy, and science, all of them together, certain questions crop up in my mind.

Fazlu Let me know what your questions are.

Araj Sir, is Allah embodied or disembodied?

Fazlu Of course He is disembodied.

Araj And the life within us?

Fazlu That's disembodied, too.

Araj What differences are there between the two disembodied things then?

Fazlu (*after thinking for a while*) There's no difference.

Araj No difference between Life and Allah?

Fazlu (*after a long brooding pause*) Are all your questions of the same type?

Araj Try me.

Fazlu Forget your thoughts and queries and do something. Come to the

Tabligh Jamat,[49] and stay there for forty days. If the Holy Allah wishes, then you shall find your answers within yourself.

Araj If a child cries from hunger, what's the use of putting him off to sleep? After he wakes up, he will surely start crying again. If I could myself provide answers to my questions, all my worries would have been over by now.

Fazlu How many questions do you have?

Araj Many, Sir.

Fazlu Do you have a list of them?

Araj Yes Sir, I have. Please let me bring the bundle of papers from home.

Fazlu I don't have much time today. You can send them over to my office. I'll answer your questions at the earliest opportunity.

Araj That would be great, Sir.

Fazlu Is there any toilet in the neighborhood?

A person enters.

Person Sir, use my home toilet, please. (**Fazlul** *starts walking. The others follow him.* **Fazlul** *stops.*)

Fazlu Do all of you need to relieve yourselves along with me?

Person We'll just show you the place, Sir.

All exit. At this juncture, the **2nd officer** *from the Police Station comes in with a* **Constable**.

2nd Officer Beware, beware, and don't try to escape. Cordon off the whole area.

Constable Are you mad, Sir? How can I do the job alone?

2nd Officer I am looking for the Matabbar of this village. Who amongst you is a Matabbar?

Constable What a question to ask! You should have brought a sketch of the man. Here, all are ordinary. Is the Matabbar an ordinary person, too?

Karim (*enters*) Mr. Officer-in-Charge …

Constable You've made a mistake. This gentleman here is not the Officer-in-Charge; he is the 2nd Officer.

2nd Officer Why do you talk so much for nothing?

Karim Mr. 2nd Officer, there are only two Matabbars here. One is by deed; the other is by name. Whom have you come for?

2nd Officer We have heard that he is in the habit of asking weird questions. And ... there's a sort of weirdness in what you say. You, please come with me. Our Superintendent of Police wants to meet you.

Karim Now I know who you are searching for. I'll go and bring him soon.

Constable On this pretext where do you plan to go, mister? Do you think I am an idiot? Do you have any idea of my length of service? For eighteen years I have been in this job as a constable. You can't give me a slip so easily, can you? Not that easily.

Karim My guess seems correct. Tell me the name of the person you are looking for.

2nd Officer Araj Ali Matubbor.

Karim You have come looking for Araj Ali Matubbor, then why do you ask for the Matabbar of the village?

Constable When his name ends with "Matubbor," then the matter is clear, Mr. Matabbar.

Karim No, that doesn't necessarily make the person a Matabbar. His name is not "Matabbar," but "Matubbor." That is in fact a title to his name, though uttered at the end. A family name often has a title. Do you understand?

Constable You'd better make the higher authorities understand this difference. I had said earlier ...

2nd Officer What?

Constable No, Sir. It was you who had once said that a Matubbor by name must be a Matabbar of his village.

Karim You please wait. I am sending for him. (*He speaks to a young man offstage.*) Enter through the back of the house and get Araj fast. (*The man offstage says "Yes, sure!"*)

Constable I suppose you haven't given him any plans to escape?

Karim Araj is not the escaping type. But why are you looking for him? Has he done anything wrong?

2nd Officer No, he has done no wrong. The Superintendent of Police wants to meet him; so we have come to take him there.

Constable Sir, will you come this way, please? (*Moves away to a vacant spot.*) The S.P. has ordered us to bring him in handcuffs. But you are saying that you have come to invite the man for a meeting with him? Why don't you take the orders of the higher-ups seriously, Sir?

2nd Officer If you understood that, you would be the 2nd Officer.

Constable The higher authority denied me promotion for a minor dereliction of duty. Why do you add salt to the wound? You could just clarify why you were altering the orders of your boss, period.

2nd Officer Once the people of this village come to know that we are here to arrest one of their own, they may resist us. If they resist, then no guns and batons will help. They will beat us down to a pulp. This is a strategic move. We shall arrest him as soon as we are on the boat.

Constable That's wonderful! You are a discerning man. Look, I was getting worried for nothing. But you should have told me this earlier. Hey … hey … (*He sees* **Araj** *coming.*) There he is. Sir, the accused is here.

2nd Officer Ah! If you call him the accused, we stand exposed!

Constable No, I won't say it again. Never again. Sir, the person whom S.P. Sir has invited is right here.

Araj *enters.*

Araj I heard that you were looking for me?

2nd Officer So, you are Araj Ali Matubbor?

Araj Yes.

2nd Officer You have already met Magistrate Fazlul Karim, right? He has told the S.P. about you. That's why the S.P. Sahib wants to meet you. Please take the trouble to come with us.

Constable Just walk up to the river bank; we shall take care of you from there.

The band of singers begin their song.

Song
  Araj Ali thinks, thinks high and low.
  He's been summoned, why, he had to know.
  Araj Ali thinks, thinks high and low.

None can tie him down, he's tied to truth,
Bind him with logic, or nothing forsooth.
S.P. Sahib summons him; but why, he had to know.
Araj Ali thinks, thinks high and low.

Scene Eighteen

The **Superintendent of Police (S.P.)** *and* **Araj** *are on stage.*

S.P. You are a Communist, aren't you?

Araj What does a man have to do to become a Communist, Sir?

S.P. First, one comes in contact with the Party.

Araj Over the last two days your constables have dug through my entire life—past, present, and even future. Have they found my connection with any party whatsoever?

S.P. No, they have not.

Araj Then how can I be a Communist, Sir?

S.P. Have you read Marx and Engels?

Araj I suppose the papers that you hold in your hand, have been given to you by Mr. Fazlul Karim? Those were written by me, Sir. Have you read them all?

S.P. No. But I've read most of them.

Araj In whatever you have read thus far, did you find any reference to Marx and Engels?

S.P. No, I did not.

Araj Then Sir, how can I be a Communist?

S.P. All right, I accept that you are not a Communist. But a serious charge still remains against you, that of treason. You have been inciting innocent villagers against long-held religious beliefs and therefore against the law and order of the land.

Araj I have not incited anyone, Sir. I only try to share with others whatever I have learnt from books on science and philosophy.

S.P. What have you studied of science?

Araj Geology, Biology, Astronomy. These books are also taught in schools and colleges. If I tell people something from these books, then what's the harm, Sir?

S.P. Who have authored these books?

Araj Ramendra Sundar Tribedi, Sir Jagadish Chandra Bose, Khagendra Nath Mitra, Rabindranath Tagore, Amal Dasgupta, Debiprasad ...

S.P. But all are Hindus! Do they write anything against Pakistan?

Araj No Sir. But they try to get at what is Truth.

S.P. What is Truth?

Araj That which can be proved.

S.P. Hmm. Who gave you these books?

Araj Many people, Sir. Barisal Public Library, Shankar Library—I go to such places to study. Professor Kazi Golam Kadir of B.M. College, Mr. Morris of Mission Library, they are all like my friends. They help me by lending these books.

S.P. But you are a mere peasant. You have studied till Class II. How could you be friends with such people? Especially Mr. Morris? He is a Christian. Does he talk religion with you with the intent to convert our people to Christianity?

Araj Sir, you are an S.P. And to become an S.P. you certainly had to read many books authored by Christian scholars? While reading those books, did you ever feel they were written with a view to turning Muslims into Christians?

S.P. You argue too much!

Araj Is that bad, Sir? Logic is the real thing. Without reasoning and proof how do you know what is right and what is wrong?

S.P. I fail to understand if you are really guilty or not. I am in a great dilemma now.

Araj There can never be two truths about a subject, existing at the same time. Either I am guilty, or I am not. That's it. When you cannot prove my guilt, then I am not guilty. Do you accept this?

S.P. But what Fazlul Saheb said was serious enough. You have kind of challenged the faith of the people. And if the book that you have written is published, it will strike a great blow to the religion of the land. But because you are yet to get it printed, you can't be pulled up for trial on that ground right now.

Araj Then Sir, please let me go.

S.P. After going through what you have written and after paying heed to whatever Fazlul Sahib said about you, I have come to the conclusion that you are a very dangerous man. You look for reasons in everything. But one thing you have to bear in mind, Mr. Matubbor, that in religious matters faith is greater than reason. Never try to go against the faith of the people. I am going to release you, but on one condition.

Araj What's the condition, Sir?

S.P. You have to give an undertaking that though you may read as much as you like, you will not preach what you read. The manuscript that I have in my hands will never be published, and you shall write no books, henceforth. If you still do, or if you preach the public in an assembly, then a criminal suit will restart against you. Are you ready to give this undertaking?

Araj If I don't give it, Sir?

S.P. You will be taken into custody for three months, beginning now, and in these three months, the necessary proof will be gathered against you to keep you behind bars for as long as I desire.

Araj *thinks over it for some time.*

Araj All right, Sir. So be it. I shall not spread around the knowledge I glean. I shall not write another book, or get it published.

S.P. Very good.

Lights dim.

Scene Nineteen

Araj *is alone on stage. Enter* **Talebul**.

Talebul How are you, Araj Ali?

Araj I am fine, Sir.

Talebul That's a lie, Araj. You are not fine. I keep track of everything you do. Didn't I tell you once that without Allah's grace you'll never succeed in anything you do? You shall never get anyone on your side?

Haven't my words come true? Now you are bound hand and foot by your own undertaking. The Christian libraries are also closed to you. You can't see the esteemed masters and professors in town. The Khodatallah[50] has tied you up with His ropes.

Araj I can't find any such ropes! It is the Government that has pinned me down. Is the Government Allah, Sir?

Talebul *Tauba*, *Tauba*, why should the Government be Allah? It's a medium. The medium of Allah. There's time yet, Araj. Recite *Tauba*.[51] Come back to the Divine Path.

Araj So that you get your reward in Paradise, right? That's the only reason why you're asking me to read *Tauba*, isn't it?

Talebul You needn't worry about my fate. If you read *Tauba*, you'll also go to Paradise.

Araj You are vainly trying to hold me from my work, Sir. Whatever I earned over the last eight years, I have distributed equally amongst my ten children. Now I have nothing that I can call my own. Not here, nor hereafter. I am happy ... But I have some dreams yet. From now on, whatever I earn through my work shall be used to build a library in this village. And I shall try to arrange scholarships for poor students.

Talebul You'll build a library in the village? Your library will remain unused. The books will gather layers of dust; not a single person will enter that library. If you don't come back to the Path of Allah, no parents will accept your scholarships for their children, no matter how poor they might be. Read *Tauba*.

Araj What grave sin have I committed, Sir, that you are repeatedly asking me to read *Tauba*?

Talebul The list of your sins is too long. The entire Lamchari village is shaking under the weight of your sin, and you can't find your sin? Go home. Get ideas of libraries and scholarships out of your head. The *Tauba* comes first. You'll find no salvation otherwise. Now go.

Lights dim.

Scene Twenty

Masked dancers dance. Dark night. **Araj Ali***'s wife comes on stage. She is searching for someone. She has grown older. Her hair is turning grey. Her clothes, mannerisms, and speech tell of her advancing years.*

Lalmone Where are you? Where have you gone? Just a while ago you were sitting here ... Esharon's father, hey Esharon's father![52]

An elderly **Araj Ali** *walks slowly on to stage.*

Lalmone Where were you?

Araj Just there.

Lalmone Where?

Araj Suddenly I saw out there a firefly going round and round over the same spot. I felt its two tiny wings had perhaps caught against something. Its companions all flitted away. The lone firefly, blinking its light, was trying hard to free its wings. My heart wept for it. I ran to set it free. The closer I went, the more the light took on a greenish tinge. Then it looked almost like a ball of fire and grew in size. When I went up really close, I saw that I was mistaken. It was no firefly. It was the light of a lamp lit in the house of Vasan Kamla. Who knows why the lamp was burning in his house at that time of night?

Lalmone Today your mind is so restless that it seems to be fluttering like the wings of the trapped butterfly. Since your return from the Barisal Magistrate's jail, you have passed most of your time sitting quietly in this yard. But I have never seen you so perturbed. Esharon's father, what's wrong?

Araj Nothing, Bibijan. You go to sleep.

Lalmone You come, too.

Araj I'll come when I feel sleepy.

Lalmone (*after a long pause*) When you spoke of the firefly with its captive wings, I don't know why I felt that you were talking about yourself.

Araj What did you say, dear? The firefly was me? Then what is it that clips my wings? Which invisible net ... (*Pause.*) Bibijan,[53] it's past midnight. Go to sleep.

Lalmone *rises and goes inside.* **Araj Ali** *sits there for a while. Then he* *stands up and grows restless. He takes some papers out of his drawer and his pen. Slowly he removes the cap of the pen and begins to write. After a while,* **Lalmonessa** *comes back in and snatches the pen away from his hand.*

Lalmone What are you doing? Are you writing again?

Araj I must write what I feel people should know.

Lalmone Seeing you so restless I knew that you were burning with the desire to write again. But you will put yourself in danger by doing so; you will ruin the whole family.

Araj You compared me to a firefly with two clipped wings. Do you know what the wings are stuck to? It's fear; I am caught in the net of fear. But I must not fear anyone. There are many things I need to tell my people. Please give my pen back, Bibijan.

Lalmone No. You should not invite danger for all of us.

Araj What danger? All I owned I have distributed among you all. You have no want now.

Lalmone Yes. You have provided for us all, and secured our future. But is that all that binds us together? If you are in danger, am I not in danger, too?

Araj But all my life I have yearned for truth and found some. If I keep it to myself, if I don't share it with others, then that will be the worst sin ever! Please give me back my pen, dear.

Lalmone In whose heart would you sow the seed of truth? Who is waiting for the light of truth? What Maulana Talebul Mokam said is right. No one is or will ever be with you in your search for truth. Your relatives, your neighbors—all will turn away from you. And at every step Satan-Iblish[54] will play his game of death with you. Hasn't it always been this way?

Araj Maulana Talebul Mokam has won you over, too, I see? I have really lost my dear wife. I stand defeated. Now I feel that death, when it comes, is welcome.

Araj *hangs his head in distress.* **Lalmone** *is deeply agonized. Her eyes brim with tears. She wipes her tears.*

Lalmone Swear on my life that you shall not write a single more line.

Araj *sinks down gradually, sitting on the floor. He feels his whole body* *going numb.* **Nakai Chandal** *walks past him, saying, "What is Bau wind, Araj? Did you ever find the answer?"* **Araj** *struggles to rise, but he dashes up against an invisible wall, and falls down. He groans.*

Lalmone What's wrong with you?

Araj A huge curtain, Bibijan. From the ground it rises high up, as high as you can see, a huge curtain. Just like the bioscope screen. Black grimacing faces are squirming about on it. Their eyes are red. With disdain they tell me, "We are as old as the ancient world; you can't drive us out." I will, dear wife, I will drive them out. I beg of you, Lalmonessa Bibi, please let me break the vow I had made to you and write. Bibijan, I have to drive the *Bau* wind off the people's minds. Please let me write. I'll write books that my people will read gathering in each other's yards. Then the huge screen with the squirming faces on it will vanish at the wink of an eye. Please let me write …

Lalmone No one can stop you from anything that you decide to do. You write whatever you like.

Lalmonnessa *helps Araj into his chair.* **Araj** *starts writing.* **Lalmone** *goes in.* **Araj** *keeps writing till the break of day.*

Early morning. **Kazi Golam Saheb** *comes in.*

Araj Isn't it Kazi Golam Kadir Saheb? How are you?

Kazi I am fine. Came around to see you. Haven't met you for about a couple of weeks.

Araj It's great that you have come, Kazi Saheb. Had you not come today, I would have gone over myself. See, this is my latest essay. I wrote it over the whole last night.

Kazi You have started writing again? What about your undertaking?

Araj I was feeling very restless. Can't afford to remain scared of a piece of paper my whole life. My mind wouldn't be at rest unless I wrote. I was suffocating within. This essay is the fruit of that pain—"Superstition and its True Meaning." You take it.

Kazi Why do you give it to me? Keep it well hidden. Otherwise, you might be in danger.

Araj I am giving it to you for safekeeping. If it is with you, there are two advantages. It will be in the safe hands and your comments, after you have read it, will help me improve on it. (*He breaks into laughter.*)

Kazi Ah, I came to see this genial laughter.

Araj Today I laughed after ages. Here, take it.

Kazi   Do you know what I feel at this moment, Matubbor Saheb?

Araj What?

Kazi I feel as if I am Galileo's favorite pupil, Andrea. In my hand is the manuscript of *Discorsi*. It has fallen upon Andrea to take it out of Italy and spread the message across Europe. But don't worry. I won't do that. Apart from a few very close people, like Shamsul Haque, I shall not share this essay with anyone else. (**Araj** *is somewhat saddened.*) What's wrong?

Araj No, nothing as such. Only a few people will see my piece. But those who really need to see and need to know will never get to see it.

Kazi Don't be sad, Matubbor Saheb. A big change is in the offing. Our liberation from West Pakistan is just round the corner. Once we gain freedom, who is there to stop us? Not only in this country, but your essay will be read by people all over the world.

Araj Kazi Saheb, I also wait with bated breath for that moment. When will our Liberation come about? Liberation!

Song of Liberation.

Song
>   Lift off your anchor, boatman,
>   Unfurl your sails, boatman.
>   Tides are high in the river.
>   Tides are high in the river.
>   Heyia ho, heyia ho.

Scene Twenty One

Some days have passed. The office of the Al Amin Press. **Araj** *is seated, reading the proofs of his book.*

Araj Jabbar Mia Saheb, hey Jabbar Mia Saheb. Please come here once. (**Jabbar** *comes in.*)

Jabbar Yes—is there any major error?

Araj I can find no errors. That's why I called you in. Now I understand why the Al Amin Press is so renowned. Your compositors do almost error-free work. Only they are a bit weak with their "n's." Every time they have spelt "pranam" with a soft "n."[55]

Jabbar Don't worry. I'll read the proofs again after you finish, and before I send it for printing. I have given my word to Shamsul Haque Saheb that there will be no printing errors in this book. I will see it through myself. Won't Haque Saheb be coming?

Araj He has a couple of classes. He will come after that.

Jabbar You are really fortunate, Matubbor Saheb, to have made Haque Saheb's acquaintance—such a great personality.

Enter two young men looking like mullahs.

1st Person Assalamulaikum, Jabbar Saheb.

Jabbar Walaikum assalam. How are you?

2nd Person Fine, by the grace of Allah. How is your health?

Jabbar I am all right.

1st Person How about the job? Is it done, or still pending? We told you that the job was urgent.

Jabbar The composing is over. Wait, I'll bring the proofs.

2nd Person Marhaba, marhaba![56] Bring it fast.

Jabbar *goes out.*

1st Person (*looking at* **Araj**) You are perhaps Araj Ali Matubbor of Lamchari village, aren't you? Heard of your reputation as a surveyor. Our boss is very happy with your work.

2nd Person We have also heard that in spite of being an ordinary farmer, you are deeply concerned about your community. Now, you are trying to build a library in the village, aren't you? But a library in a village—will it be to educate the cattle? If you build a mosque instead of a library that would be a pious deed and you shall be rewarded for that in Heaven.

Araj Building another mosque in our village will not be a pious act, Maulana Saheb.

2nd Person (*shouting*) Building a holy mosque is an act of sin, you mean? What you are saying is sheer blasphemy!

Araj Our Lamchari is such a tiny village. There are already eleven mosques there. In some of them, on Jumma[57] days, *muslis* are not available. If I build *another* pukka mosque, then the mosque next door will become irrelevant eventually. If I become the cause of a mosque's forced closure, then won't Keramon[58] note it down as a sin? Tell me.

2nd Person Then choose the village next to yours.

Araj That village is no different in this respect.

2nd Person Then the *next* village.

1st Person Mian Nausher Gazi, we haven't come here to argue with him. We are here to do our own job. We heard that you are getting a book published, "The Quest for Truth?" Does the Truth need to be searched for? We have always known that Truth is self-evident.

Araj I see that you know many things about me. But I don't know yet who you gentlemen are.

1st Person You are publishing a book on Truth, and you don't know the men in the world of Truth? But how would you know? Your days are spent reading books.

2nd Person (*takes away the proofs from* **Araj**'*s hands*) Matubbor Saheb, I have read books weighing more than seven or eight times your body weight. Even then, I have not ventured into the writing world. What do you know of Truth that you are publishing a book on it?

Araj Maulana Saheb, a book cannot be valued by its weight. If it were, then Rabindranath's *Gitanjali*[59] wouldn't have got the Nobel Prize. It would have been won by P. M. Bagchi's *Panjika*![60]

1st Person You talk too much. Do you know that in Allah's durbar[61] every word will have to be accounted for? Please stop. What Truth does your book search for?

Araj The Truth that is not superstition, or any imposition.

1st Person That's wonderful! Can we see the book?

Araj It is not all printed yet.

2nd Person The portion that is … (**1st Person** *shuts him up by putting his hand over his mouth.*)

1st Person (*takes* **Araj**'*s proofs in his hand*) The portion that's left must not go in for printing right now.

Araj Sir! What did you say?

1st Person No. What I meant to say is that first let us read the portion that has been printed, to see whether the whole book is fit for publication.

Araj WHAT HAVE YOU COME HERE FOR?

2nd Person The reason why … (*He is stopped by* **1st Person**.)

1st Person The reasons are noble, indeed. In your book, there is libelous and provocative content. The matter has come to the notice of our Superior. He wants to examine such contents, and so we are taking this copy to him.

Araj But what connection is there between his scrutiny of it and my printing?

1st Person Permission. The question is one of permission. If these portions of your book are damaging enough to the Muslim community, then he may not grant you the permission to publish it at all!

Araj Then, before you leave, you must also hear what I have to say on this. I will not wait for your Superior's permission. I shall carry on with the printing.

1st Person Be quiet! Without Sir's permission there will be no further printing!

Araj But why do I have to obey you when what you say is unlawful?

1st Person It has to be like that. (*Grabs* **Araj** *by the throat.*) Otherwise you will go to Hell. Say "I shall not do anything other than land survey work! I shall not read or write any book!" Till you say so, you'll not be released! You'll die like this!

One of them throws him to the ground and kicks him. The other tears off **Araj**'*s shirt. The voice of* **Golam Kadir** *is heard from outside.*

Kadir (*entering*) Who is there? What are you doing?

The youths run away. **Kadir** *comes over to find that it is* **Araj**.

Matubbor Saheb, you! Why were they beating you like that? (*Looks outside.*) Jabbar Mian Saheb! Are you there? Come here quickly! (**Kadir** *helps* **Araj** *to his feet.* **Shamsul Haque** *and* **Jabbar** *come in running.*)

Kadir and Jabbar What has happened?

Kadir Some people were beating up Matubbor Saheb. Had I not happened to arrive here, he would perhaps have been killed.

Jabbar Now I really have to stop the printing. They were professional killers. If I continue to print, they will not spare Matubbor Saheb.

Araj My book will not be printed then? What if I die? My book must be published.

The Band starts singing.

> To take Truth to all, Araj Ali's all set.
> He made it to the capital, to print the book,
> Araj got it done; Araj got it printed.
> Araj had a dream to educate Lamchari,
> So did he start building a library.
> Araj brought in light, light Araj gave;
> During his lifetime
> He made for his own grave.
> Listen to his last words, Araj the brave.

Lalmonnessa *and the* **Compère** *join the others on stage.* **Araj** *comes to stand in the center.*

Araj My father had ten *bighas* of land. That, too, was taken away by a greedy money lender. Our modest homestead had to be auctioned away. My Mother suffered a lot to bring me up. I took a photograph of her face as she died and that made many of you refuse her the last rites. Everybody has to leave some day. That is the law of nature. It is almost time for me to depart now. During my lifetime, I had my burial done. How? I kept my hair, teeth, and nails in a jar, and then had them buried. You must be wondering what sort of a burial that might be. But why? A person's last remains are buried in his grave. I also had my last remains buried. I'd have nothing left with me hereafter ... I have spent everything building up a library, and creating some scholarships for our poor little ones. Now I donate my body to the Barisal Medical College. After much consideration, I have taken this decision. It will not be changed. All the accounts are here in this notebook.

Araj *hands over a notebook to the* **Compère**.

Compère (*reads out the deed*) Recipient on behalf of the Government of Bangladesh, Respected Principal of Barisal Sher-e-Bangla Medical College. Donor, Araj Ali Matubbor (Village—Lamchari; District—Barisal; Religious affiliation—Mussalman; Occupation—farming). By this document, I pledge to donate my body, after my death, to the

Barisal Sher-e-Bangla Medical College, for the noble cause of medical science. My family members have no objection to it. Let it also be known that my two eyes shall go to the Eye Bank. Hereby, I, in full senses and good health, and voluntarily do complete and sign this deed of donation. December, 5 1981; 19th Aghrahayan,[62] 1388. Signed, Araj Ali Matubbor.

The end

Acknowledgment

Mosharraf Karim wrote the lyrics of the songs used in the original Bengali version of the play.

Notes

1   Araj Ali was born in 1900 and died in 1985.
2   The ninth month in the Bengali calendar (mid-December to mid-January).
3   Taro root.
4   One species of jasmine.
5   A two-string musical instrument popular in rural Bengal/Bangladesh.
6   Islamic greeting.
7   Reciprocation of that greeting.
8   This implies class inequality: a lower-class person is not greeted thus.
9   Glory to God!
10 An Arabic phrase to appreciate God for a person or a thing.
11 Bengali year (1912, by the Gregorian calendar).
12 A Bengali adage.
13 The second Bengali vowel, or the second letter in the Bengali *Swarabarna* alphabet (আ).
14 The twenty-fifth Bengali consonant, or the twenty-fifth letter in the Bengali *Byanjanbarna* alphabet (ম).
15 (Var., "Bhabi") Wife of an elder brother or an endearing and respectful address to a married woman.
16 The chief executive of a Zamindar (landlord).
17 Husband's brother or cousin (male).
18 Master.
19 The Bengali alphabet book.
20 "Junior" is used in this order in most South Asian countries.
21 Watchman.
22 Soldier.
23 Mother (-in-law).
24 The learning of Arabic was/is considered obligatory (*wajib*) for a Muslim to understand the Quran, originally written in Arabic, and the recitation of

the religious text without understanding its meaning was/is not considered a meritorious act. During the reform of Islam in colonial/pre-partition India, the recitation was taken as more important than the understanding of meaning for a section of Muslims who did not know Arabic, but must learn the language. Mankeer and Nankeer, angels who test the faith of the dead in their graves before the Day of Judgment, were/are believed to give them meanings of the Arabic words unknown to them until their death.

25   A local police station.
26   A bard.
27   Unit of measuring land.
28   Father.
29   An affectionate, respectful suffix to a female name during address.
30   In some parts of South Asia, turmeric paste (*haldi*) is applied over the bride's face and arms (basically to make her skin glow) a day before wedding, and henna (*mehendi*) designs form part of the bridal make-up.
31   People in rural Bengal used to, and many still do, chew betel leaf (*paan*) with areca nuts, and flavored tobacco (*zarda*), especially after lunch and dinner.
32   A Hindu funeral custom, people carrying the dead to the crematorium keep chanting the name of Hari (Lord Krishna) all the way.
33   A daughter-in-law.
34   Wife.
35   A close neighbor, or a male friend, is often addressed as "brother" in large parts of South Asia.
36   Sister's husband.
37   A lakh is one hundred thousand.
38   "Lungi" is a long piece of cloth worn around the waist by many South Asian men. "Kurta" is a long loose shirt worn with it, or with pajamas.
39   Ishwar Chandra Bandopadhyay (1820–91) was a key figure of the Bengal Renaissance. He received the title "Vidayasagar" (lit. "ocean of knowledge") from the Sanskrit College, Kolkata (Calcutta).
40   *Jari gan* (song) is an indigenous music form in Bangladesh, thematically drawing mostly on Islamic legends.
41   Washing the body of the dead before burial is part of Islamic last rites.
42   Disciples.
43   A Sufi guru.
44   "Hadish" (var. Hadith) is a collection of Prophet Muhammad's teachings, apart from the Quran. "Shariyat" (var. Shariat/Sharia) is a body of Islamic laws prescribing duties and punishments for a Muslim.
45   Noah.
46   Infidel.
47   One of the two famous (Hindu) epics from India. It is said that Valmiki was a robber before his transformation into a sage-poet.
48   Literally, a leader.
49   Formed in 1927 in north India, Tabligh Jamat is an Islamic religious

movement primarily aimed at spiritual reformation. Here it refers to one of its occasional congregations.

50   Allah.
51   Prayers of repentance.
52   Traditionally, South Asian wives do not take the names of their husbands out of "respect."
53   Wife.
54   In Islam, the devil is known as Iblis(h).
55   There are two "n's" in the Bengali alphabet (ন, pronounced with tongue on the teeth, and ণ, with tongue on the roof of the mouth).
56   An Arabic/Islamic greeting meaning "welcome." Here it means "Great! Great!"
57   Friday, the day for prayers in the mosque.
58   A scribe who is believed to record the sins committed by a Muslim.
59   Bengali writer Rabindranath Tagore's *Gitanjali* (1912) earned him the Nobel Prize for Literature in 1913.
60   A handbook for practicing Hindus, mentioning details of the day, time, and manners for observance of auspicious occasions.
61   The Holy Court of Allah.
62   The eighth month in the Bengali calendar.

Plays from India

The Djinns of Eidgah

by
Abhishek Majumdar

Gar firdaus bar roo-e zameen ast, Hameen ast-o hameen ast-o hameen ast.
(*If there is a paradise on earth, it is here, it is here, it is here*)
—Emperor Jahangir on Kashmir, quoting Sufi poet Amir Khusro

Characters

Abbajaan *Father to* **Bilal** *and* **Ashrafi**. *Aged between 45 and 50.*

Ashrafi *A young girl, aged 14. Suffers from post-traumatic stress disorder.*

Bilal *A young boy, aged 17. Ashrafi's elder brother and a star footballer in Kashmir.*

Dr. Baig *Head of Government Psychiatry Hospital, Srinagar. Male, aged 60.*

Dr. Wani *A doctor at the same hospital as Dr. Baig. Female, aged 27.*

Junaid/Pareen *Dr. Baig's son, a* **Djinn** *now, stuck in limbo after his death as his father refuses to read the final prayers for him. A boy who took up arms against "Indian Occupation." Male, aged 25.*

Khaled *Bilal's friend and a fellow footballer. Male, aged 17.*

Mushtaq *A young man, ex-footballer, who is also a guide to the rising football players in Kashmir. Works with protesters to organize large protests during curfews. Male, aged 30.*

S1 *A soldier in India's Central Reserve Police Force (CRPF). Male, aged around 45.*

S2 *A younger CRPF soldier. Male, aged between 20 and 25.*

Notes on the stage setting of the play: *The settings of the rooms have been suggested keeping real rooms in mind. However, the play can also be performed in an empty space with minimum furniture.*

Dr. Baig's *room could be done with just three chairs and a partition.* **Ashrafi**'s *house with only a mattress. The CRPF picket with only a picture of a god on a wall and barbed wire. The mortuary with many suggestions of bodies.*

The playwright recommends the maximum use of empty space, and of set-pieces that are almost transient in nature, as an essential ingredient of the play.

Scene One

A deep red Kashmiri carpet on stage. Another red carpet of exactly the same design but much larger suspended at an angle in the space. The carpets have floral designs on them. The carpet on the floor has **Abbajaan,**[1] **Ashrafi** *and* **Bilal***, sitting on their knees, looking at each other and smiling. Their clothes are spotlessly white.*

There are two pillows on the carpet. One small and another slightly bigger. They are both green in colour with black lace-work around their borders. The scene is lit in blue. The light must bounce off the clothes of the actors. The suspended carpet is lit to bring out the redness of the red.

Abbajaan *gestures to the children, suggesting that they should get their pillows. They get their pillows and put them on* **Abbajaan**'s *lap as he sits cross-legged. They lie down facing up, looking at him. He smiles.*

Abbajaan Which one?

Ashrafi The one in which … … the one about Hamza and the flying lamps.

Bilal No … no … no (*Hits* **Ashrafi** *on the head.*) We just did that one yesterday. Abbu, the one in which Hamza tries to break the illusion …

Ashrafi (*hitting* **Bilal** *back*) But Hamza tries to break the illusion in every Dastaan![2]

Bilal Yes, but he never succeeds, does he?

Abbajaan OK … OK … OK … Shhh … Now both of you close your eyes … and we will see. If you sleep, we can have everything in our Dastaan ... The flying lamps and also Hamza trying to break the illusion of war ... and if all goes well, insha'Allah even succeeding at it.

Ashrafi (*smiling and excited*) Really ... Abbu ... Can we have anything we want in our story?

Abbajaan Yes anything. Anything that you want but only if you are good children ... (*Like a proverb.*) If the children are good, the Dastaan becomes the blanket.

Bilal and **Ashrafi** (*quickly shutting their eyes*) And if the children are bad, the Dastaan becomes the chilling wind ...

Silence. **Abbajaan** *looks at them. The children pretend to shut their eyes but keep opening them to look at* **Abbajaan**. **Abbajaan** *looks at them and smiles. Looks up slowly.*

As he looks up, the children open their eyes as well and look at the ceiling.

Abbajaan Dastaan ... Dastaan ...

Bilal and **Ashrafi** Dastaan ... Dastaan ... (*They laugh out in excitement.*)

Abbajaan Long, long ago ... in a place that is much like today. In a place much like this, in the year of the Saturn ... there lived the general of the prophet/

Bilal and **Ashrafi** The king ... the prophet.

Beat.

Abbajaan And there was his general.

Bilal The gallant Amir Hamza.

Ashrafi (*pointing at* **Bilal**) HAMZAAAAAAAHHHH ... (*She smiles.*)

Abbajaan Shhh ...

The children pretend to sleep again.

Abbajaan ... and Hamza, the general of the army of the prophet was fighting the army of the devil. ... the evil Gulabuddin ... a devil who claimed, that he ... that he, may Allah forgive me ... that he was Allah ... And it was magicians battling magicians ... and sorcerers fighting sorcerers, spells falling on spells and illusions creating more illusions ... and the world was coming apart by the tricks and passions of the two armies ... Hamza's and Gulabbudin's armies of ... (*He looks at the children, checking if they have slept.*)

Ashrafi of ... Djinns ... (*She smiles.*)

Abbajaan *softly taps her on the head.*

Abbajaan Yes ... of Djinns. Djinns ... mighty creations of the Almighty ... made of scorching smokeless fire ... of pure passion and no reason ... . And the battle raged over red skies, fiery water, watery ice, green oceans, lavender mosques and a yellow ... yellow ... moon. And it was illusions fighting illusions, magicians battling magicians and Djinns ravaging Djinns.

And it is at this point in the battle that one night, Hamza's daughter, the little girl ... the little girl Fatima came up to him, in his palace ... and said

"Abbajaan ... my dear Abbajaan."

"Fatima ... my dear Fatima," replied Abbu.

"Abbu ... my dear Abbu ... my flying lamps have been stolen from the palace. I saw them move away last night, slowly, very slowly on their own ... with no one visible ... the lamps just went away one by one, over the ocean to some distant land and my room, Abbu, was plunged into Darkness. So I ran to the window, Abbu, and looked at the ocean, which was the colour of moonlight. And slowly, very slowly I saw the ocean recede, the ocean recede and the moon glide away. Glide away, away and far far away from the palace.

But just then two Djinns appeared, right in front of me."

"Djinns," said Amir Hamza.

Yes, Djinns ... Hafiz – Rafis (**ABBA** *says this pointing at himself and* **Ashrafi**.) ... Rafis – Hafiz (*Pointing at* **Ashrafi** *and then himself.*)

Ashrafi (*repeating after* **ABBA** *with the same gestures, pointing at herself and then him and vice versa*) Rafis – Hafiz, Hafiz – Rafis ...

Abba "... Gods, demons and angels all at once," she said in excitement. "And they weren't your Djinns or Gulabbudin's, Abbu ... they were mine." Fatima, who had not yet looked into Hamza's eyes, said, "My Djinns appeared and told me that you will never win the war, Abbu, nor will Gulabuddin ..." "What blasphemy," yelled Hamza. "And where are these unscrupulous Djinns of yours?" said Hamza fuming. Fatima quietly looked up and said, "The war is over, Abbu ... The war is over today. My Djinns have broken the illusion of war. They broke it the moment they remembered it is after all an illusion ... this war. When you fight you forget everything else, Abbu, and so does the evil Gulabbuddin. Both of you forget that this war isn't real, Abbu ... both of you fight as if it were. Look up at the skies, Abbu," she said, pulling Hamza. "Those two stars up there, are ... are my eyes and they will forever be up there in the sky. The moment your eyes meet my eyes, you will break the illusion too. Abbu, whenever you look for my eyes in the sky, you shall find them and they shall remain there forever and ever." Having said this she looked up at Hamza ... and Hamza looked at his daughter's face. There were two holes where her eyes should have been and up in the sky were her two stars. Hamza cried out aloud and held his daughter tightly.

"That evil Gulabuddin has taken my daughter's eyes," he said. "I shall gouge out the eyes of every single child in his kingdom." Saying which, Hamza got onto his magic horse and with his magic soldiers and his Djinns, went on war with Gulabuddin with a rage that the world had neither seen before nor has felt since then. The battles raged again and again ... but Fatima's eyes keep lurking in the sky.

And even tonight ... if you look up at the sky ... you will find Fatima's eyes waiting for her Abba to break the illusion ... to break the illusion by his eyes ... meeting her eyes ...

In the name of Allah the Almighty ... may the queen of sleep bless you with pleasant and beautiful dreams ... Shabba-khair[3] ...

He looks at the children. They are fast asleep. He bends and kisses both of them on the forehead. Places his head gently on **Bilal**'*s head.*

Scene Two

Bakshi Stadium.

Day one. Morning.

Khaled *and* **Bilal** *are in the changing room. They are packing their clothes, shoes, etc. in the kit bag after training. It is a dirty, broken-down space. Has a window without glass and from the window one can see soldiers' uniforms, drying on a clothesline.* **Bilal** *is standing and looking at the sole of his shoe.* **Khaled** *is wiping sweat off his body with a towel.*

Khaled   I have noticed this about you, Bilal ...

Bilal What?

Khaled Whenever we play on the campus of the girls' college, you tend to break your sole.

Bilal Bullshit.

Khaled I love that sudden burst of additional force in your kick and them going (*Imitating.*) Beeelaaal ... Bilal ... Beeelaaaal ... Bilal. (*Laughs.*)

Bilal Khaled, this is serious. They won't even consider me for the selections without boots. It's in the rules.

Khaled Heena ... or was it Hamida ... what was her name?

Bilal Khaled ... I will kill you. What are you going on about?

Khaled That girl ... what's her name? The one with the shrill voice.

Bilal Khaled, I AM SERIOUS!

Khaled About her?

Bilal *shakes his head.*

Her father is a Maulvi in the mosque, they will stuff your boots in your ass and play football with your balls!

He laughs, pretends to kick a really small ball.

Oh sorry, off side!!

He laughs out. **Bilal** *laughs as well.*

They sit down on the floor. **Khaled** *takes out a coloured energy drink. He takes a sip and gives it to* **Bilal***.*

Bilal So your father's started smuggling gold biscuits to the Middle East. (*Laughs.*)

Khaled It is an energy drink, Bilal ... it will help you run when that Heena's or Hamida's father chases you.

Bilal Why does a goal keeper need an energy drink?

Khaled Why does an Argentina supporter want to go to Brazil?

Bilal Even if I do make it, Khaled, I maintain ... Argentina is more heart.

Khaled And Brazil is more World Cups!

Bilal Shouldn't matter to you … In any case you are crazy about that robotic German club.

Khaled European football, Bilal … that's where my future is.

Bilal (*laughs*) You will make a terrific linesman in Europe. With a whistle in one hand and this coloured drink in another. Running up and down with complete dedication and ENERGY. (*Reading from the bottle, laughs.*)

Khaled European football is all TECHNIQUE … (*Mystifying the word.*)

Bilal Europeans play to not lose, South Americans play to win …

Khaled You should play for India … Indians play to run around the ball.

Both of them laugh out loud.

Bilal *looks at his shoe again.*

Won't last … not till day after.

Bilal Two days?

Khaled Unlikely.

Pause.

Bilal *pulls out a piece of paper from his bag.*

Bilal (*reading*) 10 kms … shot, dribble and pass drills and then the game … (**Bilal** *looks worried.*) and in the middle of all this, the stupid curfew. How will I get this fixed? Does anyone even remember what the curfew is for anymore?

Khaled Because the Indians want you to remember that you are not supposed to disturb the (*Sarcastically.*) *'peace talks'* with the sons of bitches while their soldiers breathe down your neck.

Bilal I am not talking about the Indian Army curfew … I am talking about (*Pause.*) yours …

Khaled 800,000 soldiers, Bilal … do you even know how much that is? My Abbu says it's more than the number of American Soldiers in Iraq and Afghanistan put together … can you imagine? And it's not my curfew, it's the people's curfew.

Bilal It's not the people's curfew, it is the Hurriyat Curfew. The Hurriyat[4] might be a political party you worship but it is not the "people".

Khaled Really …? Then who is the people … you are the people? You?

Pause.

Bilal Do you know the timings for tomorrow?

Khaled All day except four to five in the evening. In the morning is the Army curfew and in the evening … ours.

Tomorrow afternoon/

Bilal (*sternly*) I won't be there.

Pause. **Bilal** *looks at* **Khaled**.

And neither should you.

Khaled Tomorrow is big, Bilal. Don't/

Bilal Day after is big.

Khaled Your father would be ashamed of you.

Bilal No. He would be proud.

Khaled People will spit on you.

Bilal I won't be around for people to spit on me.

Khaled So it's all about you now.

Bilal Yes.

Pause.

And it should be about you too.

Khaled Tomorrow/

Bilal Khaled, I don't care if people spit on me.

Khaled You don't care … about Kashmir?

Bilal I am Kashmir. And so are you. Play well the day after.

Bilal *is about to leave.*

Pause.

Khaled If you need shoes, you can borrow mine.

Bilal *turns around. Smiles at* **Khaled**.

We should ask them to keep our trials separate.

Bilal (*looks at his shoes*) I'll manage. My shoes will/

Khaled Won't last … and no one else will give it to you …

Silence.

The boys have been noticing you … you weren't even there yesterday after practice for the protest and the procession, so it hasn't gone down well with most of them.

Bilal I was there.

Khaled Yes … as long as it was naturally moving towards your house. I am not talking about getting seen in the procession, Bilal. I am talking about being in it.

Mushtaq *walks in.* **Mushtaq** *is slightly older than them. He is not the coach but he is a senior player who helps the team.*

Mushtaq Ohho … the bright lights of Kashmiri football in one room …

Khaled Mushtaq Bhai.

Shows him **Bilal***'s shoes.* **Mushtaq** *takes one, looks at it.*

Mushtaq This won't last. Not another session.

Khaled Mushtaq Bhai, will our trials be together?

Mushtaq Depends on Coach Saheb and the foreign selector.

Khaled We just have one pair of shoes.

Mushtaq (*looks at the shoes*) OK. I will speak to Coach Saheb.

Takes out two slips from his pocket. Gives one each to both of them.

Here, these are your maps and timings. It will tell you when and where should you join the procession tomorrow. Memorize it and then chew the paper.

Khaled Today?

Mushtaq It's impossible today. We need to meet this evening to plan further. At the old school. I hope both of you will be there. (**Bilal** *and* **Khaled** *look at their slips. To* **Bilal**.) No excuses this time, Bilal. OK? It's right in front of your house.

Bilal *stands quietly.*

Why did you disappear from the procession yesterday?

Bilal The curfew/

Mushtaq The curfew was only for you, in your backyard? I could stay and raise my voice, Khaled could stay and raise his voice … Youngsters are looking up to you. The team is now in the international eye. And you are running away … just running away like a coward.

Bilal I have a sister to take care of.

Mushtaq And we don't have anyone. (*Pulls him over towards window.*) See. Look at that. This is your stadium. You play here. You practise here, look at them. What are they doing here? (*Showing him the soldiers' costumes.*) Don't you feel ashamed, Bilal, when you have to enter your own stadium like a thief, from the back gate, because some bastard in a green helmet can just stop you and threaten to shoot you for merely doing what you love doing the most? Don't you feel free, when you run, when you fall, when you scrape your shin, when you sweat, when your eyes water, when you win or when you lose? Look at them. It's not their game. This is yours.

Pause.

Play it …

Bilal *stands with his head hung low.*

Khaled He will come, Mushtaq Bhai.

Mushtaq This is Kashmir's hero! Who sits in his house, while a funeral procession gets shot at, right in front of his house. (*To* **Khaled**.) Does he know what happened yesterday in the afternoon … after he fled? (*To* **Bilal**.) Do you?

Silence.

Bilal My sister Ashrafi collapsed when she heard the crowd passing by. When she heard bullets, I held her tightly for forty-five minutes, as she shook in my arms, with her head dug into my chest.

Perhaps she needs me more than your sister needs you Mushtaq Bhai or Khaled's sister needs him … because although she is fourteen her mental age is that of a nine to ten year old. An age at which she travelled with our Abba's body on her lap, after he was shot dead in a bus. And all they were doing that day Mushtaq Bhai, was that they were going for a wedding, dressed in new clothes … (*Pause.*) at an age when young girls love to wear new dresses, Mushtaq Bhai … my sister Ashrafi is afraid of them …

I am sorry, Mushtaq Bhai, Allah knows that if I get selected I can get her treated in a good hospital somewhere outside. My selection can go a long way to help us make something of our lives.

I can't take chances, Mushtaq Bhai, for her sake. And mine.

Mushtaq Also, yesterday, in the afternoon, the soldiers in front of your house shot at the funeral procession you fled from … the funeral of a seven-year old. In the shootout, they killed his brother, who was twelve. They killed his brother and imposed a curfew so that people could not gather and the child could not be buried. His mother will be sitting with his head on her lap for another twenty-four hours before her son can be buried. Chances are, you will meet her soon in the same hospital. There is a lot that happens in Kashmir, every afternoon, Bilal … so before you bullshit with me, always remember, Bilal Naeem, jersey number six, Kashmir's star right out, right leg goal scoring machine … that special as you may be … Khaled's sister or my sister or anyone else's brother or sister, does not need us one bit less than your sister needs you.

Silence.

Are you meeting the doctor today?

Bilal (*tentatively*) Yes. In the afternoon.

Mushtaq Take this letter (*Gives him a letter.*) and give it to the doctor. Ask him not to go for talks with the Indians. I can't believe he has agreed even after this. (**Bilal** *takes it tentatively.*)

Look at me.

Bilal *does not.*

(*Loudly*) Look at me!

Pause.

Mushtaq *comes close to* **Bilal** *and holds him.*

Insha'Allah, you will make it, Bilal. Insha'Allah you will be the star of Kashmiri football and reach where no one else did. And I am there with you, isn't it?

Bilal Ji Mushtaq Bhai.

Mushtaq But for Mushtaq Bhai to be proud of his star Kashmiri players, there needs to be a Kashmir … no? A proud Kashmir. Give this letter, Bilal … please. Don't let that doctor humiliate us by going for the talk. One day you will be proud of yourself, believe me. Hmmm ...?

Pause.

Bilal I will give it Mushtaq Bhai.

Bilal *and* **Khaled** *remain standing quietly.* **Mushtaq** *hugs* **Bilal.**

Mushtaq (*smiles at both of them*) In the evening. Old school.

Bilal *and* **Khaled** Ji.[5]

Mushtaq I will speak to Coach Saheb about not keeping your trials together. Give him your shoes, Khaled, but hide a nail inside.

Khaled *picks up his bag and is about to leave when he finds that* **Bilal** *is still looking at the soldiers' clothes on the clothesline.* **Khaled** *slaps him on the head, they stand together and keep looking at the military uniforms.*

Scene Three

Day one. Afternoon.

The Government psychiatry hospital in Srinagar. **Dr Baig***'s room.* **Dr Baig** *has placed his chair in front of his desk rather than behind it.*

There is a bench on another side of the room on which **Dr Wani** *sits with a notepad in her hand. She takes notes as the session proceeds. A partition separates this room from the outside. Outside on a bench is* **Bilal** *waiting for his sister with* **Mushtaq***'s letter in his hand.* **Ashrafi** *enters the clinic with her doll.*

Baig (*loudly*) As-salamu alaykum, Ashrafi Begum/

Ashrafi (*coldly*) Walekum asaalam, Doctor Saheb.

Ashrafi *sits coldly in front of the doctor. She looks at her doll and mumbles to it.* **Baig** *smiles at her. Gestures towards the stool in front of him.* **Ashrafi** *sits down.*

Wani (*in a voice that adults use to speak to children*) As-salamu alaykum, Ashrafi.

Ashrafi *takes her doll. Makes the doll look at* **Wani.**

Ashrafi (*to the doll*) She is talking to you. Go on, speak to her.

(*Imitates* **Wani**. *In the same adult-speaking-to-child voice.*) Walekum asaalam, Doctor Saheb.

Wani *smiles and opens a writing pad. She notes things as* **Baig** *and* **Ashrafi** *speak.*

Baig (*looks at his watch; making her comfortable*) Yes, on time today.

Ashrafi *spreads her hand out.* **Baig** *takes out two small toffees from his drawer, places them next to each other.*

Éclair or Sugar toffee?

Ashrafi *puts out the other hand as well.*

No, not both. One for getting here on time. And the other when we start playing. OK?

Ashrafi *nods.*

So, we were talking about a bus ride. The last time/

Ashrafi Doctor Saheb. You did not give me the school bag you promised.

Baig Oh. Is that why you are upset with me?

Ashrafi Yes. (*Pause.*) No. The school bag. (*Looks around.*)

Baig OK.

Silence.

Ashrafi, I will give you the school bag. But for that schools have to open/

Ashrafi You. Why did you close the schools?

Baig I did not.

Ashrafi You did. I know.

Baig No. Who told you that?

Ashrafi I know. But if I tell you, you won't believe me, Doctor Saheb.

Baig Why won't I believe you?

Ashrafi Because you don't know. If you knew you would have known.

Baig Ashrafi … OK. Look. I did not close the schools. I want the school to be open. For all of you to go out and play.

Silence. **Baig** *is looking at* **Ashrafi**.

Shall we start the bus ride?

Ashrafi OK.

This is my bus, I am the driver.

She turns the chair around.

I am driving. Wooon … woon … (*Makes sounds.*) From their home in
Mirpur to a wedding … (**Baig** *is looking at her intently as she playacts
the bus ride.*) … yes. No no … this won't go there. Of course it will.
Five rupees. You have. Good … So, I am driving there … there comes
Ashrafi and her father … the gallant Jamaal of Mirpur. They get in, they
sit down and then I keep driving … I drive they are sitting … they are
sitting over there …

Baig *gets up and just stands outside the make-believe bus, trying to get
in. Waving his hand at the driver.* **Ashrafi** *looks at him but does not stop
the make-believe bus.*

The bus does not go where you want it to go.

Baig (*smiles*) Why don't you try playing Abba, I will play Ashrafi.

Ashrafi (*gets up*) OK but quickly. We need to get home. Bilal has to go
for practice.

Baig Where is Bilal?

Ashrafi (*taking another chair and making a place to sit in the bus*) At
home. He was not on the bus with us.

Baig OK. But where is he now?

Ashrafi Now, I am on the bus, and he is not on the bus.

Baig No Ashrafi, see. Now we are in my room. And we are *pretending*
that you are in a bus. Right. So this is happening for real, (*Gesturing
towards his room, desks etc.*) and that is not happening now (*Pointing at
her make-believe bus.*) Right?

Ashrafi For you, because, Doctor Saheb, you are not in the bus. I am
in the bus. This is happening for real. Come, come in to the bus. I really
have to go early today …

Baig OK, so I will play Ashrafi/

Ashrafi No you can't play me. I am here in the bus.

Baig Then Abba.

Ashrafi (*agitated*) No, no, no, no … you can't … (*She seems really upset.*) Don't keep spoiling my game, Doctor Saheb. My bus. It's my bus! Play something else. This man or … this family of seven. Don't be part of my … I don't … Now I can't remember.

Baig But you remember more than this, Ashrafi. Don't you? Just the other day we almost reached the wedding.

She sits down, starts crying. She is angry and weeping.

Ashrafi You are not in the bus, why can't you understand? Why can't you just stay where you need to be? Why can't you just watch my bus from outside? It's because of you, all because of you/

Baig *steps off the make-believe bus. Goes back to his chair.*

Baig (*calming her down*) OK. OK. Look, I am outside now. I am not in the bus. See …

Ashrafi *looks around. Still crying. Picks up her doll. Says something to the doll, looks at the doctor, talks to the doll again about the doctor and sits facing away from* **Dr Baig**.

Ashrafi The bus cannot go on, there is a curfew.

Baig Yes, there is a curfew.

Ashrafi I have to get home before the curfew starts.

Baig Yes.

Ashrafi *looks at* **Wani** *hoping that she understands what she is talking about. She looks back at* **Dr Baig**.

Ashrafi I have to get back home before the curfew starts, Baig Sahab. I heard the timings on the radio.

Baig You mean … NOW … as you are here with me, Dr Baig?

Ashrafi *smiles and nods cheekily.*

Yes. Yes of course.

Ashrafi (*smiles*) What? What did you think, Doctor Saheb?

Baig I thought you were talking about the bus, Ashrafi.

Ashrafi Which bus? This bus? (*She starts laughing.*) You are mad, Dr Baig. You are mad.

I know, you are mad.

She keeps laughing.

Wani *and* **Baig** *look at each other.*

Baig OK ... Ashrafi. You can go home now. We will meet again tomorrow. OK?

Ashrafi *does not respond. She stretches her hand out again.* **Baig** *smiles, gives her the other toffee.*

Khuda Hafiz, Ashrafi Begum.

Ashrafi Allah ... (*Looks at her doll.*) Hafiz ... (*Smiles and begins to move out.*)

Baig (*calling out*) Bilal ...

Bilal (*comes in urgently*) Yes ... yes, Doctor Saheb.

Ashrafi *holds* **Bilal***'s hand and stands. In his other hand he has* **Mushtaq***'s letter.*

Shefu ... you go and sit there on the bench, OK? I will meet Dr Sahib and come ...

Ashrafi *does not leave him.*

I can see you from here, Shefu ... and see, if you bend like this you can also see me ...

Ashrafi *shows him her teeth.*

Very nice Shefu ... now go and/

She sticks her tongue out.

Yes ... yes, Shefu ... it's all neat and clean ... you are a good girl ... now sit there and I will be back ... OK?

Ashrafi *nods and shows him her doll.*

Bilal Yes ... go and sit with Hafiz ... OK?

Ashrafi *walks away.* **Bilal** *walks in. He stands in front of* **Baig**. **Baig** *looks at the letter in his hand for a moment.* **Bilal** *is about to speak when* **Baig** *pulls out a newspaper from his briefcase. Keeps it on the table.* **Bilal** *looks at it, hangs his head.*

Baig Yes ...

Bilal *does not say anything.*

Bilal (*showing him the newspaper*) Yes … Don't you have anything to say? When is your football trial?

Bilal Day after, Baig Sahib.

Baig (*surprised*) On Eid?

Bilal *nods.*

Wani *and* **Baig** *look at each other.*

Is this what you should be doing, Bilal? This?

Picks up the newspaper, reads:

"The pride of Kashmir, the football team was seen at the funeral procession last evening around Eidgah. Along with the protestors, the team joined in with stone pelting and sloganeering. And …" (*Mumbles.*) … and yes here you are. Pride of Kashmir. Here. On this page. Is this what it's all about? Is this why you have left everything behind, and moved to Srinagar with your sister?

Bilal *puts the letter back in his pocket.*

Bilal (*looking down, tentatively*) Dr Sahib, I was …

Baig Bilal. You cannot afford to be stupid right now. If required, don't come back together with the other boys from practice. I was shocked to see you at that procession yesterday.

Wani (*looks up*) Doctor Saheb … you were?

Baig Yes, I was there. Returning from a patient's, when one of these … these (*Pointing at* **Bilal**.) boys threw a stone at my car …

Wani Your car? Oh … Doctor Saheb … were you hurt?

Baig (*ignoring her, going up to* **Bilal**) This valley needs heroes, Bilal. Fulfilled ones. Not the ones who were promising and did not finally get anywhere. (*Shakes his head.*)

You can be, fulfilled. You can leave with your sister and give her a good life. You cannot afford to mess this up right now, Bilal. You understand, don't you?

Bilal *nods.*

Go … before the curfew starts again. I don't even remember which one is about to start now!

Pause. **Bilal** *is about to bring the letter out but stops.*

Bilal Allah Hafiz, Doctor Sahib.

Baig Allah Hafiz, Bilal.

Bilal *leaves.* **Baig** *sits down.* **Wani** *is silent. Tense silence between them.*

Wani Baig Saheb … the boys stoned your car?

Baig Yes. They did. How did the whole city know about this, all of a sudden?

Wani It was on the television, Dr Baig. A news channel did a story on the people from the valley who have been selected for the talks with the Indians.

Pause.

The ones who have declined … and the ones who will be talking. People are already on the streets about the shooting of that seven-year-old boy and his twelve-year-old brother, and now this thing about the … the … peace talks … the list announced the same evening as the killing of a child in cold blood … Dr Baig it has really made some people angry. And perhaps in their anger they …

Silence.

Baig Anger … Sometimes, I start believing the Indians. Maybe, we won't be able to handle this place, if it were given to us.

Wani *sits quietly.* **Baig** *looks at* **Wani**.

Oh … of course, I forget.

Wani Doctor Saheb, the boys—(*Stops abruptly.*) They should not have stoned your car.

Baig No, no. Why not? Even you don't think I should talk to the Indians, isn't it?

Wani I never said that.

Baig Wani, I have known you long enough to be able to read your *Silence.*

Pause.

You were the only person who did not come to my room, yesterday after I heard from the ministry. Which is why Wani, you are the last one to know that my car was stoned by Kashmir's latest heroes. Kashmir's children.

Pause.

Wani Baig Saheb, forgive me but I am not sure if there is any point in talking to the Indians.

Pause.

Baig You are not sure, Wani? Sitting here, in this hospital, you are not sure if we should speak or not? Look at this place. The only psychiatry hospital in the entire valley. With five doctors ... just five, (*Laughs sarcastically.*) you and I have to be miracle workers in here.

When I was stepping in today, Wani, I saw the number on the register ... Forty-five thousand one hundred and seventy-eight ... forty-five thousand ... the sum total of the bravery and passions of our occupier and our revolutionaries ... their report card on our register at the entrance. That many people have walked in through that gate just this year and it's not even Eid ... and five of us in here. Two are my students including you and two are yours ... these are our chances. We are doctors, Wani ... our job is to heal. People want revolution. Where will we keep it? We don't even have enough benches for our patients to sit on.

Pause.

Wani When is it, Doctor Saheb?

Baig Day after tomorrow.

Wani Eid?

Baig (*smiles*) Yes, they want to meet on Eid.

Wani (*laughs*) These Indians. (*Pause.*) I can't tell what is more worrying, Dr Baig ... When they are openly hostile or when they are pretending to be friendly!

Scene Four

Dr Baig *stands outside the Eidgah at a slight distance. Suspended Time. Between Life and Death.*

The **Djinn** *appears inside. He is painted green and golden. His face is not clearly visible but there is a disfiguration to it. It is like a hole, slightly larger than the size of a revolver bullet.*

There is a sound of the Islamic prayer for the dead, "Fateha," behind, but it seems unclear and muffled. The sound is layered with the sound of a father telling a young boy a story in Urdu. The child laughs and makes noises of wind; sword fights, rain etc. on the sound track. The soundtrack layers these three sounds but the child's sounds are clearer than others.

Dr Baig *takes very slow steps towards the gate. The* **Djinn** *walks to him as if mirroring his pace.* **Dr Baig** *goes really close and as the face of the* **Djinn** *becomes more visible, he stops. The* **Djinn**'s *stomach is visible and it looks burnt.*

As soon as **Dr Baig** *stops, the* **Djinn** *appears restless. He keeps looking at* **Dr Baig** *intently and tries to spread his arms open as* **Dr Baig** *recedes.*

The sounds reach a crescendo.

Scene Five

Day one. Late afternoon.

Ashrafi *and* **Bilal**'s *house. A small room with an old television without the back so that its picture tube is visible. A mattress. A carpet.* **Ashrafi** *is doing "make-up" on* **Bilal.** **Bilal** *is watching a football match. The window is open. Clock on the wall. A radio. Same day. Afternoon.*

Bilal (*looks at the clock. Irritably*) How could you get it wrong, Shefu?

Ashrafi You can get it fixed tomorrow, Bhaijaan.[6]

Bilal And what if it doesn't happen? How will I play?

Ashrafi Sit straight. (*Turns his neck*)

Bilal (*checks a slip of paper*) The curfew time has not changed. You heard it all wrong on radio.

Ashrafi How do you know?

Bilal I asked Khaled. On the phone.

Ashrafi Then you should have asked Khaled Bhai, in the first place, Bhaijaan, I am not him, I have things to do of my own. OK?

Bilal (*looks at* **Ashrafi**) Shefu, you have to stop watching television.

Ashrafi *does not look at him, she keeps doing his make-up.*

Look at the way you speak. Even to Doctor Saheb. No one in the valley speaks to him like that. My god, Shefu! If Ammi were here, she would give you two tight ones ...

Ashrafi If Ammi were here ... (*She mumbles to Hafiz.*) she would let me go wherever I wanted ... whenever I wanted ... with Hafiz ...

Bilal *looks at* **Ashrafi** *as she continues to apply make-up on his face.*

Bilal Your Hafiz!

Ashrafi Hafiz has also told me several other things, Bhaijaan ... about that doctor.

Bilal Oh (*Laughs.*) really ... like what?

Ashrafi That the doctor is mad ... that he is a kafir, an infidel, which is why he never enters the gates of the Eidgah. He goes there every evening, and stands outside.

Silence.

Bilal Shefu ... what do you know about the Eidgah?

Ashrafi That which everyone knows.

Bilal What?

Ashrafi That it is a graveyard of the martyrs. And in there are the Djinns. Living Djinns.

And they are all living there, in that world.

Bilal You and your Hafiz ... (*He looks at the clock.*) ... OK, I have to go.

Ashrafi Bhaijaan.

Bilal No, no. Make-up, after I come back from the team meeting, OK? Mushtaq Bhai will kill me if I don't go today. OK? (*As* **Bilal** *prepares to leave* **Ashrafi** *begins to panic.*)

Ashrafi But Bhaijaan, how will you have the meeting. The curfew is till eight.

Bilal There is no curfew that side.

Ashrafi Tomorrow. Have the team meeting tomorrow, Bhaijaan.

Bilal Shefu, the team needs to plan, for the selections and everyone needs to meet, OK?

It's not in my hands.

Ashrafi Bhaijaan ... please don't go out in the curfew ... please Bhaijaan. I will ...

Bilal *looks at her. Starts to wipe the make-up.*

Bhaijaan no, no don't wipe the make-up, please. You are my only model. Bhaijaan ... Bhaijaan ... (*Screams.*)

Pause.

Ashrafi *is flustered. She sits on the floor.* **Bilal** *stops. Looks at her, goes close to her and holds her.*

Bilal Shefu ... Shefu ... see ... I am here, for real ... I am. You can feel my face with your hands ... I am here. (*Puts* **Ashrafi**'s *hands on his face. She seems to calm down with this gesture.*)

Ashrafi (*holds him tightly*) You are my only ... my only ... model Bhaijaan.

Bilal *laughs.*

Bilal And you are also my only beautician, no?

Ashrafi *is still shaking.*

OK ... OK ... Shefu, you know if I get through this football trial what will happen?

Ashrafi You will go away.

Bilal Yes, and you will also come with me to Brazil. We will be completely, completely ... free. We can go wherever we want, whenever we want ... you can go to school ... everyday.

And I will play the World Cup (*Laughs.*) and you ... you will become a master beautician!

Ashrafi Abba? Will he come with us? Where will he be?

Bilal He will be ... in his world.

Ashrafi Which world?

Bilal Abba is fine, Shefu. In his world. In the other world. OK?

Ashrafi *nods.*

Ashrafi And Hafiz?

Bilal We will take your Hafiz as well. Promise.

Ashrafi *looks around.*

Ashrafi Bhaijaan, will you be gone for long?

Bilal I will come back in no time.

Ashrafi Bhaijaan ... will you?

She pulls two pillows. A big one and a small one.

Bilal (*nods softly*) Sleep and before you know I will be back.

She lies down. He sits next to her and begins to tell her a dastaan.

Dastaan ... dastaaan ... which one?

Ashrafi (*immediately*) The one in which Hamza /

Bilal Sends the flying lamps?

She nods and both of them laugh.

OK ...

He strokes her head and she closes her eyes.

Long long ago, in a land much like ours, in the year of the Saturn, in the kingdom of heaven, there was the general of the king ...

Ashrafi The king ... the prophet ... the king the prophet ... Bhaijaan, did a boy die yesterday?

Bilal What?

Ashrafi Didn't a boy die yesterday Bhaijaan ... right here ... somewhere close by? Did he go to Allah, Bhaijaan, or has he now become a Djinn?

Bilal (*nervously*) Shefu ... what are you talking about ... who told you that a boy died yesterday?

Ashrafi (*holding her doll*) Hafiz ... us Hafiz rafis ... Rafiz Hafis ... long long ago in the year of the?

Pause.

Bilal Saturn ... at a time much like this there lived/

Ashrafi His mother (*Starts laughing.*) ... she thinks he is dead, Bhaijaan. She is sitting with his head on her lap.

Bilal Shefu ... Shefu ... I don't know what you are talking about ...

Ashrafi It's in the dastaan, Bhaijaan ... when Djinns die people think they are dead, the armies of Gulabbuddin and Hamza think that they are dead but ... have you ever been to the funeral of a Djinn?

Bilal No.

Ashrafi and will you?

Bilal No ... don't know ... Shefu, shefu ... go to sleep. What are you saying?

Ashrafi Will you?

Bilal Sometimes you sound like other people.

Ashrafi You're not telling me the dastaan, Bhaijaan.

Bilal I am, Shefu ... sleep. If the children are good the dastaan becomes the blanket and if the children are bad ...

Ashrafi The dastaan becomes the chilling wind ... Bhaijaan, do you think that the boy, he felt cold when he died. Is death hot or cold Bhaijaan?

Bilal Shefu, go to sleep, Shefu.

Ashrafi Will you go for his funeral or will you stay here Bhaijaan ... tomorrow ... what will you do Bhaijaan ... are you with the Djinns or are you with the enemies of Hamza ...

Bilal and as Hamza's eyes are to meet.

Ashrafi Fatima's eyes.

Bilal (*rapidly*) Fatima's eyes hanging in the air, if Hamza's eyes meet Fatima's ... that day/

Ashrafi They will never meet, they will ... will you get me your shoes, magicians battling magicians battling magicians.

Bilal *holds her tight and embraces her.*

Silence.

Bilal Sleep, Shefu ... sleep ... shhhh ... shh ...

Kisses her on the forehead.

May the queen of sleep bless you with good dreams. In the name of Allah the merciful ... Shabba Khair.

He puts **Ashrafi** *to bed. She is fast asleep. He sits next to her. On one side of him is* **Ashrafi** *and on the other his football boots. He looks outside but holds her and keeps sitting.*

Scene Six

Day one. Night.

The bunker of the Central Reserve Police Force (CRPF) close to the Eidgah. Same night. The gate of the Eidgah is visible. This is the complete form of the gate that is visible between the **Djinn** *and* **Dr Baig***. It's not very brightly lit.* **Soldier 2** *(***S2***) is ringing a small bell and praying to pictures of Hindu gods on the walls.* **Soldier 1** *(***S1***) comes running in, looks at him in shock. Keeps his gun aside, and slaps him on his head.* **S2** *stops and salutes.*

S2 Sir!

S1 *slaps him again on his head.*

S1 Don't 'sir' me, I am the same post as you.

S2 Still sir, you are older.

S1 (*takes his bell*) What is this?

S2 Sir, today is Tuesday.

S1 So?

S2 Good day for Lord Hanuman.[7]

S1 Here. Next to the Eidgah, when everyone is breaking their fast for Ramzan, you are thinking of Lord Hanuman!

S2 Sir, this is our country, we can … /

S1 *slaps him on his head again.*

S1 This is not our country. We are sitting here, OK? And this has got nothing to do with Lord Hanuman anyway. Just stand guard and watch out for movement.

S2 *stands guard, unhappily. On the way to the window of the bunker he apologizes to Lord Hanuman quietly.*

S1 They are not there.

S2 In the school?

S1 No.

S2 Behind the mosque?

S1 No ... no.

S2 Then they must be home.

Pause.

S1 All of them? All the boys?

S2 Yes, sir, they must be tired of planning for tomorrow (*Laughs.*)

S1 These boys from the mountain; they don't tire that easily.

S2 You really think they will come till here tomorrow.

S1 I am sure. In hordes. They would have, yesterday itself, but the procession got shot at, at Lal Chowk itself. Tomorrow not only will they get here, they will get here with stones in their hands and blood on their hands.

S2 Saheb, when will our shift change?

S1 Not till these things get over, I'm sure.

S2 But will we have back-up by tomorrow?

S1 Hopefully.

S2 If they come here ... I will ... I will shoot.

S1 They will skin us alive. Don't do anything stupid.

S2 By the grace of Lord/

S1 Shut up! Will you shut up and look?

Pause.

S2 Sir, don't mind me asking, but you are not Hindu?

S1 Yes, I am.

S2 So ...

S1 What?

S2 If you are Hindu, you don't pray to/

S1 I am Hindu but I am not stupid ...

S2 A true Hindu cannot get hurt by stones, sir.

S1 *looks at* **S2** *in disbelief.*

S1 Good. Stand in front of the bunker tomorrow morning then.

Pause.

S2 Sir, how long have you been here?

S1 Three years in Srinagar. This picket is new, though. About six months old.

S2 Why sir … here? (*Looking around.*) Where are the militants here? It's just houses all around … isn't it? What can possibly happen/

S1 Stay here for two more days and you will realize what can happen over here.

S2 What sir … you are making me a little nervous, I must say.

S1 You see that gate? …

S2 Yes … sir.

S1 What does it say? Read it?

S2 (*tries to read*) It's in Urdu …

S1 Underneath that … look at the gate … that's in English.

S2 (*reads*) LEST YOU FORGET, WE GAVE OUR TODAY FOR YOUR TOMORROW … Who has given … this is a martyrs' graveyard, Saheb?

S1 Yes … good. You are not as dumb as I thought you were.

S2 *quickly goes close to the photo of the god, rings the bell, puts a red 'tika' (a mark) on his forehead and comes back and stands.*

You are … not very smart after all. Erase it … are you stupid?

S2 *looks at* **S1** *in disbelief that being a Hindu* **S1** *is asking him to erase his "tika."*

S1 You want to stand guard next to the Eidgah, surrounded by god knows how many of these bloodthirsty boys with a red tika on your forehead! What are you … Lord Hanuman's disciple or Lord Hanuman himself!

S2 This will ward off the evil, sir. Mine will work for both of us, but I suggest you also apply some. It will be more foolproof! These graveyards are full of ghosts, sir ... I am telling you ... all kinds of ghosts are/

S1 Shut up ... you idiot. They have posted us here so that there is no trouble. Things do not go out of hand. So that even if they get provoked or heated up in some funeral procession, with all those slogans pumping their blood onto their foreheads, we can control the population ... the "awaam." Do you know what that means ... to control them ... not to provoke them further by standing here with a red tika on your head? God ... why do I get posted with idiots ... always!

Ashrafi *appears in front of the gate of Eidgah. Just her silhouette is seen. She sits down outside the gate and appears to be speaking to someone who is inside. She seems to be talking, mumbling, laughing.*

S2 *notices her. Abruptly takes aim and loads his gun.*

What ... what are you doing?

S2 She is meeting someone, Saheb ... I was right ... Saheb ...

S1 Who? Can you see anyone?

S2 She is laughing, Saheb. I am sure she is, you don't know these people, Saheb, they are ...

S1 Shhh ... shh ... what's wrong with you?

S2 I know these people, Saheb. Saheb, you shoot her.

S1 What?

S2 Yes Saheb.

S2 *picks up a gun and gives it to* **S1**.

S1 What ... are you/

S1 *pushes* **S2**, *and the latter falls.*

S2 Saheb, I will forget who you are ... you are just same post as me ... don't.

He picks up the gun and tries to go towards the window himself. **S1** *hits him again.*

S1 What's wrong with you?

S2 It's a curfew, she can't/

S1 It's OK. You can't shoot her for/

S2 I know these people, Saheb, I have seen … even their children …

He gets up again to shoot. **S1** *hits him even harder and snatches his gun.* **S2** *is bleeding.*

(*Loudly. In panic.*) What are you doing Saheb … she will blow up. She will blow up on our faces and we will be in shreds, like cloth, lying around … you don't understand … These people are mad … she is … is …

S1 *holds him by the collar.*

S1 I don't know about her but you are mad. Completely mad. Tomorrow morning, the first thing I do is to report you to the commandant.

S2 I will report you. You are standing here and fighting with a man, of your own post to defend a girl who has broken the law. You have broken orders, we can shoot. We must shoot.

We can shoot anyone we like. Anyone we suspect. You are mad, all you old soldiers are mad … you deserve it … deserve this … this hell … not us …

S1 *comes charging at* **S2**, *slaps him hard on the back of his head.* **S2** *falls on the floor.* **S1** *loads his gun and points at* **S2**.

(*Closes his eyes. Loudly.*) My god … oh my god … what are you doing? Will you kill me … why … but what did I do?

S1 SHUT UP!!

Silence.

I will kill you if you are stupid. I can afford insanity, OK? But stupidity, no. Not here. I will not be lynched by a mob of boys because of an idiot like you.

S1 *goes to the window of the bunker and keeps observing* **Ashrafi** *closely.* **Ashrafi** *comes out of the bunker with her wooden doll, she faces the soldier.* **S1** *smiles at* **Ashrafi**. **Ashrafi** *smiles at the soldier.* **Ashrafi** *leaves.*

Scene Seven

Day two. Morning.

Bakshi Stadium. None of the equipment that was there in a previous scene is present in the same place. Outside the room, on the other side, where all the military uniforms can be seen hanging on a clothesline, footballs, kit bags, a pair of goalkeeping gloves and a huge pile of jerseys are kept.

Khaled, **Bilal** *and* **Mushtaq** *are present in the room.* **Mushtaq** *is sitting in one corner looking out. An eerie stillness.* **Khaled** *and* **Bilal** *do not have their jerseys on.* **Mushtaq** *gets up, takes a steel mug that is lying around and throws it in the direction of the military camp. He comes back and stands next to* **Bilal** *and* **Khaled**.

Mushtaq We'll practise. Come.

Khaled *and* **Bilal** *look at him.*

He removes his shoes and makes a goal post.

Bilal Coach Saheb?

Mushtaq He cannot come today. I heard from him this morning.

Khaled Why?

Mushtaq They are looking for his son.

Pause.

Come (*to* **Bilal** *and* **Khaled**) We will play.

Bilal (*tentatively*) Just the two of us?

Mushtaq You and Khaled are the only real chance we have of sending someone to a decent club abroad … out of this … this prison of a stadium. (*Pause.*) You don't turn up for meetings I ask you to come for, Bilal, but I still need to make sure you do justice to your game. Isn't it? You boys are wimps. Two of you are sitting here without your shirts on in shame and the others are hiding on being asked to surrender their equipment. We would have torn at those Indians.

Khaled (*goes towards* **Mushtaq**) We will play, Mushtaq Bhai … for our team and yours.

Mushtaq Yes, you must and you must come for the procession, later in the day today. For that twelve-year-old martyr, may Allah be with him. It is going to be a huge protest.

Khaled Is that why …

Mushtaq Yes. The bastards want to show us who is in charge.

Khaled (*to* **Bilal**) It's going to be massive … Three battalions are covering just ways from Lal Chowk to the Eidgah. Apparently, even women and young girls are coming out of their houses.

Mushtaq Kashmir has pledged that it will bury its son where it wants today.

Pause. **Mushtaq** *looks out towards the soldiers.*

Bilal Our practice …

Mushtaq (*turns to* **Khaled** *and* **Bilal**) You will practise … the more they try to stop you the more I want you to practise. This isn't a game … you know that, don't you? I have stood here, year after year recalling that day when the Indians locked the stadium and took two of our best boys into custody.

Rizwaan and Rasool. The best. We never saw them again.

And you know what the real story is … it has nothing to do with militancy. None of the boys of our team crossed the border to Pakistan or trained in weapons. It was a protest, here in Bakshi Stadium by a bunch of sportsmen, merely demanding that the military camps be moved out of the stadium. And guess what did the Indians do? The peaceful, peace-loving Gandhian sons of bitches … they came in and beat Rasool and Rizwaan, our two star players, to a pulp a few days before the Asian Games trial. Locked the stadium and … .

Man is a beast, and that over there … is the worst beast of them all. A kind of man who was ruled by others for over 300 years and is here now to rule someone else. There is nothing … nothing more dangerous, believe me, than a ruler who has been a slave before. And there it is, staring at you … with your equipment under the nozzle of its gun. (*Pause.*) and our boys, a bunch of wimps … have gone away after turning in their jerseys; jerseys which have made them who they are today. (*Pause.*)

Bilal They haven't gone anywhere, Mushtaq Bhai … see (*He takes him to the window and stands.*) there … behind the gate … can you see the boys? They are just not allowing anyone else in anymore.

Mushtaq So, what are they waiting for?

Bilal For practice …

Khaled And then to go for the procession. (*Looks at* **Bilal**.) They are waiting outside, so that even if the practice does not happen, the procession against the army curfew can/

Bilal But right now, it's the practice that matters.

Silence.

Mushtaq We will practise. Now … (*Looks into his bag.*) here, Bilal … you're number six.

Mushtaq *throws a brush dipped in green paint to him.*

Bilal Ji, Mushtaq Bhai … (**Bilal** *paints it on his body gladly.*)

Mushtaq And here Khaled … take seven … idiot … the only goalee in the whole planet who wears number seven.

Khaled It's my lucky number, Mushtaq Bhai. (**Mushtaq** *paints seven on* **Khaled**.)

Mushtaq Sure … Lucky number … that's why you are sitting here without a jersey in the middle of a stadium with one more player and the captain of a disbanded football team.

Bilal Mushtaq Bhai … we don't have a ball!

Silence.

Mushtaq You have your brain … and your feet … you two have played enough football in your life to imagine the ball if it's taken away. Haven't you?

Pause.

Close your eyes.

Khaled … walk to the goal post. If this were the field, where would the goal post be?

Khaled *closes his eyes and walks to a place that he thinks is the goal post.*

Now take position. Bilal … you start charging from the left flank … and I will keep calling out names …

Khaled Ji.

Mushtaq Pass … Bilal to Basher … Basher to Majid … Majid to Bilal … back pass … Bilal … run down flank … cross to Basher, Basher heads …

Khaled *jumps up and mimes catching the ball.*

They smile. **Khaled** *and* **Bilal** *still have their eyes shut.*

Once more ... Basher runs down right ... back passes to Majid ... Majid makes ball for Bilal ... Bilal shoots ...

Khaled *dives exactly in the direction in which* **Bilal** *shoots.*

Khaled *opens his eyes,* **Bilal** *opens his eyes and they laugh out loud.*

Good ... Now play with your eyes open ... I will call and you just play all the moves we have practised ... let's practise all the moves that we have done ...

Music plays and the boys practise. Needs to be a complete sequence.

Bilal ... I have asked Coach Saheb to keep your trial separately from Khaled's.

Bilal Shukriya,[8] Mushtaq Bhai.

Mushtaq *nods at him and smiles.*

Khaled *walks up to him as* **Mushtaq** *goes to talk to other boys.*

Khaled I hope you are staying back, Bilal.

Bilal No Khaled, I am not. I have to go home. Shefu is alone.

Khaled *slaps him hard.* **Bilal** *falls on the ground.*

Mushtaq Let him go, Khaled.

Khaled You don't even care about football, do you? They take everything away from you and still ... still it doesn't make you angry enough.

Pause.

Your session will be before mine. I will get the shoes early, don't worry. You can play and become whatever you want to become, Bilal ... just don't come in front of me.

Pause.

Bilal I don't want to imagine my equipment and my team all my life, Khaled. Do you get it? Is it too unreasonable a desire?

Khaled No, Bilal ... it's too reasonable. A bit too reasonable for us. Don't you think?

Pause.

Go Bilal. Go away before I start despising you. You are my friend and insha'Allah you will be the star of Kashmiri football one day. I don't want to look down upon you, the way I so want to … at this moment. Get out of the stadium before I genuinely start hating you.

Bilal *leaves.* **Khaled** *and* **Mushtaq** *remain standing, looking at him leave.*

Scene Eight

Day two. Morning.

An hour after the previous scene.

Dr Wani *and* **Dr Baig** *in* **Dr Baig**'s *office.* **Wani** *is injured. Her white coat is soiled with blood and her head is bleeding.* **Dr Baig** *is trying to stop the bleeding with cotton.*

Wani It's OK, Doctor Saheb.

Baig I don't believe this.

Wani It's OK, Dr Baig.

Baig Sit still, Wani.

He ties a bandage and sits in front of **Wani**. *He is shaken.* **Baig** *looks at* **Wani**. *Smiles. Goes close to her. Touches her forehead with affection and sits at the table holding her lightly.*

Wani It was also my fault.

Baig No it wasn't. I should have asked everyone to stay at home. Till this meeting with the Indians gets over. I am sorry, Wani. You are like my own … my daughter if I had one. I am/

Wani It's my duty, Doctor Saheb …

Baig This place has made me stubborn. (*Pause.*) You are young, Wani. A young woman.

Don't be like me. Stay at home on such days.

Wani Doctor Saheb, I have stayed at home a little too long.

Dr Baig *looks at* **Wani**.

(*Smiles.*) I even took my son out, today (*proudly*). The processions, the barricades. He enjoyed it.

Baig I hope you are not telling him ...

Wani No, Baig Sahib ... I am telling you.

Baig What?

Wani That I don't want to be here anymore.

Baig What?

Wani Yes, Baig Sahib ... forgive me but what is going on outside the compound of this hospital right now is so ... so brutal that I don't understand my role inside the safety of these walls anymore.

Baig Don't be stupid, Wani. You are one of the only qualified doctors here. One of the five psychiatrists. What are you talking about?

Wani Maybe I will practise psychiatry, Doctor Baig, but outside. Outside where I can see what is really going on ... and also show the world to my son.

Baig Wonderful ... not only have you lost your senses, now you are also taking your son out to processions and protests ... telling him all of kinds of half-baked, ill-thought, ill-informed/

Wani (*smiles*) Doctor Saheb, you will be surprised. I haven't told him anything, but my eight-year-old son stuck his head out of the window of the car today. Around Lal Chowk.

And the moment I was about to pull him in, he looked at a soldier straight and screamed, "Azaadi." And I, I did not pull my son back in. I let him keep his head out. He kept it high, he looked people in the eye. He felt the wind on his face. On his own. Without his mother.

Silence.

Baig Mother ... is this what you want to raise? Is this your idea of a child, Wani?

Wani I am a mother, Baig Saheb. A child is not an idea for me. It is a real thing.

Baig You must be teaching him all this nonsense.

Wani No. I am not. Perhaps he has his own reasons. His own reasons to be angry.

Pause.

Baig If we have no reason to be angry, we will go insane, for that is our only memory of ourselves. (*Pause.*) Grow up, Wani. This thing needs to end somewhere. We can't keep teaching our children the same thing over and over again. We have to look ahead.

Wani But I am not teaching him anything.

Baig Then how does he know? How does he know all this at this age? What does a child know about politics? What does a child care for? You people are ruining Kashmir, not ruining, killing it, with your need to be *heroes* in front of your own children.

Wani You're right, Baig Saheb, my son knows nothing about politics, but sometimes when I see him, I wonder if this whole thing is not about knowing at all. It's human instinct. To be free. Even birth, Dr Baig, is an act of freedom. A child cries out loud, and wails and fears that she will die, and only very, very slowly, learns to breathe. But a child still wants to be born. To be free. Freedom, Baig Saheb, is perhaps larger than reason. Larger than reason, religion, the mind or medicine. Perhaps it is just pure human instinct.

Silence.

And ... and ... your family, Dr Baig. May Allah be with them. Forgive me for speaking out of turn, if we were free, they would have lived. Perhaps.

Silence. **Dr Baig** *looks at her in anger.*

Baig How is that? How is it, that of all people, you know if my family would have lived or died, Wani? What do you want to say ... no really. What is it?

Your son takes his head out of the car and like a complete idiot you allow it, and I am supposed to learn what from it?

Wani Doctor Saheb, I didn't mean to say anything like that ...

Baig No ... Wani ... you think I can't see it in your eyes. You think I can't see it in the eyes of every single person who has been looking at me with contempt or disgust for the last fifteen years. My son Junaid ... loses his way. Goes across the borders, trains in some godforsaken camp and comes back with a changed name ... "Pareen ... Pareen, the star of the east." A glorified murderer. Is it my mistake that he turned out to be a militant?

Wani Doctor Saheb …

Baig A freedom fighter!! Oh I forget, a freedom fighter! A boy who does not care about his mother and father and … (*Breathlessly.*) becomes a freedom fighter. Who teaches our children this idea of freedom? Their parents?

I did not even know, Wani, at which point did he chose to give up his name, at which point did he decide to go and train in a camp full of Afghan and Syrian mujahideen … and now people look at me as if I killed him. Their hero! Everyone wants a hero in their neighbour's house, isn't it?

Every leader … every single separatist leader of this godforsaken movement has sent their children away to study in England or America, and here you are … THE PEOPLE … population … the bloody "awaam" … the common bloody man and now the woman: a bunch of fools, killing your children over this ill-thought, ill-motivated celebration of murder!

You, Wani … have your son by your side … I have held my son's burnt dead body … burnt in molten plastic in my hands … his organs stuck to my hand … and even now when I rub my palms together to wash my hands … I can only feel his bile … soft … green but burnt …

And he wasn't killed by any Army or Police. You know, Wani … that burnt bile of his which still haunts me was burnt by his own boys. His own Mujahideen.

So don't you dare tell me, that if we were free, my family … would have lived.

Silence.

Did you?

Wani Yes, Baig Saheb. I could not resist it.

Baig You …

Wani Yes. My son was holding on to my left hand, and with my right hand I threw a stone.

Baig Do you know, Wani, what effect it can/

Wani I know what effect it will have on his mind, if he grows up thinking that his mother never raised her voice. He is a child of today, Doctor Saheb. He won't let history pass him by.

Baig Don't you dare talk like an illiterate, Wani. Being my student, don't talk like a bloody villager, an illiterate, violent, godforsaken kafir, an infidel who quotes the Quran like an idiot, who knows nothing, neither about science nor about religion, a bloody villager ...

Silence.

Wani It's relieving, Dr Baig ... to see that even you have your prejudice. Even the Almighty does not treat everyone equally, from what I know. I am glad that considering you look down upon our anger so much, there are things that still make you angry, Baig Saheb.

Silence.

Baig Saheb ... I just don't want my son to be hiding on the outskirts of Srinagar, in some medical college when the whole city is in flames.

Baig You have lived. That's why you take it lightly. When you were in college, Wani, sitting in medical college, safely on the outskirts of Srinagar, don't forget that thousands of boys were killing each other in the name of jehad. Thousands were killed not by any armed forces but by each other. For guns, for money ...

Wani Doctor Saheb, I am your student. I always will be. But if I have an opportunity, I will throw a stone again. I loved it.

Baig I know what this is, Wani ... glorification ... glorifying other people's sorrows and making of them public events. You people are not allowing that mother to bury her son for two days now ... do you realize that? For two days she is watching his body rot ... smelling him as his corpse decays. Two whole days.

It took me seven to bury Junaid. Seven days after he was floating in the River Jhelum and that ... that was three days after he was burnt to death. My last memory of my son is not one of a glorified warrior ... no ... that is yours and the rest of Kashmir's, of everyone who is buried there at the Eidgah.

My last memory is the smell of him rotting, the shit, the bile and urine inside his body smelling through his pores. Or was it his soul that was smelling so bad those seven days, Wani? Desperate to get out of the limitations of his biology and the politics of his people.

This is what you are giving that mother. You people, the public ... are no less violent than the Army. You can leave.

Silence.

Wani Thank you, Dr Baig ... I have learnt a lot from you.

Baig No, Wani ... I am not living with that guilt. There must be some other imperfection in me, otherwise how is it possible that all my children become so unrecognizable one day.

(*Looks at her.*) My students have all turned out to be just fine.

Wani You know what your problem is, Baig Saheb? You are a great doctor but a poor storyteller. You have one story about everything ... about the hospital, Junaid, Pareen, Wani and Kashmir. Even if someone tells you another story you can destroy it with reason. I really wish we had another Dr Baig in the valley. Someone who could read your mind and heal you.

Show you more than one possibility to your Dastaan. Something you do very well with others.

Silence. They look at each other.

Baig (*preparing to leave*) I am not your father. You don't have to be with me forever.

Go ...

Wani Baig Sahib, the city is in flames ... and since your name is on the list, I think you should stay indoors.

Baig Thank you for your concern, Wani ... but I just have to get to Ashrafi's place ... I am sure that in these conditions she won't be able to make it to here.

Fifteen years ago I thought I was shaping young minds. Clearly I need to start younger.

Scene Nine

Day two. Afternoon.

Ashrafi *is sitting in her room. She is mumbling to her doll.* **Dr Baig** *enters. He notices her from a distance as she mumbles.*

Baig As-salamu alaykum, Ashrafi Begum.

Ashrafi (*tentatively*) Walekum a saalam, Doctor Sahab.

Baig Where is Bilal?

Ashrafi He has gone for practice. He has his selections tomorrow and then we are going to Brazil.

Baig (*smiles*) OK … good. That is really good. Has he told you when he is going to get back?

Ashrafi He will come back after playing.

Baig OK … should we play as well?

Ashrafi Us? What can we play?

Baig Let's see … what we have got here. (*Gives her a bag.*)

Ashrafi *looks into the bag and pulls out little toy figures, like GI Joes. There are soldiers, people, guns, aircraft etc.*

Ashrafi (*looks at the doctor in anger*) Is this my age to play with toys?

Baig No, no, we are not playing with toys. We are playing Djinns.

Ashrafi Djinns?

Baig Yes, you and I can be like Hafiz.

Ashrafi *looks pleased with the proposition.*

Ashrafi Us Hafiz (*pointing at herself*) …. and … (*Thinks.*) Rafiz (*Pointing at the doctor.*)

Hafiz – Rafis … Rafis – Hafiz …

Baig OK … Hafiz (*pointing at her*) and Rafis (*pointing at himself*) …

Ashrafi This (*pointing at a carpet which she spreads on the floor*) is Kashmir and that is Amir Hamza. Looking out at the world. (*She looks far.*)

Baig Where?

Ashrafi There … over there … you can't see him because you are a Kafir.

Baig I thought I was a Djinn … a Djinn in the army of Amir Hamza … the general in the army of /

Ashrafi Yes, the general of the army of the prophet, the king …

Baig (*excited*) OK … good.

Ashrafi But how do we play Djinns?

Baig Both of us take out things from the bag … and call it whatever we want.

Ashrafi And when we call it something, we make it that?

Baig Yes.

Ashrafi We call something, something and we build the world around it … we create the world in our calling.

Baig Yes.

Ashrafi Just like the Djinns …

She is excited, her body is shaking with excitement.

Baig Yes …

Ashrafi *picks the first one out.*

Ashrafi My flying lamp.

Baig The magician Amar Ayyar.[9]

Ashrafi *laughs.*

Ashrafi My receding ocean.

Baig The moonlit moon.

Ashrafi My bridge of smoke.

Baig the … the … you have to tell me more of the story.

Ashrafi How can I tell you more of your story, Rafis … your story, you make as your dastaan moves along.

Baig My story or the Djinns' story?

Ashrafi Your story of the Djinns or the Djinns' story of you … who is telling whose story?

(*She laughs.*) My blue mosque in the middle of a …

Baig My …

Ashrafi My paradise.

Baig My …

Ashrafi My magic mirror for fallen magicians.

Baig My … scooter.

Ashrafi My hair.

Baig My briefcase.

Ashrafi My nails.

Baig My hen.

They laugh.

Ashrafi My absolute power.

Baig My wife, my child.

Ashrafi My complete night.

Baig My potato field.

Ashrafi My Sunflower's guide to staying awake.

The sound of the procession gets louder outside the house.

Baig My watch.

Baig My glasses.

Ashrafi My Water's book of staying wet.

Baig My house full of flies.

Ashrafi Sky full of vultures.

Baig My bus to the hospital.

Ashrafi My light.

Baig My third grandchild.

Ashrafi My grandfather.

My father's bicycle.

Baig My …

Ashrafi *gets more involved and picks out objects in quick succession.*

Ashrafi My father's back. My father's/

Baig My father's?

Ashrafi My//

Baig My son's watch.

Ashrafi A clock my father looked at every morning.

Baig A clock my son//

Ashrafi A fly in my father's cup of tea.

Baig My son's back.

Ashrafi My father's plate full of food.

Baig My son's last meal.

Ashrafi My father's//

Baig My father's?

Ashrafi I wipe.

Baig I erase.

Ashrafi I wake up. I check my book. My sunflower's guide to staying awake.

Baig My father's?

Ashrafi The last curfew. My father's bus.

Baig The last curfew, your father's bus.

Ashrafi The Djinns outside, on both sides of the road …

Baig The Djinns outside …

Ashrafi And in-between, my father …

Silence.

Abbajaan …

Ashrafi *stops.*

The **Djinn** *appears in the room visible only to* **Baig**.

Scene Ten

Baig *and the* **Djinn** *in the same space as* **Ashrafi**.

Time suspended. Between Life and Death.

Baig You … you are a ghost.

Djinn You … you are the ghost, Abbajaan. Blind, burnt, battered and now betrayed.

Baig You are the one who was betrayed, Junaid. Betrayed by your own boys/

Djinn You are right Abbu, I was. The Junaid in me was betrayed, but by you. The Pareen never was!

Baig Don't make up lies for yourself. For you to go on and on … at least in death, be truthful. If not to me, to yourself at least.

Djinn You should not have traded me.

Pause.

Baig No one can watch their son go there.

Djinn There were many boys. We were all prepared.

Baig Who prepares for being beaten up naked and being dipped in a pool of oil, who prepares for electric shocks in the penis … (*Closes his eyes.*)

Djinn I was Abbu. We all were.

Baig I can't be speaking to you. You are dead. This is insane.

Djinn Just … Just like the others. The moment it's your fault, we are insane. The moment it isn't simple, it's just madness. (*Pause. Looks around.*) These boys/

Baig These boys are fighting, out of anger. Anger at themselves/

Djinn No Abbu. No. (*Pause.*) They are fighting for their Djinns. For hundreds of thousands of Djinns, who are still around … It's not a war of right and wrong. For cars and jobs. Of books and blankets. It's a war of the living and the dead. Between those who are fighting for tomorrow and those who are laying down their lives for eternity. These boys, Abbu, will keep coming back, again and again.

Pause.

Baig They wrapped you in plastic, and burnt you alive. And still you/

Djinn They were our boys, too. It hurt, but you know what my last words were.

Baig Yes, I heard. (*Pause.*) Shoot me, I have gone too far. (*Pause.*) You were scared. It's completely normal to be scared. I was just trying to save my son/

Djinn You tried to save Junaid, Abbu. In doing so you killed Pareen.

Baig Pareen ... that's who you are? Not my son ... not my son Junaid.

Djinn (*proudly*) Pareen, the star of the east. A maker of men. A leader of boys/

Baig Pareen, a misled boy. A mujahid[10] ... the day you joined them/

Djinn Why Abbu ... why do you find it so difficult to believe that there was a boy, deep deep inside your son who was more than just your son. Who was not a coward like you? Who could stand up and fight even then for what was right ... what was just ... what was ... (*Pause.*)

Do you know Abbu, why we change our names when we take up our arms?

Baig So that you can cheat yourself ...

Djinn No Abbu ... so that we always remember we are more than our father's sons. So that at the time of justice our hands do not tremble under the weight of the names our fathers have given us ... we have only one father ... that father ... the one and only ... in the name of the merciful ... in the name of Allah ... !

Baig Don't you dare, don't you dare make Allah your shield. I know the likes of you.

Pause.

What do you want from me?

Pause.

Djinn Don't speak to the Indians Abbu ... humiliate them, insult them, blow up on their faces.

Baig You cannot be saying these things to me ... No son asks their father to blow up on people's faces ... I am not your Abbu ... you mean nothing to me.

Djinn I am your son.

Baig Junaid, my son. Pareen ... a ... a violent mind.

Djinn Every evening you come here, Abbu, with prayers on your lips ... prayers that you never recite ... and every evening you stop outside. Everyone's Abbu has come and gone and it's only you who does not set me free.

Baig I don't come here every evening to say my prayers ... for you.

Djinn Then why do you come here every evening, Abba Jaan.

Baig To see, if my Junaid is here. But every evening I find Pareen.

Djinn It was you, Abbu, you who gave me my name. Junaid ... a warrior ... a warrior of/

Baig Of peace. The day they changed your name, they changed your soul and left you here.

Here. In-between, as nothing, as dust, as ...

Djinn All of us are ... All of us are in-between.

Baig Mad, you are mad, even in your undoing you are mad ... insane ...

Djinn It surprises me. A doctor of the mind, you know so little about insanity, my Abbajaan.

Silence.

Baig *shuts his eyes.*

Baig I can't be speaking to you ... you are dead ...

Djinn You are not speaking to the dead Abbu ... you are speaking to the living ... you are the one who is dead. You are speaking to your own desire, Abbu ... you are speaking to your Djinns ... Pure passion, made from smokeless fire, Allah made the Djinn first, Abbu ... you are talking to the first creation of the Quran.

Baig Don't you dare teach me the Quran ... you cannot be the Djinn of someone ... if you are a Djinn, you cannot be a soul; if you are a soul, you cannot be a Djinn ... there are no Djinns of the dead ... souls are souls and Djinns are Djinns ... and boys are boys and sons are ...

Djinn How can you want everything so neatly Abbu ... in this madness, in this chaos, in this churning ocean of violence, not only have our lives got mixed ... so have our deaths. Our stories, our gods and demons and angels ... have all collided in this infinite churning of passion. Don't expect reason from a world gone wrong, Abbu ... don't wish the universe into an understandable falsehood ... this is real, Abbu ... and reality cannot be that simple.

Pause.

You wanted to save Junaid ... But you don't realize that when you killed Pareen, there was no Junaid left in me. No Junaid left, in your house.

Baig Then I made a mistake, a huge mistake. (*Pause.*) Now I don't even know whose Djinn you are. But whoever you are, it was a mistake. A huge mistake. You should have rather died by an army bullet, than being burnt by your own boys. Burnt in molten plastic, with your insides clinging on …

Djinn For Allah/

Baig Don't take his name with your infidel 'kafir' soul … The Quran forbids the burning of even a rabid dog. You know nothing about God. And there is no god that you can call your own. You are right, it's not a war for books and blankets. It's a war of the godless. The godless fighting the godless.

Pause.

Ashrafi *is seen sitting on the floor of her house. Her eyes closed as she feels her doll. As she recites the following verse like a prayer,* **Dr Baig** *and the* **Djinn** *recede.*

Ashrafi
    The threadbare setting of the sun
    The last dwindling rays,
    The final scream of the boys of snow
    The way they die,
    On tables and mats.
    The last song of their lungs
    The need to breathe
    The urge to open one's eyes
    Everyone wants to live in the end
    Everyone wishes another breath.

Scene Eleven

Day two. Evening.

An evening before Eid.

Ashrafi *and* **Bilal** *are at a mortuary of a government hospital in Srinagar. The mortuary is on the first floor of the hospital. The room is dark.* **Bilal** *and* **Ashrafi** *are just outside the door of the mortuary.* **Bilal** *switches on the torch of his cell phone.*

Bilal Yes.

Ashrafi Is this it?

Bilal Go home, Shefu. I am telling you.

Ashrafi No, Bhaijaan. You are not coming out alone in the curfew.

Pause.

Bilal *looks around.*

Bilal Shefu, there will be bodies inside.

Ashrafi I know Bhaijaan. (*Pause.*) But you will also be there.

Bilal Shefu …

Ashrafi Hmmm …

Bilal I am scared.

Pause.

Ashrafi You must say your prayers for Khaled …

Bilal Yes.

Bilal *slowly opens the door of the mortuary. They go in and slowly start walking around the mortuary trying to find* **Khaled**'s *body.*

Ashrafi (*smells something. She finds it repulsive*) … This

Bilal Shhh …

He gives her his handkerchief. She covers her nose.

Ashrafi Why is it smelling?

Bilal *bumps into something.*

Bilal Stale.

Ashrafi What?

Bilal The bodies.

Pause.

Ashrafi *covers her nose even more strongly with the handkerchief. Turns around and is about to leave.* **Bilal** *grabs her from the back.*

Bilal What!

Ashrafi I can't bear the/

Bilal You'll get used to it. (*Pulls her back. Sternly.*) I have been here before. I know it.

Ashrafi *suspiciously looks at* **Bilal**. *They continue to look at the bodies. Hopping over the ones on the ground. Uncovering their faces.* **Bilal** *is more definite in his search than* **Ashrafi**.

Ashrafi We should go back.

Bilal No.

Ashrafi What if he isn't here?

Bilal He has to be. I know.

Ashrafi How do you know?

Bilal Shit.

Ashrafi What?

Bilal Women. (*Pause. Looks around.*) All of them.

Ashrafi *looks around at the uncovered faces. She is about to throw up.* **Bilal** *covers her face.*

Bilal Swallow it.

Ashrafi What!

Bilal Swallow it, we can't leave anything behind.

Bilal *covers her face strongly.*

Bilal (*still holding the handkerchief*) I did it. (*Pause.*) I came with Khaled when his brother was killed. Swallow it once, it won't come back.

Bilal *holds her strongly as she swallows it.* **Bilal** *is relieved.*

Bilal No sweat, no saliva, no blood, no vomit. Nothing.

Ashrafi *nods.*

Bilal The men …

Ashrafi This.

She is looking at a body whose face she has uncovered. **Bilal** *uncovers some more.*

Bilal Here on.

He frantically begins to look. Both of them look. **Bilal** *trips on a body on the floor and falls. His cell phone falls on the ground, its torch throwing light on another dead body.*

Ashrafi Bhaijaan … Bhaijaan …

She is scampering on bodies nervously. She looks through them slowly. She can't hear any sound or see anything.

Pause.

A moment of silence. They just look at the bodies. **Bilal**'s *voice: Shh … shh …*

Ashrafi Bhaijaan (*In sobs, out of fear.*) … .

Silence.

Suddenly **Bilal** *turns and picks up the light and points at her face from nowhere.*

Bilal Shh …

Ashrafi *hugs him. Breaks down with her face dug into his chest.*

Bilal Let's finish this quickly and leave.

Ashrafi (*shaking her head*) Let's go Bhaijaan. Let's go …

Bilal Look … (*Makes her feel his face.*) … I am here.

Ashrafi Bhaijaan, please let's …

Bilal Khaled is my friend. I have to. Don't I?

Ashrafi It's too late Bhaijaan. He is dead.

Bilal *holds her tightly.*

Bilal (*softly*) Shefu … I need his shoes.

Ashrafi What …

Bilal Yes … I need his shoes, don't I?

Ashrafi We are here for his shoes!

Bilal Shh … I need them, Shefu. You know. More than anyone else.

Ashrafi *looks at him in disbelief.* **Bilal** *continues to search.* **Ashrafi** *follows him.*

Shaken.

The boys.

Bilal *uncovers one. Uncovers another.*

Majid, Rafiq, Riyaaz ...

One, two, three ... Oh God.

Ashrafi What?

Bilal *sits down on his haunches.*

Ashrafi What Bhaijaan ...?

Bilal Majid, Rafiq, Riyaz, Basher ... one two, three, four ... they lined them up and ...

(*Pause. Gathers himself.*) Khaled, seven ... (*He counts.*) five, six ... six? This must be him.

Ashrafi Seven ...

Bilal This is him. (*Pause.*) I am six.

Bilal *and* **Ashrafi** *look at each other.*

Ashrafi Let's leave, Bhaijaan ...

Goes towards the body. Uncovers the face. **Bilal** *looks at it, holds the face.*

Ashrafi Is it ...

Bilal *nods. He covers the face. Suddenly some noises are heard from outside.*

Bilal Go ... go ... check the door.

He shows the light. **Ashrafi** *goes and looks down the window.*

Ashrafi Downstairs ... come Bhaijaan ... we must/

Suddenly we hear **Bilal** *gasp. He has removed the sheet from the other side of* **Khaled**'*s body. He breathes heavily and continuously gasps.*

Ashrafi What ... Bhaijaan ...

Bilal He has no ... no ... feet.

Ashrafi What?

She runs towards him. **Bilal** *has uncovered two other bodies.*

Bilal Basher, Riyaaz ... no ... no feet ...

Bilal *begins to throw up.* **Ashrafi** *forces the handkerchief on his face.*

Ashrafi (*dragging him*) Come Bhaijaan ... come ... leave it ... we will find other/

Bilal No feet, Shefu ... no feet ... They have no feet.

The light of his cell phone goes off. They exit the room gasping.

The **Djinn** *appears in front of* **Ashrafi.** **Bilal** *remains on stage looking at the dead bodies.* **Bilal** *is between the* **Djinn** *and* **Ashrafi.**

Djinn Your highness ... (*Smiles.*) Your Bhaijaan ... our general.

Ashrafi What?

Djinn It is time, your highness. For Hamza to return. To return as your beloved Bhaijaan.

Ashrafi *looks at him doubtfully.*

Ashrafi Let someone else be Hamza ... Let someone else ... not my Bhaijaan.

Djinn I am not doing a thing, your highness, you are making this up. It's your story ... I am not even here, your highness. Your brother Bilal, is leading from the front, because that is the way you want it to be.

Ashrafi No, I don't want Bilal to go anywhere. And I don't want you to become him or him to become you.

Djinn That is what you say, your highness, not what you feel deep down inside. I am everything you feel deep down inside. Your Djinn appears as your deepest desire ... your darkest secret, your strongest wish. You have made Bilal from me. You have made me from Bilal.

Hafiz ties the black cloth around his face. He is about to leave.

Ashrafi But what if my deepest desire is wrong, Hafiz? If my desire is not my deepest desire. If I want something simpler. Something, more basic, more easy. What if it is not about freedom, not about war; my deepest desire, Hafiz, is to cut out magazines and show my Bhaijaan, and his to be able to tie my hair! We don't want our deepest desires. Our deep desires are not our own ...

The **Djinn**, *who has his face covered, turns around and looks at* **Ashrafi.** *He comes close to her, takes off the cloth from his face. Kisses her on the forehead. He picks up a stone and begins to recede.*

Ashrafi (*speaking to empty space*) No Hafiz … no … don't do that … please, Hafiz.

Bilal *gets up with a stone in his hand.*

Ashrafi Bhaijaan … no Bhaijaan

Bilal *comes closer. Pulls her to a corner and they hide.*

Bilal Shefu.

Ashrafi Bhaijaan.

Bilal (*screaming*) Shefu … who are you talking to … there's no one there … there's no one there, just stop talking all the time … just stop it Shefu.

Ashrafi *looks at him as he leaves her hand.* **Bilal** *looks down, picks up some stones and comes out of the hiding.* **Ashrafi** *remains hidden in a corner. He throws stones, one after another at the window of the mortuary in rage. Whistles are heard.* **Ashrafi** *begins to pull him. The sound of soldiers, running towards them. Their boots, guns and sticks. As the sound gets closer,* **Bilal** *stands and waits for them even more decisively.* **Ashrafi** *pulls him with all her might. He throws a stone at the soldiers.* **Ashrafi** *pulls him back into the corner.*

Ashrafi Come Bhaijaan … let's go … run Bhiajaan … they will take us in, Bhaijaan … what are you doing, Bhaijaan … this isn't you, this is the Djinn. This isn't you Bhaijaan … what are you/ (*Screaming.*)

Bilal Run Shefu … just run away and go straight to the clinic … go Shefu …

Ashrafi What are you/

Bilal They shouldn't get you, Shefu … just go … go …

Bilal *pushes* **Ashrafi**. *She refuses to move.* **Bilal** *slaps her hard. She stands shocked.*

Do it, Shefu. Just go. Listen to me alright. I can't be with you forever. I am tired of you. You are insane. Do you get it? Just get lost!!

Ashrafi Bhaijaan … Bhaijaan … this isn't you speaking … it's the Djinn … Bhaijaan, he is making you/

Bilal *holds her by her hair and pushes her away. She falls. They are both panting.*

Silence.

Bilal This isn't the Djinn, Shefu. There are no Djinns. All those boys, you saw up there, they are real boys. Real boys cut into pieces. This is me ... for real. And I need to do this ... Go Shefu ... Go ...

Bilal *is in absolute rage and* **Ashrafi** *begins to slowly move away in fear.*

He tries to come closer and lift her but she gets scared of him and quickly gets up and runs away. **Bilal** *remains standing in the corner. Watches her go away. He then comes out and stands facing the soldiers who are running towards him. He screams and picks up stone after stone to throw at them. Sounds of bullets.*

Flashes of light.

Blackout.

Scene Twelve

Day two. Late evening.

The CRPF bunker next to the Eidgah. **S2** *sits in front of an electrical heater, stirring instant noodles.* **S1** *is trying to catch a frequency on his wireless.*

S2 When is our next supply coming, Saheb?

S1 Shh ...

He is trying to listen to the messages on the wireless which are unclear.

S2 We will starve like this, Saheb. What is this thing? (*Picks up the packet.*) Did I join the force and risk my life to eat instant noodles? In my village, Saheb, we had so much/

S1 Shut up ... shut up ... I know what's there in your village and what's not ... so just shut up

(*Pause.*) I don't know. I can't pick up a single frequency. What about you?

S2 No, Saheb.

S1 I have never seen you use your wireless? Where is it?

S2 It's in my bag, Saheb. Safe.

S1 Idiot. What is it doing in your bag? What do you think it is ... your wife's photograph, that you have saved it for a lonely day? Bring it out.

S2 (*feeling shy*) I am not married, Saheb. I will get married, this time when I go home.

S1 Good. Very good. Now can we please try catching a frequency on your wireless? If no one comes with supplies, we will starve in two days.

Loud sounds of procession are heard. Deafening. They take their guns quickly and stand guard. They are unable to see anyone but the procession sounds are clearly heard.

S1 *and* **S2** *stand tense.*

S1 Don't shoot. OK?

S2 We should just kill some of these assholes and put an end to these funerals!

S1 (*looks at* **S2** *in disbelief*) They are not here.

S2 Then?

S1 They are in the other lane, behind the houses. They are going around right now, from house to house.

Pause ... the sounds continue.

Oh ...

S2 What, Saheb?

S1 They haven't buried that boy as yet.

S2 But I thought/

S1 They haven't ... they won't do it till they get here.

S2 You shoot, Saheb ... you shoot, then they won't come here.

S1 If we shoot they'll come here immediately.

S2 Crazy ... crazy assholes. Motherfuckers, sons of bitches ... bastards.

S1 Shut up ... just shut up and/

Suddenly the sounds fade away. They stand quiet. **S1** *is relieved when the sounds go away completely.* **S2** *falls on the ground shivering.* **S1** *comes and stands next to him. Gives him a glass of water.* **S2** *takes it abruptly and splashes the water on his face. He is sweating.*

S1 It's OK. What? ... what is it?

S2 *is still in a state of shock.*

Which sector were you in before this?

S2 Rajouri.

S1 Rajouri! You … you were in Rajouri? (*Laughs.*) Isn't there an operation every night in Rajouri?

S2 Ji … ji, Saheb.

S1 Then …

S2 These children are insane, Saheb. I am telling you. I have seen them. Those militants are at least people. But these are all ghosts. They don't have eyes. They have something else.

Something else, that no one can see through … even when they die their eyes don't shut, Saheb. No matter what you do/

S1 (*suspiciously*) Have you seen them die?

Pause.

S2 Yes … yes, Saheb … I have.

S1 Where?

S2 I have buried some of them with my own hands, Saheb. And one of them, a little girl … of seven I think, her eyes just wouldn't shut. (*Pause.*) I shot her thrice after she died. *Pause.*

Twice on her eyeballs … finally … just to get away from that ugly … ugly stare …

Silence. **S1** *keeps looking at* **S2**. *He goes and sits next to* **S2**. *Just pats him on his back in a placating manner.*

S1 Isn't Rajouri the place, where … where it happened? The … commandant who …

Silence.

S2 Yes Saheb. (*Pause.*) I saw him do it. That night he went insane. He was so angry with everyone. His child had died back home, and he did not get leave to go back.

He went into the village and shot three children, and then in one of the houses, he … he raped a mother … in front of her daughter.

S1 Were you there with him?

S2 Not when he left the barrack … But by the time our next senior
officer took some of us into the village to look for the commandant, he
had already shot this woman's elder son and he was making the younger
daughter sit and watch … the …

S1 And did you try to/

S2 No, Saheb. It was an order. My father served the force, my
grandfather had served the force … he asked me to keep watch outside,
I stayed at the door.

S1 And the girl?

S2 Three days later, Saheb … I was standing at my post and I saw
two men and a young girl walk towards the camp … they were not
Kashmiris, these men.

The girl was wearing a hijab … they came close to the camp and the
men left. The girl just walked closer and closer towards the gate …
towards my post and I thought she wanted something. Water or food …
I stepped out with my water bottle … went close to her and suddenly
she took her hijab off, and I saw, Saheb … it was this girl … she had
mad eyes, insane … she was looking at me like she would burn me with
her eyes … and I started running back to the post and she … she started
to run behind me … this little girl … Saheb … was chasing me to my
own post, to an entire barrack and then she made it to the sand bags and
just … just … (*Closes his eyes.*)

S1 What?

S2 She blew up Saheb … right in front of me … into pieces … and a
part of her head fell right in front of me. (*Pause.*) That night I was asked
to bury her, and I saw her eyes … they just wouldn't close … I prayed,
and prayed to exorcise her ghost but she would not go away … she was
dead but her eyes were alive … she kept staring at me, Saheb … I shot
her in the eyes … and her head … but her eyes just would not shut …
and as I was burying her, I just kept hearing sounds from their mosques.
Their god was keeping her head alive … just her head … they are
demons … these …

S1 Just pray to Lord Hanuman that either they bury that child elsewhere
or the force gets us out of here.

Silence.

S2 How did they get this close, Saheb?

S1 The patrol is receding. Two battalions have already been called back.

S1 *goes to the pan and starts stirring it.* **S2** *is nervous.*

Come, it's ready …

S1 *takes two aluminium plates and serves the instant noodles.* **S2** *keeps sitting still.* **S1** *places* **S2***'s plate in front of him.* **S2** *keeps sitting quietly.*

S2 The strange thing is you know what, Saheb?

S1 What?

S2 My unit sent me to a doctor. He made me tell him everything. And then he made a report that said, I was imagining everything. I hated his voice … the sound of him … he was pretending to be my father but calling me insane …

S1 What does the report say?

S2 That I am overworked and I need to go home …

S1 Then you should.

S2 But I was not imagining it, Saheb, I saw it.

S1 *begins to laugh. Not hysterically but trying to conceal his laughter.* **S2** *looks at him.*

S1 You saw it … (*Laughs.*)

S2 *hits* **S1***'s plate of food and it falls on the ground.*

S2 What are you laughing about?

S1 Are you crazy … what are you doing?

S1 *tries pick the food up and put it back up on the plate.* **S2** *kicks his plate away again.*

S2 No, tell me first what the fuck are you laughing about? Is this a joke to you … my imagination!

S1 Listen, I understand you, now don't test me. Don't waste food or I will kill you.

S2 *kicks* **S1***'s plate again.*

S1 *gets up and hits* **S2** *hard.* **S2** *falls on the ground.* **S1** *hits* **S2** *again with the back of his gun. He is shocked and badly hurt.*

Silence.

S2 *slowly gets up and sits.*

Now eat … if you waste food, I will kill you myself. I don't pray but I don't waste food and water. These are your gods right now. These instant noodles, this bottle of water, your automatic and me. And if your other god … your wireless … does not tell you anything soon … you are short of a god … and then it's really bad news. There are several ways in which we could die in the next few hours. Starving each other doesn't need to be one of them.

S1 *starts eating.* **S2** *looks on. He quietly joins in. Both of them eat in Silence.*

Scene Thirteen

Day two. Night.

A bench inside the Police Station in Badgaum, on the outskirts of Srinagar.

On one corner **Ashrafi** *sits, looking away and mumbling. Her doll is in her left hand. Her right hand is lightly held by* **Dr Wani**.

Dr Baig *enters after meeting the police officer. He looks at* **Wani**. *A moment of silence. Comes and sits down next to her. He appears flustered and breathes heavily.*

Silence.

Baig We can meet him now. He's in a solitary cell.

Silence.

Wani Is he …? Have they hurt him?

Baig (*rhetorically*) What do you think, Wani?

Silence.

Wani You do not need to do this, Dr Baig. I can meet him and/

Baig I need to, Wani. This time I need to. (*Pause.*) I should have done this a long time ago.

Back then, I did not have the courage to see my son in prison, but this time …

Wani We should not have brought her along, perhaps.

Baig Without her they won't let us see him.

Wani And what are they saying?

Baig They'll keep him here till the end of the talks. He is apparently a 'high-risk' prisoner!

Tense silence. **Wani** *looks at* **Dr Baig** *in horror.*

Wani Dr Baig, we have to get him out. You have been called from the ministry, you can get him out.

Baig He is here on the orders of the ministry. They showed me a letter.

Wani Saying?

Baig Saying Bilal Naeem is a high-risk prisoner. He needs to be arrested for precaution and kept in prison till the talks are over. It is an official letter. Signed, government of Jammu and Kashmir …

Pause.

All the cells are full of boys who have been taken in on precautionary grounds, before the … the talks.

Wani He has been kept in a solitary cell … Do they suspect that he is … I mean do they really think he is a high-risk prisoner? Baig Saheb, we have to do something. If they have a letter from a ministry, they won't take chances, would they, they will … they … will just … Dr Baig.

Baig They have kept him there, separately … because of me, Wani.

Wani *looks at* **Dr Baig***, comes closer to him and sits, holding his hand.*

Wani Or maybe because youngsters look up to him? You cannot blame yourself for this, Dr Baig.

Baig Can't you see, Wani … they are trying to put pressure on me before the talks. The inspector … that bastard in there is showing me a list and asking me to identify potential antisocial elements. (*Sarcastically.*) I have a reputation after all … (*Pause.*) and this boy is paying for it.

Looks at **Wani***.*

They will kill him?

Ashrafi *looks at* **Dr Baig***. Silence. She keeps looking at him intently, as* **Dr Baig***, completely unaware of the stare, looks flustered and* *keeps looking into thin air in the direction of the prison.* **Dr Baig** *is seen to be mumbling things to himself. He is almost an adult mirror of* **Ashrafi.**

She slowly walks towards **Dr Baig.** *Stands in front of him. Gently gives him her doll. He holds it, looking at her. She embraces him. For the first time* **Dr Baig** *holds her.*

Ashrafi Doctor Saheb, I will do whatever you want. Play every game and come on time.

Will you take me to my Bhaijaan? Just once …

Silence.

Baig I will … I will, Ashrafi …

Ashrafi You can have my Hafiz, Doctor Saheb … you can have him, too. He told me you play Djinns every night, every night at the Eidgah. Here he is, Dr Baig, you keep him. You can take him along and play with him. We can go together. You and I.

Baig I will, Ashrafi … I will get your Bhaijaan home.

Ashrafi Can you take me to him … please, Doctor Saheb/

Baig I will, Ashrafi … I will … I promise.

Dr Baig *gestures towards* **Wani,** *for her to sit with* **Ashrafi. Wani** *gently holds* **Ashrafi,** *sits down with her on the bench.* **Dr Baig** *gets up. Looks inside. Waits. Walks in purposefully.*

Inside, is a prison cell. In one corner which is dimly lit, lies **Bilal.** *Naked. He can be seen in partial light. There is a bulb in one corner of the room which lights his face and his body partly. He does not come into light in the beginning.* **Dr Baig** *stops and tries to look at him.*

Baig (*hesitantly*) Bilal …

Bilal *does not reply.* **Dr Baig** *bends over to see. He goes and sits next to the cell on his knees.*

Bilal …

Bilal *recoils fast and disappears into darkness.*

Bilal, it is me … it is me … Dr Baig …

Bilal *slowly brings his face into light. He is badly bruised. His lips are swollen and one of his eyes is completely busted.*

Bilal ...

Bilal Doctor Saheb ... Shefu reached you ... didn't she?

Baig *nods.*

I had to let her go, Baig Saheb, otherwise ... otherwise they would get her too ... and then ...

Baig I understand, Bilal ... I understand. Don't worry, she is fine.

Bilal *seems to want to stand up and come closer but struggles.*

Bilal are you/

Bilal They did that to me, Baig Saheb ...

Baig (*in horror*) They ...

Bilal They inserted a wire into my ... my penis, Baig Saheb. And gave me ... shocks in my ... I cannot ... I am bleeding, Baig Saheb ... from ... I am scared, Baig Saheb.

Baig (*unable to hold his voice*) Bilal ... Bilal ... my ... my son ... you are/

Bilal Everyone's been killed, Baig Saheb ... Basher, Majid, Riaz ... Khaled. And they chopped their feet ... Khaled has no feet, Baig Saheb ...

Baig Oh ... did Ashrafi see it too?

Silence.

Bilal She did, Baig Saheb. I did not know ...

Baig I understand, Bilal. I understand.

Silence.

Bilal Are you still going to speak to them, Baig Saheb?

Pause.

Baig I will get you out, Bilal.

Bilal Three boys were killed here, right in front of me. They won't let me go.

Baig I will speak to the people in the ministry ... OK ... don't worry, I will/

Bilal Baig Saheb ... will you take care of Ashrafi?

Baig Yes, Bilal, I will. But I will also get you out ... I promise ...

Bilal Baig Saheb ...

Baig Yes, Bilal.

Bilal Just promise me one thing, Baig Saheb.

Baig Yes ... yes tell me Bilal ...

Bilal You won't trade me for someone else ... (*Silence.*) ... and get someone else in ...

Pause.

Baig I won't. I won't ... my son ... I won't trade you for anyone.

Pause.

Bilal I am sorry, Dr Baig, I had to ask you. Everyone in the station was talking about it.

About, how you traded your son for another boy when he was caught.

Pause.

Baig Are you hurting?

Bilal I want to see Shefu, Baig Saheb ...

Baig (*flustered*) Yes ... yes of course ... but don't worry I will get you out ... whatever it is.

Bilal Baig Saheb, I know it. They will kill me before dawn. (*Pause.*) I heard what the inspector told you. My cell is right behind his desk. See. But you shouldn't/

Baig I won't tell them about anyone else, Bilal. They do this all the time. Catch someone and then get someone else. I know, that the boy they are asking for is ... (*Unconvincingly.*) innocent.

Bilal (*sternly*) I know him, Baig Saheb. He is Coach Saheb's son. I know where he is.

They asked me about him but I did not tell them anything. Which is why they've let you come in.

Baig You ... know him! What are you saying Bilal, you know where he is ... I can't believe you have started keeping track of the whereabouts of Mujahideen nowadays! ... it's a disgrace, if you know people like ... like ... (**Baig** *appears flustered and undecided.*)

Silence.

Bilal (*sternly*) He crossed over last week ... To a training camp in Muzaffarabad but you don't know why or how? You know nothing about him because he hasn't come to your clinic, Baig Sahib. But isn't it possible that he is also worthy of as much understanding as your patients? Don't trade him. They won't find him but will kill one of his brothers and set me free. Set me free and then kill me on another day. I don't want my freedom at someone else's cost.

Pause.

Baig *looks at* **Bilal** *in disbelief. In anger. Gets up slowly, begins to go. He takes off his phiran and throws it to* **Bilal**.

Baig I don't want Ashrafi to see you like this. She has to live ... and live with better images.

You are wrong, Bilal. Once again you are wrong. Your great sacrifice, (*Mocking him.*) your act of bravery is still at someone else's expense. If not for yourself, for her you could have/

Bilal For her, I should have stopped myself from throwing a stone? I should have come back from the mortuary, unaffected, unmoved, stoic, like a rock as if nothing has happened?

Pause.

You are blind, Baig Saheb. Absolutely blind. You are treating our minds ... I wish I could treat your soul. Even now, you are just angry with me, since I know about a boy who has gone to a training camp in Muzaffarabad. A boy you know nothing about. Even now, I am absolutely sure, your instinct is to treat his mind but not stand up against the mind that creates him. Why are you curing our anger, Baig Saheb ... why? Cure our children, Baig Saheb, but not their anger ... please!

Silence.

Dr Baig *keeps looking at* **Bilal** *in disbelief.*

Forgive me Baig Saheb, for speaking to you like this ... you will take care of Shefu, won't you ...

Baig I will ... you know I will ...

Dr Baig *turns around and walks away. He comes out where* **Wani** *and* **Ashrafi** *are sitting. He gestures to* **Wani** *to send* **Ashrafi** *in.* **Wani** *gets* *up to go with her.* **Dr Baig** *stops her and gestures to send her alone. He sits down distraught but stern. Visibly disturbed.*

Ashrafi *walks in.* **Wani** *stands between* **Dr Baig** *and* **Ashrafi.**

Ashrafi *comes and stands in front of the cell with her doll.* **Bilal** *sits under the bulb in his room, wearing* **Dr Baig**'s *phiran, smiling.*

Ashrafi Bhaijaan …

Bilal (*in a storyteller tone*) Shefu … Welcome to your Bhaijaan's cave … hahahahahaha!!!

Ashrafi Bhaijaan … what happened to your face?

Bilal The lions of Hamza have been fighting with the lions of/

Ashrafi Bhaijaan … are you hurt?

Bilal (*trying to get her back to the story mode*) The gallant warriors on the gallant horses, rose up from their cavalries and flew up and up in the sky till the lightning from the stars/

She comes close to the cell to see and then extends her right hand.

Ashrafi Are you hurt, Bhaijaan?

Bilal *stops the story and comes close to* **Ashrafi.** **Ashrafi** *touches his face. He wreathes in pain. She withdraws. He looks at her and brings her hand closer again.*

Ashrafi Did they beat you up, Bhaijaan?

Bilal Yes, Shefu. They did … are you alright?

Ashrafi Yes … (*Pause.*) why did you do it Bhaijaan?

Bilal I am sorry, Shefu … I just had to.

Ashrafi You should not have, Bhaijaan … we would have been free in two days …

Bilal We wouldn't have been, Shefu. We might have been able to get away from here but we wouldn't have been free.

Pause.

Shefu, I am sorry … I … hit you/

Ashrafi If you hadn't I wouldn't have gone away Bhaijaan … you saved me. I ran to the clinic and that doctor … he was still there, he took me home. (*Looks at the doll.*)

Bhaijaan … you know what Hafiz told me? Just now, as I was waiting outside …

Bilal What did Hafiz tell you, Shefu?

Ashrafi That you will become the moon.

Bilal This Eid?

Ashrafi Yes … will you?

Bilal *comes closer and looks into Shefu's eyes and now feels her face.*

Bilal A Half-moon …

Ashrafi Half-moon – half-man …

Bilal Half and half.

Ashrafi Half-man-half-Djinn … half and half.

Bilal Half-light and half-darkness. (*Laughs.*)

Ashrafi Half-Bilal and Half-Shefu. (*She laughs.*)

Bilal Half-football player.

Ashrafi And half-Ashrafi Naeem's model. (*She laughs.*)

Bilal Half … the moon circle … in the sky.

Ashrafi I had a dream last night, Bhaijaan.

Bilal Hmmm …

Ashrafi Abba came to meet me. That doctor, he made me see him today.

Bilal He did? (**Bilal** *smiles.*) And then?

By now they sit holding each other across the bars and appear comfortable.

Ashrafi Abbajaan came to me today … the first time after he died, Bhaijaan, and you know what he said?

Bilal What?

Ashrafi I will never go away, Shefu … never. I am a star and your Bhaijaan will become the moon this Eid. And forever we will be there, and appear on every single Eid. (*Smiles.*)

Bilal Yes, Shefu. (*Laughs.*)

Ashrafi You will die, Bhaijaan?

Bilal (*smiling*) Yes. Yes Shefu. I will.

Ashrafi You know what happens when we die?

Bilal We go to Heaven ... "Jannat" ... or Hell. "Dozakh" ...

Ashrafi No, Bhaijaan ... Abbu told me the other day what happens.

Bilal Really?

Ashrafi In the last moments of one's life, one gets a dream, he said. This is the dream we have always wanted to see. "Actually, we are dreaming people", he said. We live in-between dreams and not dream in-between life.

Bilal Shefu, you are talking like a Pir Saheb ... like a saint. (*Laughs.*)

Ashrafi Abbu says, our entire life is about this dream. This one that we want to see.

Everything we live takes us closer to it ... and in the end if we see this dream, it is Jannat.

(*Pointing up.*) If we don't it is Dozakh. (*Pointing down.*) ... We don't go to Heaven or Hell

Bhaijaan ... this dream itself is it. Death is the dream at the end of life, and life, the dream at the end of death ... it's just that.

Bilal So, did Abbu get to Jannat or Dozakh?

Ashrafi Abbu ... he died so quickly, he did not see a dream, he said. He is with us, Bhaijaan, always. But I know you will see your dream ... you will die in peace. And then become ... the half-moon.

Ashrafi *pulls* **Bilal** *closer, kisses his eyes. Gives him her doll.*

Keep my Hafiz with you Bhaijaan ... he will make the pain lesser.

Bilal It seems like you are older to me, Shefu. (*Smiles.*)

Ashrafi I am, Bhaijaan ... I am very old. I am as old as this land itself. If they get the land, I will become the moon, if they get the moon, I will become the sun ... they will never get me, Bhaijaan ... they will never get us. We will all becomes Djinns ... Djinns ... at the Eidgah.

Bilal (*in storyteller mode again*) Made of fire, dust and smoke.

Ashrafi (*in the same storytelling mode*) Allah made Djinns before he made Men.

Bilal And set them free to be pure passion …

Ashrafi Pure passion … no reason, no thought … everything that man wants to be.

They laugh.

Bilal Our Abba told us wonderful stories, Shefu … didn't he?

Ashrafi Our Abbu told us the truth … the truth of in-between …

Silence.

Ashrafi *gets up.*

Don't be afraid Bhaijaan … you won't die, you will just change. From man to moon.

Bilal I know. (*Smiles.*) Shefu they won't even give you my body … you will never see me again.

Ashrafi As this … (*Touching him. She smiles.*) You always insisted, Bhaijaan … this is you … for real. (*Imitating him.*) In real … you are something else. Something much larger … I won't miss this Bhaijaan … I will say your prayers at the Eidgah. I will say your prayers to the sky …

Bilal *pulls her closer and kisses her hands.*

Allah Hafiz, Bhaijaan.

Bilal Allah Hafiz, Shefu … Allah Hafiz.

Scene Fourteen

Day two. Late night.

S1 *and* **S2** *at the CRPF barrack. In the background there is a sound of a young girl reciting the "Fateha," the prayer for the dead.* **S2** *has an injury on his head from the attack by* **S1**. **S1** *is sitting on the chair trying to listen to something on his wireless on which some distorted sounds are heard. Looks irritated and angry.*

S2 (*trying to look out*) Saheb, if commandant Saheb comes please don't make a complaint against me … please, Saheb.

S1 Wasn't he supposed to come today?

S2 Yes ... Yes, Saheb. Perhaps he will. Later at night ...

Pause.

S1 Switch on your walkie-talkie ... now.

S2 *switches it on. He tries turning it on but there is no signal. He tries desperately. Says "hello hello."*

S1 We are off.

S2 What?

S1 Yes that's it. What did they tell you about this posting? Why were you sent here?

S2 Saheb (*Nervous.*) this is my punishment posting, Saheb. After the doctor's report, they sent me here on punishment, saying there is no "action".

S1 No action! Of course.

S1 *is looking around.*

S2 What, Saheb? I am feeling/

S1 This is where all the action will be. Everything. Can't you see?

S2 *also starts looking around.*

S2 What, Saheb?

S1 We are on our own. And the only picket in the middle of a completely residential area.

And that too right next to the Eidgah.

S2 So ...

S1 They didn't come, because they want us to shoot at the boys. And then the boys will stone us, and before tomorrow, before Eid, before the talks begin it will be clear, that Kashmiri boys are killing Indian soldiers.

S2 *nervously paces inside the picket. Keeps looking out. Picks up his gun.*

S2 Why should they stone us, what did we do to them?

S1 Why should we kill them, what did they do to us?

S2 We are bloody standing here in this cold, away from home to save these …

S1 *picks up his gun and shoots the two walkie-talkies. Loud sound. A still Silence.*

S2 *completely panics at the sound of the gunshot … he coils to one corner of the picket.* **S1** *looks at him in surprise.* **S2** *gets up suddenly and in one move comes and hits* **S1** *hard with the butt of his gun.* **S1** *falls.* **S2** *snatches his gun and vehemently starts kicking his face and body.* **S1** *bleeds as he tries to fight back but* **S2** *beats him up in rage.*

Dr Baig *appears outside. At the gate …* **S2** *notices him and rushes out.*

S1 What are you doing? Are you crazy, where are you going?

S2 *hits him again, very hard.* **S1** *lies bleeding.* **S2** *comes out in the open, screams out at* **Dr Baig**.

Dr Baig *stands unperturbed outside the gate of the Eidgah, looking inside.*

S2 Oi … ei …

Dr Baig *turns around. Looks* **S2** *in the eye.*

Silence.

S2 *points his gun at* **Dr Baig**.

Oi … hands … hands!

Dr Baig *looks puzzled.*

Hands … behind your head. Walk.

Dr Baig *does not place his hands behind his head. He remains standing, unmoved.*

Oi … ei … hands … hands. (**S2** *loads his gun.*) …

S2 *walks up to* **Dr Baig** *and pushes him hard.* **Dr Baig** *falls on the ground.*

S1 *comes out, struggling to stand.*

Baig What is the matter with you?

S2 Can't you hear me? Should I kill you? You bastard, bloody … how did you get here?

Dr Baig *looks at* **S1** *as he struggles to come closer. He is bleeding all over.*

Baig What are you/

S2 *places his gun on* **Dr Baig**'s *head.*

Baig If you could shoot, you would have … long back.

S2 *slaps* **Dr Baig**. *Hard.*

Dr Baig *is stunned.*

S2 Don't be smug with me, alright? I am here to guard you, you asshole … just tell me, how did you get here?

Baig I got here walkin … like you saw. There is no curfew at this hour and I am not a teenager to be kept away on precautionary grounds!

S1 Oi … what are you (*To* **Baig**.) Are … Doctor Saheb. Sorry, Doctor Saheb. (*To* **S2**.) Listen, everyone here knows him, OK. He comes here every evening, his family is/

S2 (*points the gun again at* **S1**) Shut up …

Dr Baig *gets up and starts walking towards* **S2**.

Where are you coming? Go … go/

Baig Listen … son, it's ok. Just keep your gun down.

S2 Don't come towards me … I am telling you, I will shoot you.

S1 Shit.

S2 What?

S1 Now we have to kill him, you idiot. If you let him go out, he will tell everyone what's going on here. And in no time/

Baig Don't worry, I have nothing to tell anyone.

S2 Oh … so now you are scared for your life, you bastard.

Baig I am scared for yours, Son. I am speaking to your people tomorrow.

S2 *slaps him again. Holds him by his collar. Makes him kneel right in front of the gate of the Eidgah.*

S2 Sit here. Just fucking sit here, OK. I can't stand it. When you assholes get smart with us.

What do you think, we are enjoying this? This is my idea of a life? You bastard, you are talking to my people. Well talk to them. Talk to them if you/

Baig Shoot me. Go on.

S2 *points his gun. Again.*

Baig Yes, go on …

S2 *tries hard. His face goes red. His eyes water. He sweats. He sits down on the floor. Holds his rifle.* **S1** *watches in amazement.*

I know. You can't. You are scared, of the sound of bullets.

S1 *laughs at* **S2**.

S1 He's scared of the sounds of bullets … really … you are (*Laughs.*) No wonder … punishment posting.

Baig It's a common disorder, in soldiers. Especially like you. It's alright.

S1 Great. Now we are surely dead. I don't have a gun and you are scared of the sound of bullets. Excellent. (*Starts laughing.*)

S2 *walks up to* **S1** *and hits him again. Really hard. A few blows with the back of his gun.* **S1** *screams and falls bleeding badly.*

Baig What are you doing? (*Screaming.*) Why are you … ! (*Breathes heavily.*) Let him go … listen … I can get you out of here. If you leave with me, no one will touch you around Eidgah.

You will be safe.

S1 (*struggling*) We have to kill him now. Doctor Saheb, I am sorry, I have nothing against you personally, but we can't trust you.

Baig We, who is we? You and I are at gunpoint here. He is not.

S2 Shut up. Just shut up. Both of you.

Baig You are making a huge mistake, son …

S2 *charges at* **Dr Baig** *again. Is about to hit him.*

S2 Listen, don't make me hit you again and again. OK. I am not your son. Don't call me that.

Baig I am trying to help you … you are disturbed … you need some rest … some time away … listen …

S2 *grabs* **Dr Baig** *by the collar.*

S2 Listen, asshole, don't play this trick on me. I know your type. Don't pretend to be large. I can't stand saints in such places. I maybe scared of the sound of bullets, but I could stab you or strangle you or burn you to death. I am the one being large here. So stop feeling good about yourself at my expense.

Loud speeches from the mosque.

(*To* **Dr Baig**.) What are they saying?

Pause.

Baig They are saying, the child will be buried on Eid and as of now the Imam has not spotted the moon.

S2 But the moon is surely there.

Baig It is. But if the Imam does not see it, we have to wait another night for Eid.

S2 (*to* **S1**) So, if there is no Eid, they will keep circling us another day with that corpse?

They won't have the meeting and no one will come.

Baig Maybe not.

Silence.

S2 *sits down on the floor dejected and not knowing what he should do. He desperately gets up and walks around to find a way out of the place.*

Baig You Indians want to meet on Eid.

S2 (*snaps*) What do you mean by "Indian," you asshole? What are you?

Dr Baig *remains quiet.*

S2 You are not Indian? Then why am I protecting you … your children … your mother? Why am I protecting you?

Baig I am not Indian. And you are not protecting my mother.

S2 *goes up to* **Dr Baig** *and hits him hard. Takes out a small book from his jacket, holds it in one hand and in the other hand holds his knife.*

S2 OK … come here. (*Pushes him down to the floor.* **Baig**'s *face is covered in mud.*) Can you read this? This?

Baig No.

S2 You can't, because this is in Marathi. Not in Hindi. I am Maharashtrian. But I am also Indian. OK? You asshole. Get your facts right.

Baig I am Kashmiri. But I am not Indian. If I were Maharashtrian, I would be.

S2 *slaps him hard again.* **Dr Baig** *falls on the ground.*

S2 He is mad. This asshole. And he calls me a lunatic. Look at him.

S1 Don't start this fight now. Kill him or let him go. But don't get into this/

S2 You. Maybe I should kill you first. I had my doubts. Right from the beginning. Maybe you are also one of them. Maybe you are not Hindu. Maybe … (*Takes a knife.*)

S2 *goes towards* **S1**. *Places his knife on* **S1**'s *stomach.*

With his other hand **S2** *unzips* **S1**'s *pants. Pulls his underwear.*

S1 *and* **S2** *are sweating.* **Dr Baig** *is lying in one part of the picket. Everyone is breathing heavily.* **S1** *is in a state of shock.*

Baig You are sick. Totally sick. (**S2** *looks at* **Dr Baig** *enraged.*) You don't understand, this war is not about gods at all. It has nothing to do with/

S2 *gets up, grabs* **Dr Baig** *again. Drags him to the gate of the Eidgah. Pulls out a small prayer bell from his pocket and places a knife on* **Baig**'s *neck. Keeps the guns on the ground.*

The speeches from the Mosques are distant but charged up.

S2 Fold your hands. Go on asshole. Fold your hands. Yes, even if they are tied. Fold your hands, close your eyes and repeat after me … start … fold your hands (**Dr Baig** *hesitates.*) no … why this war is not about gods, isn't it … then … what's the problem?

Baig You are making it about gods but it's not. I am not forcing you to pray to my god … /

S2 (*places the knife on his neck*) What did I tell you? Don't do this shit with me. You are not forcing me to pray to your god? Will you let me stay here, if I pray to mine? Will you allow it?

I still have your neck on the blade of my knife, and if I did not, who knows you might have had my neck on your blade. And you know what, whenever someone chops someone's head off ... both of them, take their own gods' names at the end. Those are everyone's last words.

Baig Both of them just scream. Everyone just screams at the end. The name of the god, yours or mine, is just an excuse.

S2 *holds* **Dr Baig** *by the hair. Pushes him down on the floor. Makes him kneel down in front of the picture.*

S2 OK, please me. Your Imam has not spotted the moon, so your god is not coming out for you tonight. So go ahead and pray to mine. Mine is always there you know. Moon or no moon. Go on.

S2 *presses the knife on* **Baig**'s *neck. It starts to bleed.*

S2 *begins to ring the bell. Loudly. He begins to chant, when all the mosques together, do the evening "azaan." The sound is deafening.* **S2** *closes his eyes. Presses the knife and tries to ring the bell even louder and faster, as loud as he can. The azaan gets louder.*

Dr Baig *does not say the prayer even though his neck bleeds.* **S2** *keeps looking at* **Dr Baig** *in rage, till* **S2** *collapses, sits next to* **Dr Baig** *and starts to cry. He wails loudly. Lets out a scream.* **Dr Baig** *immediately comes closer. Embraces him.*

They sit still.

Silence.

S2 *opens his eyes. He can see* **Ashrafi** *approaching from the Eidgah. He is silent and stunned.* **Ashrafi** *is wearing a Hijab.*

Baig (*facing the other way, holding him*) You will be fine ... you will be ... my son ... you will be. (*He shuts his eyes.*) You don't need to kill anyone my son ... remember the story your Abbu told you ... in the sky one night there will be Fatima's eyes ... forever and ever ... and after that the moon will come out ...

Ashrafi *keeps walking towards* **S2** *from within the Eidgah.*

And as long as Fatima's eyes are there ... she will keep watching you ... forever and ever ... and ... (*He holds him.*)

S2 *pushes* **Dr Baig***, picks up his gun and shoots him.*

Silence.

Ashrafi *is unfazed. She removes her veil. Her eyes are visible. She looks straight into the soldier's eyes.*

S2 Go ... go away or I will kill you. I promise you. You ... (*To* **Dr Baig**'s *dead body.*) Tell her ... tell her to go away or/

S2 *panics on realizing that he is speaking to a dead body.*

Ashrafi *stares coldly at* **S2**.

Just close your eyes ... I am telling you ... you just close your eyes or ...

He points his gun at her.

Ashrafi *bends down, picks up a stone.*

Ashrafi Shoot me ... and I will come back again ... and again ... and again ... (*Slowly but decisively like a chant.*) And again and again and again ... shoot me ... and I will return ... again and again ...

S2 *points the gun at* **Ashrafi**. *The morning azaan is called loudly from the mosque. As the azaan plays,* **Ashrafi** *just keeps looking at him and says "again and again ... and again"* ... *under her breath as if it were a chant.* **S2** *puts the nozzle of the gun in his mouth. A loud gunshot.*

Blackout.

Epilogue

Suspended Time. Between Life and Death.

S1 *and* **Ashrafi** *are on either side of the gate.*

Dr Baig *is now inside the Eidgah. The* **Djinn** *is in the same clothes as* **Dr Baig**. *But painted.*

A big red carpet between **Dr Baig** *and the* **Djinn**.

Djinn Abbajaan ...

Baig Not you ... Not now.

Djinn It's time.

Baig Not yet ...

Djinn Yes.

Baig Pareen. Not with you ...

Djinn Abbajaan ...

Baig Don't call me that, Pareen. For me you are a Kafir.

Djinn How blind can you be? At least now, at the end, at the very end stop hating me. I am here, as I was meant to be. Perhaps I can say my prayers for you, as you never said yours for me. Perhaps then, Abbajaan, we won't be Djinns anymore. Perhaps then, we really will be free. Neither ghosts, nor Djinns, nor souls trapped in this madness ... but free ...

Pause.

Baig (*somehow turns his head towards* **Djinn**) Do you know why you are here my son?

Why are you still a Djinn ...

Pause.

Djinn Because I chose to be.

Baig You didn't choose, my son. No one can choose this in-between.

Djinn You chose Abbu. You are the Djinn ...

Baig On the day of judgement, if Allah asks me, am I right or wrong ... I will ask him in turn (*Pause.*) ... .why didn't you say anything about us in your book? We, the people of in-between ... what do we chose, where do we go? Am I a Kafir or am I not ... where do I begin my faith, my maker ... by healing my children or by fighting their war? What if oh Merciful ... your book was for simpler times ... on judgement day, what if I am prepared but you don't find the chapter for my world.

Pause.

Junaid ... my son ... I just want you to know ... Since ... these are my last words ... your Abbu loves you.

The **Djinn** *recedes slowly as he recites the "Fateha," the prayer for the dead.*

Silence.

The end

Acknowledgments

The Djinns of Eidgah has had a long journey and in this journey it has collected several debts. Many people have made the play possible, and although it might not be possible to have everyone's name here, I am deeply indebted to all those voices that made this voice possible.

Thanks to Rajit Kapur for making this possible. Without him nothing would have happened.

To Shernaz Patel and Rahul da Cunha and everyone else at Rage Theatre. To all the other writers of Writer's Bloc at Vasind. This play is yours. Special thanks to Irawati Karnik for being a wonderful friend and a constant dramaturg.

Thanks to Anmol Vellani and Sunil Shanbagh for giving it direction that only they could have at an early stage. Thanks to Syed Humayoun, Showkat Motta, Dr Ashraf, Dr Mushtaq Margoob, Dr Amit Sen, Dr Shalija Sen, Irfan Hasan, Ishfaq Hussain, Ashwath Bhat, Anand Vivek Taneja, Bilal, Khalid Wasim, Rizwaan Khan.

Thanks to Dr Hameedah Nayeem for being such an inspiration.

Special thanks to Rukmini Sen and Suvojit Bagchi.

Thanks to those three CRPF soldiers who cannot be named. No one can share their lives like you did.

Thanks to those countless freedom fighters who again cannot be named. No one can share their life like you did as well.

Thanks to Carl Miller for being the greatest friend a writer can have.

Thanks to Elyse Dodgson for believing in it much before I did. Thanks to Vicky Featherstone for being the dramaturg that she is. Special thanks to Richard Twynman for going through all the highs and lows of this play for two years. Thanks, Richard, for your mind and for your friendship. Special thanks to Ayesha Dharker for all the love and thought she has given to this play over the years. Thanks to all the actors in London who have informed this play through the workshops and in its production at the Royal Court Theatre. This play could not have been written without your thoughts, ideas and embodiment of characters through the various stages of development.

Special thanks to the cast and crew of *The Djinns of Eidgah* in Mumbai.

Special thanks to Mahmood Farooqui for reviving the Dastaan Goi. Special thanks to Sunil Khilnani for "The Idea of India."

Thanks to Joyeeta Bandyopadhyay, for being the first and most important storyteller in my life. To Pallavi Krishna for making the Dastaan worthwhile and for continuously nudging and guiding the play in several ways.

Thank you, Chris James, for all your hard work and support for this play.

And finally, a very special thanks to Abbaji and Tabrez Alam. Without you, the world would not have revealed itself to us mortals. I hope wherever you are, you are resting in peace. Deeply indebted to you.

The play was first produced by Rage Theatre in collaboration with the Royal Court Theatre at the Writer's Bloc Festival in Mumbai in 2012. It was last produced in London by Royal Court in 2013. This edition is a pre-production version of the staging at the Royal Court.

Notes

1   Respectful address to a Muslim father (in South Asia).
2   Persian word for 'story'—an oral tale, sometimes of epic proportions, relating the heroic deeds of an individual who protects his tribe from invaders.
3   Good night.
4   The Hurriyat Conference, with its hardliners, is currently perceived as a pro-Pakistan element or irredentist force seeking unification of Kashmir with Pakistan.
5   Yes.
6   Respectful address to a Muslim brother (in South Asia).
7   An ardent devotee of Lord Rama, Hanuman is worshipped by practicing Hindus as a deity embodying power and selfless service.
8   Thank you.
9   One of Hamza's companions.
10 One engaged in jihad in its contemporary political sense. Etymologically, it means one who fights for spiritual Islam. Plural: mujahideen.

The Far-reaching Night

by
Zahida Zaidi

Translated from Urdu by **Ameena Kazi Ansari**

In memory of the victims of communal violence:

the homeless,

the women who fell to bestial lust,

the innocent who languished in jails,

the children who lost their paradise.

The original Urdu version was published by Abshar Publications, Aligarh, in 2006.

Characters (In order of appearance)

Children as angels
Satan
Voice of God
Rajrai in saffron dhoti
Todi (pronounced "Tori") in saffron dhoti
Rathbani in saffron dhoti
Swami in saffron dhoti
A few leaders in saffron dhotis
Young men in saffron dhotis
A mob in saffron dhotis
Some commoners in saffron dhotis
A house owner in green kurta
A middle-aged male refugee in green kurta
Elderly male refugee in green kurta
Young female refugee in green kurti
Young male refugee in green kurta
Some commoners in green kurtas, skull caps, and white pyjamas
Police Commissioner
Police officers
Policemen
Poor tribals
Newsreader
Two fashionably dressed ladies
Two male well-wishers
A female well-wisher
Male guards
A female guard
A child Satan
A booming voice

Act One

Scene One

An empty expanse, in which a faint bluish light shines and small stars twinkle occasionally. Soul-stirring music is heard. A long line of lightly made-up children appears. They are dressed as angels in flowing robes of white, and wear silver crowns. On their wings, silver stars glint. Their gentle and rhythmic movements convey their innocence. They spread out in a semicircle, and raise their hands in supplication to God.

The angels' song
From each corner gleams the glory of God,
The glory of God shines from everything.
His glory the vast blue skies hide,
In the ocean's waves, his glory swirls.
Splendorous looks the universe in His light,
Up to heaven leads His light's radiant river.
From each corner gleams the glory of God,
In its lustre is bathed each particle, each speck.

Satan *enters. He is a tall, dark, well-built, confident, and haughty individual, with jet-black, shoulder-length hair, and brows and moustaches to match. He wears a black robe embroidered with golden thread. A golden crown rests on his head.*

Satan (*addressing the angels*) The same old song to the Almighty! Don't you have anything better to do?

Angels
From each corner gleams the glory of God,
The glory of God shines from everything.
The moon and stars His radiance illumine,
And lives the world on His munificence.
From each corner gleams the glory of God,
In its lustre is bathed each particle, each speck.

Suddenly, there is a stir, and a blinding radiance spreads out. The music rises to a harsh crescendo, and then abruptly stops.

The voice of God Iblees, you've arrived at an opportune moment. You were granted aeons of time, with all the freedom to sow discord and strife in the world. But now it's time for your obliteration.

Satan O, One Above All, I've no objection to this. My task stands completed. Many of my disciples and admirers have surpassed me. The powers of evil have prospered, indeed. The actors on earth are ready to stage a new play; a drama of unprecedented bloodshed waits to unfold.

The voice of God You don't wish to return to earth and direct this new play?

Satan Lord of the Universe, there's no need for me to lead this bloody drama! The creatures below have their own directors to follow! The opening scene has already been enacted. The main part will unfold soon.

The voice of God But you do look impatient to return there?

Satan Because, Ruler of the Heavens, the bloody drama is to be enacted in the land of *devis* and *devtas*, gods and goddesses, where you've often bestowed your attention and pinned all your hopes. Massacre and arson, loot and rape, murder of children and brutalization of women—they're all going to be presented.

The voice of God So, you want to participate in the performance; you want to guide the players by demonstrating your acting skills?

Satan The truth, Omnipotent, is that those people don't need my assistance or leadership. I've always entered the minds of people, one by one, and taught them. But their stage managers have trained the minds of an entire generation. I would mainly like to watch the grand spectacle!

The voice of God Who are the villains of the piece?

Satan It's all those who differ from them. In the course of their training, they've sworn to wipe out their enemies. Their target now is the destruction and decimation of all those who wear green kurtas,[1] that is, the green kurtawallahs whom they've sworn to eliminate.

The voice of God The ones dressed in green kurtas? But why?

Satan Because they are proud of their saffron dhotis! They see as enemies anyone who doesn't live their way, who doesn't eat or wear as they do. At this moment, their real enemies are the green kurtawallahs.

The voice of God You seem to have great knowledge in this regard. Shed some more light on the issue.

Satan The stage is all set. Now only a suitable moment is awaited for the curtain to go up. Lead actors are engaged in discussions on the details of action. If you're kind enough to grant me permission, I'll not only watch the terrific spectacle but also report developments to you.

The voice of God You don't need to keep me informed. I can well see what is to happen—scene-wise. Rather you can't imagine yet the extremes of savagery that soon are going to be enacted. That's because I'd set certain limits for you. But these actors are going to surpass all limits and their past records. You can go. If possible, don't allow the sensationalism to cross the limit onstage. To assist the oppressed and homeless, I am also despatching some of my representatives. They shall seek my instructions on and off. I can't control this orgy of hatred because their script is ready and its pages have spread far and wide in time and space. But I'll certainly help those actors who still try to keep the lamp of humanity aglow. All right, you can go now. And when I command, you will return.

Satan Many thanks, O Supreme Being. I am grateful indeed for your kindness.

Satan *bows in obeisance. As he leaves, the blinding radiance slowly takes on bluish tones, and the harsh sound of music changes into an enchanting melody. The* **angels** *then make an appearance, and continue their hymn in praise of God.*

Angels
From each corner gleams the glory of God,
The glory of God shines from everything.
He is the concealed, and He the revealed,
He is the secret behind all creation.
From each corner gleams the glory of God,
The glory of God shines from everything.
Each particle, each speck, is bathed in its lustre.

Slowly darkness envelopes the stage and the enchanting melody fades away.

Curtain

* * * * *

Scene Two

Earth. The "drama" begins. A big room where the atmosphere is mysterious. The lighting is muted. Center stage is a small round table on which the lights are focused. Around it are seated **Rajrai**, **Rathbani**, *and* **Todi***—all busy conversing. They are attired in expensive, saffron-coloured dhotis, and wear jewelry.* **Rajrai** *and* **Rathbani** *sport small*

golden crowns on their heads. In the course of the conversation, **Rajrai** *often removes his crown, and scratches his head. He speaks softly, opening and shutting his eyes.* **Rathbani,** *on the other hand, repeatedly tries to steady the crown on his head, and grinds out his words.*
Todi *speaks very fast and loudly, gesticulates often, and springs up and down.*

Rajrai So what do you say, Rathbani-ji?

Todi Rajrai-ji, all preparations are complete. From the far corners of the nation, zealous young men in saffron dhotis have reached my locality.

Rajrai And what more have you done in this regard?

Todi I have distributed swords and *trishuls*[2] to my workers. Diagrams of the enemy's localities have been prepared, and their addresses obtained. Thousands of tons of the precious liquid have been collected, and lie concealed in secret storehouses. We've got a detailed chart of the enemy's neighorhoods.

Rathbani You should also prepare a list of their schools and places of worship. It's quite possible that they'll choose to flee and hide in these places.

Todi Such a list is also in our possession. We've even had rehearsals of how to enter and ...

Rajrai All this should be done after due consideration and circumspection.

Todi Rajrai-ji, where's the time for all this? Preparations have been made. Our *kar sevaks* are brimming with enthusiasm. Should we let all this diminish and our efforts be washed away?

Rathbani Our friend Todi is right. Strike while the iron is hot!

Rajrai Well, I agree with what you say. But it's necessary to take Swami's opinion, too. What's your advice, Swami? (**Swami** *enters.*)

Swami All this is absolutely necessary. But everything has to be linked to religion. Only this will truly enthuse every one.

Rathbani How can we ensure that, Swami?

Swami For example, by provoking the enemy to attack our holy sites.

Rajrai Will all this really be done?

Rathbani Not really, Rajrai-ji. But it can be claimed to have happened.

Todi (*very passionately*) That's a great idea! We can stage-manage things, and then say it's the handiwork of the green kurtawallahs. Instantly, people will be aroused into a frenzy, and they'll take to streets to wreak revenge for the sacrilege. Then, our volunteers shall confront the green kurtiwallahs and …

Rathbani But our enemies are quite fearless and their impassioned slogans very effective.

Todi But our men will far outnumber them. They'll be carrying their weapons. Then, our uniformed slaves, with theirs, will also be present. They'll assist our brave hearts with skill and ruthlessness.

Rajrai Our uniformed slaves?!

Todi Yes, that's what I call policemen. Their job is to obey our orders. Should a policeman not obey his superior's orders, he should be dismissed, or …

Rathbani This question will arise later. Right now, you've got to ensure that all dissenters are banished from your locality.

Todi I've made arrangements in this regard. All officers and staff who've maintained contact with green kurtawallahs shall be transferred to remote towns and villages.

Rajrai This could be termed an obsession!

Todi What is enthusiasm if it's not an obsession?

Rathbani And you, its shining example!

Todi Many thanks, Rathbani-ji. Whatever I am, I owe to the leadership of you both. It's the miracle of your affection and training. The young bubbling spirits should find an occasion to display their skills after all.

Rajrai What is your plan then?

Todi Rajrai-ji, my dream has been a world without green kurtawallahs. Their children in the womb should not see the light of day. Their attractive women should be taken care of by our worthy workers. When these women are of no further use, they are fit to be disposed of, I mean …

Rajrai What do you mean?!

Todi Rajrai-ji, how can you not understand? You're a great leader and man of wisdom, but you are old-fashioned. In these times, everything

has changed. For example, today's generation knows that burning ... is
... a festival!

Rathbani Your words carry weight. But before this festival, shouldn't
we make preparations for its initiation? In this regard, Swami's opinion
is absolutely vital. So, Swami, tell us your views?

Swami This task should be undertaken as soon as possible.

Rajrai How soon?

Swami (*with closed eyes*) Three days from now.

Todi Well said! Well said! (*Laughs uproariously.*)

Rajrai and **Rathbani** *look at each other, smile, and shake hands.*
Swami *makes a gesture to bless them.*

Curtain

* * * *

Scene Three

*A noisy railway platform with people moving about and hawkers loudly
selling their wares. Suddenly, a train's whistle is heard, and people
silently freeze in their places. In the background, the blurred image of
a train bogey in flames. A few young men in saffron dhotis can be seen
leaping out from it and raising slogans. Then, from all sides converge
men with shaven heads, bare torsos, and in saffron dhotis; some wear
beaded necklaces. With great enthusiasm, they join the sloganeering.
Some policemen appear and try to douse the flames with water. As the
flames die down, men and women gather on the platform. The men
in saffron lay out the injured and dead on the platform. Each of the
victims is covered with a saffron sheet in the midst of impassioned
sloganeering. A crowd stands around the dead and injured. Then, some
green kurtawallahs, wearing topis[3] and white pajamas, appear. As they
bend down to see the bodies, the ones in saffron push them away, and
enthusiastically raise slogans of "Murdabad" that call for the death and
damnation of the green kurtawallahs.*

Green kurtawallah (*to* **Policeman**) Some women and children from
my family were to arrive on this train but they're nowhere to be seen.
Please allow us to check out the injured.

Policeman Move! Keep away! Let us do our job.

Man in saffron dhoti These are bodies of *sants* and *sadhus*,[4] all holy men whom you've burnt alive.

Green kurtiwallah My dear Sir, we've just arrived here from home! We've not set anyone aflame!

A few men in saffron dhotis No, you *have* burnt alive the sants and sadhus. We'll surely pay you back in the same coin.

A man in saffron dhoti, appearing to be a leader, brings in some photographers. One carries a TV camera. They photograph the bodies covered with sheets.

Green kurtawallah But, Sir, all these are not sadhus and sants. See, there're bodies of women and children here. Please let us lift the sheets and look. God forbid, some of them could be our family members.

A leader in saffron No, they're all sadhus and sants. Why can't women and children be sadhus and sants? After all, they're all involved in the rituals of faith. That's why you set afire the train coach. And now you want to desecrate their bodies. That we won't allow. Murdabad!

A few green kurtawallahs No, we did not set the fire. We're here to receive our relatives.

A few men in saffron dhotis No, this fire was lit by you. You're all agents of the enemy.

A few green kurtawallahs No, no, we ourselves are very distressed.

A few men in saffron (*to* **Policemen**) What are you doing just standing around! Why don't you arrest these men? These are extremely dangerous people. They're all enemy agents.

The men in saffron begin to assault the ones in green.

A leader in saffron Stop! Hold on! We'll certainly teach lessons to those in green, but not right now. Please restrain yourselves. (*To* **Policemen** *who are now arresting green kurtawallahs.*) Quick, arrest these people. Don't let a single one get away. Arrest them all. Catch anyone, even looking like them, outside the station. All of them lit the fire to kill the holy men.

As the green kurtawallahs begin to flee, the police assaults, and arrests some. Others are caught by the men in saffron and handed over to the police. A **leader in saffron** *makes a gesture that sets off spirited sloganeering.*

Men in saffron Green kurtawallahs, murdabad, murdabad! Revenge be taken! Death and destruction! Enemy agents, murdabad! Men in green, murdabad!

*The **leaders in saffron**, holding saffron flags, lead a procession of their sloganeering men offstage. Police, now in large numbers, take away the arrested green kurtawallahs. Silence descends on the deserted railway platform since ordinary passengers and hawkers have fled for their lives in the melee. On the platform, there are 25–30 corpses draped in saffron sheets. Suddenly, there is a slight movement under one of the sheets. A young woman emerges from under it. She is wearing a green salwar-kameez and is draped in a white dupatta. She lifts a saffron sheet nearby and peers under it. Two terrified young children emerge from there. They are twins and are dressed in green kurtas and green topis. Seeing their mother, they cling to the young woman. The young woman then lifts the saffron sheet on the other side of her and searches for another lost child amid some dead infants. Recognizing her child, she lifts it and clasps it to her bosom. As this child is dead, she quietly weeps. Then, holding the hands of her two surviving children, and covering her face with her white dupatta, she slowly leaves through the rear exit. In the background can be heard a heartrending tune. A few moments after her departure, two **leaders in saffron** and a **police officer** appear. They are conversing in a conspiratorial manner.*

First leader in saffron (*to the* **police officer**) You've done your job very well. Did any of them manage to escape?

Police Officer No, Sir. Each one of them stands arrested, whether found inside the station or outside. My brave force has thrashed them and put them behind bars.

Second leader in saffron How many did you arrest?

Police Officer Forty to fifty. Four or five are women. They're the ones who created a real ruckus and tried to save their people.

First leader in saffron That's a very small number. At least two hundred should've been arrested. And what sorts of women have been arrested?

Police Officer They're all old, or middle-aged.

Second leader in saffron Why didn't you arrest the young?

Police Officer That's exactly what we wanted to do. For this effort, we deserve a special reward! But the opportunity never came! Right from the beginning, all the young women took their children, and silently left on rickshaws, or horse-drawn *tongas*. If an opportunity comes in the future, we'll surely arrest them, too.

Second leader in saffron   Yes, this state of affairs should linger on. In the next three months, the count should rise to two hundred and fifty.

Police Officer   But that seems impossible! In this episode, all possible arrests have been made and done with. For what crime can we arrest more people later? Where'll we find evidence against them for the arrests?

Second leader in saffron   There's no need for evidence! The very fact that they wear green kurtas is evidence enough of their complicity in this episode.

Police Officer   You've set us an extremely difficult task. By arresting commoners, we arouse anger. They can even attack police posts. If, in enthusiasm, our bullets target them, then ...

First leader in saffron   No, no, there's no need to arrest common people. In fact, you should hunt out and arrest eminent folk.

Police Officer   Eminent people, that is ...

First leader in saffron   That is, eminent green kurtawallahs who wield greater influence than the ordinary folk. I mean either the leaders of green kurtawallahs, or their clerics. We can say they're all enemy agents. It's also necessary to arrest some wealthy green kurtawallahs, raid their mills and factories. We'll then announce that arms and ammunition were recovered there. That's how we can showcase them as agents of our enemy.

Police Officer   Yours is a wonderful idea, Sir. But it's dangerous to issue warrants against the wealthy as they're very highly connected. They'll get themselves released by paying large bribes and will then make life difficult for us.

First leader in saffron   No, there's no such possibility. It's absolutely necessary to prove that the hands behind the arson were these very people who are hands in glove with our enemies.

Police Officer   Even then, Sir ...

First leader in saffron   Look here, it's our government's writ that runs now. As far as this issue goes, no one will heed their pleas. Our government has also recently made laws by which anyone suspicious can be considered a terrorist and be arrested. After all, agents of the enemy are essentially terrorists!

Police Officer With your permission, Sir, may I summon my men to remove these corpses? At least today's task shall be complete then.

Second leader in saffron (*in worried tones*) No, no, there's no need to display any hurry now. We've got to check things out properly. There's no scope for any mistake. Meanwhile, go and get your papers in order. Return in an hour at the most, if you can't make it in half an hour. And make sure your report mentions at least sixty dead.

Police Officer Very good, Sir. I hope you'll keep us in mind, Sir, especially me as …

First leader in saffron There's no need to say this. Just stand by us, and you'll see how fast your promotions come. Your soul shall have *shanti*, peace, when you assist us in matters of faith. Think of it as your very own mission.

The **police officer** *salutes and exits.*

First leader in saffron Have you correctly recorded the number of bodies?

Second leader in saffron Yes, very precisely. (*In a hushed whisper.*) I'd instructed the stationmaster to record at least sixty dead, though there weren't more than thirty-five. In reality, however, the casualties were far less.

First leader in saffron But photographs have been taken.

Second leader in saffron Rest assured. I'd personally arranged for the photographers. They were my chosen men, not any riff-raff photographers.

First leader in saffron And the TV crew? I only hope they don't spoil things.

Second leader in saffron No, I'd also made arrangements for that. With great friendliness, I told the TV crew that, in addition to the corpses that were visible, there were many others that lay buried beneath the rubble. That's why it was important for them to announce that at least fifty-to-sixty holy men died in the inferno.

First leader in saffron Well, everything's gone fairly well, but what happens to those fools lying injured there?

Second leader in saffron Let them lie here. Their lives were worthless anyway.

First leader in saffron No, no, how can we let them be! It's highly dangerous! When the police return to take them away, they might create an uproar, and even go to the extent of giving statements against us.

Second leader in saffron (*drawing out a pistol*) So shall we put them to eternal sleep?

First leader in saffron *Arrey,*[5] what're you doing? They're supposed to have been burnt to death. If their bodies are found to have bullets from your weapon, then what happens? Also, some of them seem to be alive. Hearing a pistol shot, they might attempt to run. Then they'll certainly give statements against us.

Second leader in saffron What are the implications of that?

First leader in saffron A planned success will fail, and we'll rot in jail.

Second leader in saffron You speak great sense. But what are we to do with these people?

First leader in saffron We'll just have to let them go. Be very gentle with them as they'll be of use to us in the future.

Both move toward the covered bodies and peer beneath the sheets.

Both leaders in saffron (*in loud chorus*) Get up, Brothers, you're now free to leave.

Six or seven extremely impoverished **tribals**, *wearing torn and dirty vests and dhotis, emerge from under the saffron sheets. They dust themselves and wipe their perspiration.*

Two or three tribals (*in chorus*) Your lordship, may we leave now?

First leader in saffron Yes, leave very quietly through the rear exit, or walk along the rail tracks for some distance, and then make your way out. But not everyone together, walk in ones and twos.

Poor tribals (*in chorus*) And our reward, Sir, for your risky work?

First leader in saffron Yes, yes, why not? (*To his companion.*) Brother, give them their reward. They can either buy fruit and *mithai*[6] for their families, or spend it on toddy to drink and celebrate the whole night.

*The **second leader** of the saffron party gives each tribal a currency note.*

Poor tribals (*in chorus*) Only twenty rupees? Even our daily wages are more than that! We expected at least a fifty-rupee note each as reward!

First leader in saffron Here, here you are. (*Takes out fifty-rupee notes from his pocket and hands one to each of the poor men.*) Look, this is just the beginning. Keep working for us and you'll be better rewarded. We've got to severely punish the people in green. If you contribute to this, the Almighty *Bhagwan*[7] will be happy.

Poor tribals (*in chorus*) Blessings on your lordship. May we leave now?

Second leader in saffron Yes, go and enjoy yourselves. Very soon we'll invite you to the state capital. There we'll be distributing *lathis*[8] and trishuls to facilitate your job. And naturally, your reward then shall be much higher.

First leader in saffron Before leaving just see if there's any green kurtawallah amongst the dead. Should you find one, take off his green clothes, and wrap him up in the saffron sheet.

*The **poor tribals** lift the sheets and are seen changing the clothes of some.*

A poor tribal Your Honor, there is also a woman dressed in green here.

Second leader in saffron Take off her clothes, too, and drape her in the saffron sheet.

A poor tribal But, Sir, we shouldn't do this.

Second leader in saffron All right then, throw this woman's body on the railway track. It'll be crushed by the next train that comes.

*The **poor tribals** throw the woman's corpse onto the railway tracks, and, terror-stricken, exit.*

First leader in saffron So, Brother, a difficult task's been easily done. There just remains the information to be sent to Todi-ji. I now go straight to the capital city where Todi-ji and Rathbani-ji are busy making preparations for a big meeting. Please go and inform Swami that it's necessary for him to join this meeting on time.

Second leader in saffron My dear Brother, a difficult task so easily accomplished! Let's at least shake hands before you go.

Both shake hands, embrace warmly, and laugh uproariously.

Curtain

* * * * *

Scene Four

A large open space which gives the impression of being used as a stage or dais for a large meeting, the preparations for which are underway. On a small table is a telephone. A few chairs are scattered about chaotically. Two or three saffron party workers are running about, hanging up saffron flags, and displaying **Rajrai***'s photograph.* **Todi** *is rushing around, giving instructions to the workers.* **Rathbani** *stands near the small table, and is trying to make a call. As the phone seems to be out of order, he goes toward* **Todi** *and whispers into his ear. Todi very quickly pulls out his mobile and hands it to* **Rathbani***, who moves away and punches in a number. He can be seen speaking over the phone, but he is inaudible. Only his gesticulating hands suggest that he has something very important to convey. After making the call, he moves toward* **Todi** *and says something softly. Then* **Todi** *begins to look worried. They each pull a chair toward the small table and sit down. They whisper into each other's ears as a mournful tune echoes in the background. The preceding scene's two leaders in saffron rush in with a glow of happiness on their face. The first leader goes to* **Todi***.*

First leader in saffron It has HAPPENED, finally!

Todi What? How?

First leader in saffron All by God's will. Bring us some *mithai*.

As the gaze of the first leader falls on **Rathbani***, he does a quick* namaste *and touches his feet. Then he moves to stand between* **Todi** *and* **Rathbani***, bends a little, and tells them something in a very low voice. Hearing whatever it is, both* **Todi** *and* **Rathbani** *stand up in excitement simultaneously.*

Todi So, how many dead? Tell us the details.

First leader in saffron Here, listen to it yourself.

On a pocket transistor, he sets the wavelength and the news can be heard very loudly.

Newsreader News has just come in from the state capital. Just a few kilometers away, at a small railway station, a fire broke out on the Mahatma-ji Express. More than seventy Hindus, all kar sevaks[9], are reported to have been killed in the blaze. Twenty-to-twenty-five kar sevaks are injured, and the condition of some is critical. Our correspondent, who reached there immediately, reports that the fire was allegedly ignited by the green kurtawallahs who had come in large numbers, shouting slogans. Some six or seven of them had entered the compartment where the kar sevaks were seated while returning from their pilgrimage. It is also alleged that the men in green sprinkled petrol on the holy men and set them afire. Then they went out and threw burning tires into the compartment due to which the fire spread across the whole coach. Only a few emerged alive, though badly injured. Our correspondent also reported having seen more than seventy corpses on reaching the railway platform. These were covered with saffron sheets. The green kurtawallahs were trying to escape in different directions. As the police reached there in time, they were able to arrest forty-to-fifty of the green-clad terrorists. The hunt for the others is on.

*The **first leader in saffron** switches off the transistor and looks triumphantly at* **Todi**. **Todi** *nods.*

Rathbani Come on. Will you continue celebrating or plan for the next phase of action to cash in on this windfall? In Swami's opinion, it should begin before sunrise.

Todi Don't worry. Our kar sevaks and our uniformed servants are in perpetual readiness.

He claps his hands. A few workers come running.

Todi Are preparations for the meeting complete?

Workers bring a large table and place it in the center. They carry the scattered chairs and set them around the table. Then they place a vase and a microphone on the table.

Todi (*clapping his hands*) Let our kar sevaks and enthusiastic young supporters be presented.

Dressed in saffron clothes, young and middle-aged men march forward in their very own distinct style, and stand in a line on the right side of the stage.

Todi Let our men in uniform be presented.

In large numbers, policemen make their entry, salute **Todi** *and* **Rathbani**, *and stand in a line on the left of the stage.*

Todi (*to* **Rathbani**) All important players who are to participate in this program are now here. Take your place and begin your speech.

Rathbani Yes, but the masses, the believers … where are they?

Todi (*gesturing toward the audience*) They're all here, waiting to hear you speak.

Rathbani (*in a conspiratorial manner*) And, Swami? His presence is absolutely necessary here.

The second leader in saffron enters with **Swami**.

Todi Here's Swami. (**Namaste** *to* **Swami**.) As expected, Swami, you've arrived on the dot.

Rathbani Swami, namaste. (**Swami** *reciprocates.*) Without you, this gathering would be incomplete. (*Gestures to the vacant chair in the center.*) Please take your seat.

Swami No, that's your place. It doesn't behove a *sanyasi*[10] to sit there. (*Points toward the floor in the front of the stage.*) I'll sit there to listen and meditate.

Two workers carry in a four-legged chauki, or four-legged seat, covered with a saffron cloth. They put it down at the spot that **Swami** *had pointed to. He sits on it and appears lost in thought.*

Todi (*pointing to the chairs*) Rathbani-ji, please take your place so that the proceedings can begin.

Rathbani *sits on the chair in the center, and* **Todi** *sits next to him. The two saffron leaders sit on the chairs next to these two.*

Rathbani (*in a conspiratorial gesture to* **Todi**) Are those tribals from remote villages also present in the crowd?

Todi Yes, I've had them summoned from their villages. They've also been promised huge rewards. Lathis and all have also been distributed amongst them. They've eaten *puris, kachauris*, and *laddoos* made by our special *halwai*.[11] (*Quietly pointing toward a corner in the hall.*) Observe the enthusiasm on their faces!

Rathbani (*very softly*) Any green kurtawallahs here?

Todi Rest assured, the gatekeepers have been instructed not to allow any green kurtiwallahs inside. Should any try to get in despite this, they'll be thrashed and thrown outside.

Rathbani But they can always disguise themselves and get in. After all, the agents of the enemy across the border usually disguise themselves, and then intrude anywhere.

Todi Don't you worry about that. In the gathering before you, many of our partyworkers have come dressed as common people. They've been instructed to keep an eye out for suspects. Should anyone arouse their suspicion, they will thrash the man and throw him out.

Rathbani Well done! You've made preparations with great care and forethought.

Todi Thank you, Rathbani-ji. Whatever I am is due to your tutelage. You're, indeed, my guru. (*Both laugh.*) Rathbani-ji, please begin your address. Then I have mine to give.

Rathbani No, you begin the proceedings. But, before that, give these two young men the chance to speak since they have witnessed this tragedy with their own eyes.

Todi (*speaking into the microphone*) Ladies and gentlemen, Brothers and Sisters! You're all aware that we've gathered here to express our grief over a very painful incident. It occurred at a small railway station, a little distance from here. It happened on the Mahatma-ji Express. The enemies of our faith burnt alive almost a hundred of our kar sevaks. You might have heard of this from someone or over the radio. But it's not enough for those who wish to know facts. Luckily, two of our associates, our Brothers, happened to be at the site of the tragedy. They're here right now and will narrate what really happened. They will recount how, in a flash, the enemies of our religion set afire our holy men and devotees returning from a pilgrimage. So quickly were the holy people martyred that they couldn't even say their last prayers. So, I now request one of those young Brothers to place the truth before you all.

*The **second leader in saffron** gets up, does a few namastes, and then stands before the microphone.*

Second leader in saffron Ladies and gentlemen, Brothers and Sisters, words are not enough to describe what my own eyes saw a while ago. Such brutality, such atrocity, I could never imagine even in my wild dreams. From my house, I hired a rickshaw, and was going to the railway station. I had to catch a train to the capital. Suddenly, I saw a

huge procession of green kurtawallahs emerge from a nearby street.
They held green flags, and were shouting slogans frenziedly. I couldn't
hear very clearly but the few words I did hear were something like
this—"Kill! Burn! Destroy! Murdabad!," etc. Just as I reached the
station, these people also arrived, and surrounded the platform. When
the train arrived, about a dozen of them charged into the coach where
the pilgrims were seated. Sprinkling oil on their clothes, they set them
afire, and then jumped out. Then they dipped rags in oil, lit them up, and
threw them into the coach through the windows. The whole coach went
up in flames. Seeing this, I ran to the Stationmaster's room and rang
the police. When I returned, I saw that the police had already arrived.
The fire was being doused. Policemen were pulling out charred bodies
and laying them out on the platform. Our friends were covering them
with saffron sheets. The men in green were running about. Seeing this,
I was so incensed that I could've killed a few green kurtawallahs right
there and then. But seeing the scorched faces of the holy men, I was so
overcome by grief that I was about to faint. Luckily, my elder brother
here arrived on the scene and saved me. Now, hear the rest of the story
from him because I was unconscious for a long time afterward.

Todi (*in a tearful voice*) Brothers and Sisters, ladies and gentlemen,
you've heard this heartrending tale. (*Wipes tears.*) Forgive me; I'm
unable to control my emotions. (*In a more controlled tone.*) I can also
see that many of you are weeping; all those who love their holy men
are distressed by the martyrdom of people who show us the right path. I
fully sympathize with you. But the whole truth has not yet been placed
before you. So, I request my other brother to give you more details.

First leader in saffron (*getting up*) So, Brothers and Sisters, when I
reached there, I saw this younger brother faint and fall. The first thing I
did was to help him. After giving him water, I laid him out on a bench
where he lay unconscious for a long while. Then I saw that the entire
length of the railway platform was covered with the corpses of kar
sevaks. Their bodies had been burnt to a charcoal black. Their open eyes
stared upward at the sky, almost as if asking their Creator, "Why this
misery, Bhagwan, after having served you all our life? For which crime,
such punishment?" Then, on seeing the green kurtawallahs running
about and the police arresting them, I suddenly realized that God had
not punished these innocent people at all. Rather, whatever happened
was the doing of terrorists. When I glanced again at these avatars of
God, it struck me that their open eyes were saying this savagery done to
them was really an attack on our religion. Those eyes were asking me
what I could do to restore justice. At that moment I took a pledge—I

swore that the brothers of my faith and I wouldn't rest in peace until
we had punished the offenders. Till then, I'll sleep on the bare ground,
drink only warm water, shun delicious food, and eat only dry *rotis* and
gram.[12] I swore to pray night and day for the extermination of all those
wicked men who unleashed savagery on innocent souls. I also appeal
to the government to declare the harshest punishment possible for these
evildoers so that none dares repeat what they have done.

Todi (*again in a tearful voice*) What more can I say? You've all heard
this story with your own ears. (*Wipes away tears.*) I'll only say that
today I want all of us to take the same pledge as this man's taken. We
have to bring those brutes to book. But before this, I request our great
leader, Rathbani-ji, to say a few words to the good, upright people here,
showing them the way ahead.

Rathbani (*slowly gets up*) Ladies and gentlemen, you've just heard
the words of our young leaders who witnessed a tragic event and heard
everything with their own ears. What more can I add to this? But it's not
enough, my dear young fellows; it's just not enough to know everything.
We've now got to go into the depths of this tragic event. At whose
signal did the events unfold? First of all, we've got to clarify who these
men in green are. Ladies and gentlemen, you've got to understand that
they're our enemies, and they want to erase our identity. That's to say,
they want to destroy us. We've got to find out who're behind these
evildoers. And it's enough for you to know that they're also the spies
and agents of our enemy across the border. They're spread all over our
country. I might also add that all green kurtawallahs might not be our
enemy's spies, but their sympathies definitely lie with our enemy. So
the first thing we've got to do is rid our country of enemies and spies.
Then we've got to tell the green kurtawallahs to change their way of life
and adopt ours. Instead of building their ghettos, they should integrate
into our society and uphold the great tradition of this country. If they
can't do this, they're free to leave this land. But the green kurtawallahs
are unable to understand this. When I ask them to quit our land and
migrate westward, from where they receive their orders, they say there's
no place for them there. When I tell them to go eastward, where others
of their faith live, they say all roads leading there are closed to them.
Then I tell them to move northward, since many of their faith live in
the countries there. They reply they can't cross the high mountains
on the way. Now, my Brothers, tell me what should I say to them? ...
You're all silent. All right, I'll tell you. Now, if they can't go east, and
westward routes are closed, and they can't even cross the mountains in
the north, then there's just one course left to them. They should move

toward the Deccan; that is, head south. And you all know that a huge ocean[13] lies to the south of our country. So all these people in green kurtas and kurtis can simply jump into it. If they drown, all their sins shall be washed away. If they survive, they can swim to some far-flung island and settle there. They can live in this land only if they integrate into the mainstream. So, ladies and gentlemen, what I want to tell you is that this is a major attack on our religion and nation, that there might be similar attacks in the future, too. If we don't give a befitting reply, these anarchists shall find encouragement. Now I'd like you all to listen to the views of our great youth leader, Todi-ji, and reach a decision in this matter. It'll be difficult to do anything if we miss this opportunity. (*He gestures to emphasize his words.*)

Todi (*gets up*) Ladies and gentlemen, the views expressed by our great leader, Rathbani-ji, are straightforward and true. He's absolutely right in saying that either the green kurtawallahs adapt to our way of life, break their association with our enemy, or they leave our land and settle elsewhere. But it's very clear, my friends, they'll not change; nor will they jump into the ocean to cleanse their sins. That's why we need to do something about it. We also have other opponents in this country, but they're a small number and usually don't cross their limits. However, the green kurtawallahs are fearless and dangerous because of their teeming numbers. The day is not far off when their numbers shall surpass our own. We can't sit quiet; we've got to give an appropriate reply to this attack, and frustrate their future conspiracies. Can all of you please stand now and say "We shall fight for our land!"

Some in the audience stand up and enthusiastically shout the slogan. The saffron-clad young men on stage join the sloganeering.

Today, before God, and in the presence of our great leader Rathbani-ji, take the oath that you will not rest till you take action for this atrocity. Friends, you've been put to test this time. You've got to prove how much you love your religion and country. Friends, we shall supply you with everything that you need to carry out this great mission. Our workers in uniform will assist you. There's little time to think. Swami is already here and he suggests that this work begin before dawn. Begin the work with all the enthusiasm you can muster. Our trained workers, who are on the stage before you, will show you the way and assist you in everything.

Enthusiastically shouting slogans, the saffron-clad young men descend from the stage. They are joined in sloganeering by some in the audience.

Rathbani (*a moment later*) Your words have filled the people with enthusiasm, Todi! You've only got to ensure that this fervor does not diminish. Now let the curtain fall.

Todi Rathbani-ji, that fervor won't fade; it'll only intensify. Just wait and watch. And, there's no need for the curtain to fall. The mike will now be disconnected. Most of the audiences have already left. Those who remain won't hear us.

Rathbani Rajrai-ji had sent a message for this occasion. I wanted to read it, but the events suddenly came to an end.

Todi It doesn't matter, Rathbani-ji; there will be many more occasions for this message to be read out. At an opportune moment, the message shall be placed before people. In any case, you and Rajrai-ji are frequent visitors here, and will continue to address people. It's necessary that such gatherings continue in the future so that the media constantly gets interesting news to break. Now with your permission, I'd like to say a few words to our men in uniform. Their role is very vital in the time to come.

Rathbani Oh yes, go ahead. I also want to encourage them.

Todi (*addressing the* **policemen**) I've already explained what you're expected to do and what to refrain from. People's enthusiasm and passion should not get diluted. In fact, you should just observe the spectacle. In case the green-clad men attempt any confrontation, you know what to do. Another thing Should your officer or any subordinate display sympathy toward them, inform me immediately. They'll be summarily transferred, or suspended. You all can leave now.

The **policemen** *salute him and march out.*

Rathbani You've worked wonders, Todi, my friend!

Pats **Todi** *and shakes his hand. Other* **saffron leaders** *shake hands with one another and leave.* **Swami** *is lost in thought.*

Curtain

* * * * *

Act Two

Scene Five

It is night. A street can be seen. The doors of houses open on the road. White crosses are seen drawn on the doors. There is feeble lighting. Suddenly, sloganeering is heard and a large group of saffron-clad men enter. In the forefront are two leaders in saffron, each with a saffron flag. Those behind them carry trishuls, swords, and flaming torches. When this group reaches centerstage, one of the leaders stands on higher ground and gestures for silence. Then he passionately bursts forth.

Leader in saffron Folks, these are the homes of green kurtawallahs. You can see the crosses we've put on their doors. And you know what to do. Instinctively, the inhabitants will rush out. Then you will just take care of them.

The men in green try to flee. Some of the young women in green are caught by the policemen and forced into their vans. The sloganeering crowd in saffron leaves the stage. The police vans are heard starting up. Silence descends as the stage empties out. Some of the injured can be heard moaning.

Curtain

* * * * *

Scene Six

The two saffron leaders of Scenes 3 and 4 enter with a few tribals. The former carry huge cans of petrol. The latter wear dirty threadbare loin cloths, and some have angochhas (towels) thrown over their shoulders. All tribals carry tridents or lathis. On reaching a dark corner, the two leaders pause. The tribals behind them do the same. This alley is rather dim though it is daytime.

First leader in saffron (*to a tribal*) Enter this alley. The small houses of the green kurtawallahs are here. We've marked their houses with crosses. (*Each leader in saffron hands a tribal his petrol can.*) When they try to escape ... that's precisely why we've given you tridents and lathis. Do your work well. The job well done will earn you a big reward! These people have been very cruel to you. You can now pay them in the same coin. As regards their children, you needn't go out of your way ...

Second leader in saffron   And yes, this alley also has a few shops of the green kurtawallahs. You can loot them before setting them on fire. Take away whatever you wish from them. You've got to do this for a few more days. So looting eatables will keep you fortified.

Curtain

* * * * *

Scene Seven

A shopping area in daytime. The shop windows of some big stores can be seen in the background, with expensive fancy items on display. One store showcases expensive shoes and sandals; another displays smiling mannequins in pricey attire; yet another flaunts electronic items such as TV sets, radios, toasters, lamps etc. A mob clad in saffron enters, shouting slogans. Leading them are the **two leaders in saffron**, *waving saffron flags.*

First leader in saffron (*addressing the mob*)   Yes, here're the grand shops of the green kurtawallahs. They're very proud of them. Set them on fire!

The honking of cars is heard nearby, and some cars are heard screeching to a stop. Some fashionable ladies enter, clad in expensive clothes, and wearing high heels.

First lady (*to* **first leader in saffron**)   What the hell are you doing here? At least let us buy what we like. There's nowhere else you can get better shoes or jewelry.

Second lady (*pointing to the mannequins in the shop window*)   I've chosen some expensive clothes and saris there. Just give me some time to pick them up.

First leader in saffron   All right, Madam, quickly buy whatever you want. If the mob arrives, they'll pick up a fight.

Three or four ladies enter a store, the doors of which had earlier been broken by the mob.

A man in the mob (*to men in saffron, with a conspiratorial air*)   We also have some rights over these goods. Under your leadership, we've been attacking the green kurtawallahs for quite a few days now. We, too, have our families and children to take care of.

Second leader in saffron All right, you can also have your pick from these stores. But make sure you reduce them to ashes after you're done.

He gestures to some people in the mob, and three or four of them silently enter the stores. The rest stand outside, shouting slogans. Moments later, they smash the store windows. The fashionable ladies happily emerge from the stores, laden with exquisite outfits, saris, sandals, jewelry, and some decorative items. They thank the two leaders and exit. Moments later, car engines are heard starting up. The men who had entered the stores emerge carrying huge bags filled with merchandise. To the **two leaders in saffron**, *they present small gift items like wristwatches, pens, rings, chains, mobile phones, etc., looted from the stores. The two leaders quickly stuff these items in their pockets. Flames are now seen engulfing the stores. The mob smashes the remaining windows, enthusiastically shouting slogans. The leaders pat them on the shoulders. Slowly the lights fade out.*

Curtain

* * * * *

Scene Eight

An open lawn. Behind it stands a grand mansion with a large balcony, in silhouette. It becomes gradually visible. A large mob of sloganeering men in saffron enter. They carry tridents, rods, and large cans of petrol. The two saffron leaders are heading the group. They spread out over the lawn and shout "Come out, come out!" The lights should now be focused on the balcony; the crowd should be in semi-darkness. The silhouette of a police van is also visible. The house owner, an imposing fifty-year-old man, dressed in khadi kurta-pajamas and a Jawahar jacket,[14] *appears on the balcony. Some sloganeers throw stones at him. While trying to dodge these, he takes out his mobile phone and calls the police. A few armed constables and two police officers are seen standing near the van. The sound of the sloganeering diminishes and the house owner's words are heard. The lights will now alternately shine on the balcony, the policemen, and the mob.*

House owner (*speaking on the mobile*) Police station? Hullo ... hullo ... Police Officer? Hullo ... look, a mob has surrounded my house.

They're shouting slogans and stoning my home. They are carrying things like rods in their hands. Please send a force down here quickly. The mob's getting out of control.

The mob shouts, "Enemy of our religion, come out, come out! We shall wreak revenge!" The lights now focus on the police van. An officer is seen disconnecting the call on his mobile phone.

First police officer (*to* **second police officer**) Whose call was it?

Second police officer That scoundrel's (*Points to balcony.*). Thinks himself a great nationalist leader! But he's in league with our enemy.

First police officer What did he say?

Second police officer Just that a mob has surrounded his house and threatens to run amok.

First police officer What did you tell him?

Second police officer I disconnected the phone.

Both laugh. The phone rings again. After a while, the second police officer disconnects the call again. Both officers laugh aloud and shake hands. Darkness envelopes the policemen as the pool of light shifts onto the balcony. Besides the house owner, there are others on the balcony, including women and children. The man is repeatedly trying to make calls, each time asking for the police to be sent quickly to his residence. The crowd is very restive now, and stones are being pelted at the balcony. The man gestures to his family members to get back into the house. They go in, and the man then addresses the mob. The lights now focus on the mob.

House owner Please go back; otherwise, it won't be good for you.

Voices from the mob Enemy of our religion, come out, come out! We shall wreak revenge!

House owner I'm no enemy of any religion, and I've never attacked your men and women.

A voice from the mob It's people from your community who've attacked our religion. In your heart of hearts, you support them.

Another voice from the mob You strut around like a nationalist leader, but in actuality you're a green kurtawallah. And we shall surely punish you.

First leader in saffron (*to the mob*) If these people refuse to come out, set the house on fire.

House owner Don't come any closer. It won't be good for you. (*Takes out a revolver from his pocket and fires it into the air.*)

First leader in saffron (*to the mob*) There's no time to lose. Quickly set fire to the house, or they'll riddle you with bullets. Don't allow any of them to escape.

Second leader in saffron Get to work fast.

A voice from the mob What if the police arrive?

Second leader in saffron Rest assured, the police will not arrive. And, even if they do, there's nothing to worry about. They, too, love their religion and want to save it at any cost.

Some in the mob throw stones at the balcony. Startled, the house owner rushes back into the house. A few from the mob advance with canisters of petrol and surround the house. In a few seconds, flames engulf the house. Cries from within the house are interspersed with slogans from the mob. Darkness then descends on the scene.

Curtain

* * * * *

Act Three

Scene Nine

A cold winter evening. In a vacant space surrounded by dilapidated buildings, a large crowd of men, women, and children is seen. This is a refugee camp. Most of the refugees here are middle-aged or old. Their clothes are filthy and tattered. No one is wearing anything woolen, though each wears something green. The clothes of some are stained with blood. A few people have lit a small fire in a corner, and are warming their hands. Some children are playing in the dust; others are seeking warmth by huddling close to their mothers; some are crying. There is only one exit from this enclosed space, manned by armed policemen. Two men and a woman, all dressed in brown, try to enter through the exit. These three are from some welfare society, called "well-wishers" here. They are stopped by two policemen.

Policeman You can't enter.

Male well-wisher 1 We've got passes to enter.

Policeman No one's been issued a pass to enter here.

Male well-wisher 2 We've obtained our passes from the national capital, Delhi.

Policeman Our orders are to deny entry to anyone.

Male well-wisher 1 All right. Then you answer some of our queries.

Policeman Go ahead and ask!

Male well-wisher 1 How many people are here in this refugee camp?

Policeman We don't have the exact number. Must be around two hundred.

Female well-wisher We've reason to believe that the number is much higher.

Policeman What you might think is none of our concern.

Male well-wisher 2 In this cold season, why've they been kept in this open space?

Policeman Are you suggesting that mansions and palaces should have been built for them?

Male well-wisher 2 There's no need for mansions and palaces. But surely they could've been in proper tents?!

Policeman Go and speak to one of the ministers. Our job is to guard these people. And that's what we're doing.

Female well-wisher And why're these children crying?

Policeman Children don't sing *bhajans*,[15] they can only cry!

*The **policemen** smile. A few of the refugees come and stand near them. A **middle-aged refugee woman** steps forward and speaks.*

Middle-aged refugee woman I'll tell you why they're crying. They're absolutely famished. The infants are crying because their starving mothers can't nurse them.

Policeman (*pushing them back with his lathi*) Why are you here? Just shut up. These people are talking to us, not to you.

Female well-wisher But we're here to know the conditions *they* live in.

And only they can tell us. (*To the* **middle-aged woman**.) Don't you get enough to eat?

Male refugee We get food just once a day. And even that is not fit to eat. That's why so many people are ill here.

Male well-wisher 1 (*to the* **policeman**) Are there any arrangements for the medical treatment of these people here?

Policeman That's none of your concern.

Male well-wisher 1 But I have a right to know.

Male refugee My dear Sir, not a single doctor comes here. Many children have died of fever and diarrhea. Some of the old people are just waiting to die.

Male well-wisher 1 (*to the* **policeman**) Is that true?

Policeman No, this fellow's lying.

Male well-wisher 2 So doctors do visit here?

Policeman Why should doctors come here? When anyone falls ill, they're taken to hospital.

Male well-wisher 1 All right, we're leaving for now. But there should be better arrangements for feeding these people. They should have a tent to sleep in; doctors should be permitted to come here in need. It won't be good for you otherwise.

Policeman And what exactly do you mean? What do you think you can you do to us?

Male well-wisher 1 We're going to publicize all this; run the story in newspapers.

Exit the three well-wishers.

Policeman (*pushing back refugees who crowded in around the exit to see off the visitors*) If you people continue to speak nonsense, we'll throw you out of here. Then you'll be targets for the swords and tridents of the saffron hordes.

Male refugee Do throw us out. It's far better to confront the enemy and die fighting than face a living death each day.

*Three **guards** posted by the Volunteers Association for the refugee camp—two men and a woman—enter. They are dressed in blue, and are pushing a small cart filled with large packets.*

Policeman You can't enter here.

Male guard 1 We've got entry passes.

Policeman But we don't have orders to let you in.

Male guard 2 Here, we've got an order for you. (*Shows a piece of paper.*)

Policeman But what brings you here?

Male guard 2 We want to meet these people. We've brought blankets and woolens which we want to distribute to them. There're a hundred blankets and two hundred sweaters.

Policeman There are many more people here. What'll you do with just these few?

Male guard 1 Blankets will help some, and sweaters will help others in keeping warm. A single blanket can be shared by a few children.

Policeman All right, just put down all these things here. Without the Commissioner's orders, these things can't be distributed. And then, we also have families to take care of.

Male guard 1 All right, you two can have a blanket each. The remaining blankets must be distributed in our presence. There's no guarantee these things will reach them once we've left.

Policeman We can guarantee nothing.

Female guard All right, we'll speak to a senior officer then. But we're here to interact with these people. We have that right.

Policeman (*looking at the pape.*) Okay, we'll bring some of them here. You can speak with them. But we can't allow you to give any speeches here.

Male guard 1 We're not here to give speeches. We only want to meet and speak with them.

The **policeman** *calls some refugees over. The group includes a* **middle-aged woman** *holding the hand of a 5–6 year-old child, an old man, a girl, and a young woman.*

Male guard 1 (*to the* **middle aged woman**) Whose child is this? Is he your daughter's or your son's?

Middle-aged woman refugee No, Sir, he's a helpless orphan. His parents, brother, and sister were killed during the massacre. He must've hidden in some corner or under a bed; that's how he survived. And now he's attached himself to me. At night, I hold him close, cover him with my sheet, and put him to sleep. He doesn't play with children in the day, just keeps sitting near me.

Female guard Amma-ji, don't you have any children of your own?

Middle-aged woman refugee (*weeping*) Don't ask about me. Mine's a heartrending tale. I'm a widow. I lived happily with my son and daughter-in-law. They killed my son before my eyes and raped my daughter-in-law. She was pregnant. They didn't even spare the foetus when they killed her, and … I've no one now except this child. Somehow, I'm going to bring him up.

Female guard (*wiping her tears*) This will earn you blessings. We'll try and get you some work, Amma-ji.

Male guard 2 (*to the* **old refugee**) And where might your family and relatives be?

Old male refugee (*weeping*) They were also victims of the saffron madness. And poor old me, they thrashed me and let me go. I've no one now. My sons are dead; my house is reduced to ashes; there's no news of my granddaughter who was abducted. I have just one prayer—God grant me death.

Male guard 1 Uncle, have fortitude. We'll try and get some news of your granddaughter. We'll also try to get you full compensation for your burnt house. But all this will take time. You'll have to live here till then. (*Gestures toward his companions.*) They all sympathize with you. Think of themselves as your own children.

Female guard (*to a* **young woman** *who has a dupatta wrapped round her face*) Sister, tell me about yourself.

The **young woman** *only sobs loudly and does not say a word.*

Middle-aged woman refugee What account can this poor woman give of herself! What she's gone through is beyond words.

Female guard Amma-ji, really so?

Middle-aged woman refugee The devils tied up her husband and raped her. Then they burnt her house with her husband inside.

Female guard It's … . Sister, can you tell us something more in this regard?

Young woman (*removing the dupatta from her face*) What shall I say? Why should I tell you? Can you get those savages punished for their sins? Can you get me justice? Can you restore my lost reputation? Can you bring my husband back to life? Just for the heck of it should I tell you more about my wretchedness?

Male guard 1 We can't restore your husband to life. But we'll try our best to get you justice. If possible, we'll also get those villains punished.

Female guard Sister, have patience. We understand … We'll try our hardest to get you justice.

Male guard 1 (*to a* **young man**) You want to say something? Are some of your relatives also in this camp?

Young male refugee None of my relatives survived. My parents were killed before my eyes. My brothers and sisters met the same fate. They would've killed me too, but I managed to escape somehow.

Male guard 1 What do you plan to do?

Young male refugee Time will tell. I've so many friends who've been victims of the same carnage. They want punishment for all responsible for it. They seek retribution, retribution for the merciless killing of our parents, for the raping of our sisters, for looting and burning our homes, for throwing young children into fires, for completely destroying us … We shall rest only when we've avenged all this. And we're willing to die to achieve this.

Male guard 1 We'll try and get you justice.

Young male refugee What justice can you get us! (*Pointing toward the camp's inhabitants.*) You can't get two square meals for these people. They're frozen in this cold. You can't even arrange for a roof over their heads. Children starve and cry; the sick are racked with pain. There's no comfort you can offer to lessen their suffering.

Female guard We've brought you blankets and warm clothes. We're trying to find ways to lessen your misery.

Young male refugee The blankets and clothes you've brought will only be distributed with the Commissioner's permission. For appearance's sake, we'll receive some of those. Even if you distribute everything that you've brought, it'll be of no help. What we want is justice, and that you can't get us. So, we have to get it ourselves. We've got to punish all who're responsible for the barbarity. And we're willing to die for this.

Female guard You have all our sympathy. In fact, all good people are on your side. All over the land there are demonstrations and demands to bring the culprits to book. That's why we say that the retributive path must be shunned; it doesn't spare even the innocent.

Young male refugee Were those who became targets of the savagery not innocent? Were those children who were burnt not innocent? Were those women whose bodies were ravished not innocent? Were those elders whose sons and daughters were killed before their eyes not innocent?

Male guard 1 Yes, they were. The sins of the wicked cannot be forgiven. But revenge can never be a way. It's very late now; we've got to leave. We'll be back tomorrow to talk about all this with you and your friends. *Khuda hafiz*, may God keep you safe.

Young male refugee *Khuda hafiz*.

All three guards exit.

Curtain

* * * *

Scene Ten

The same big room as in Scene 2. The mood is not secretive any longer; rather it is jubilant. Bright lights shine. In the background, a raucous tune is heard. Small saffron flags hang everywhere. **Rajrai** *is hovering around a mid-sized table on which lies a large bouquet.* **Rathbani** *and* **Todi** *are seated. They are all dressed in the same attire as in Scene 2.* **Todi** *has a huge garland around his neck.*

Rathbani Very well done, Todi-ji! Things are moving on steadily, all in our favor.

Todi Yes, Rathbani-ji. All in accordance with your lofty thoughts.

Rajrai But tell us, Todi, how many green kurtawallahs remain here?

Todi Rajrai-ji, that's difficult to say. Now you won't usually see any green kurtawallahs on roads or in bazaars, schools, colleges, parks, or offices. A few remain rotting in refugee camps. These camps will also be closed in a few days. Then they'll have to find shelter elsewhere as they won't dare to …

Rathbani That's really well done, Todi-ji. You've done a splendid job.

Todi Indeed, Sir. But it was impossible without your blessings.

Rathbani (*to* **Rajrai**) Rajrai-ji, this program can now be sort of replicated in other states. The enthusiasm of our workers has not waned. We should take advantage of this.

Rajrai Yes. But each step in future will have to be taken very carefully. I'm attending an international conference next week. Should the issue be raised there, what should be my response?

Rathbani Refuse to acknowledge that anything like it ever occurred here. Just say all the stories were simply a creation of the media. Another response could be to say that when a faith is attacked with great ferocity, there's bound to be a reaction.

Rajrai Yes, I always believe that every action has an equal reaction. But the problem is that everywhere voices are being raised against us. The capital city witnesses protests every day.

Rathbani The capital's another matter, Rajrai-ji. There's no such thing here. If anything, there's an air of celebration here. Our workers are overjoyed with their success.

Rajrai (*to* **Todi**) There's no doubt about that, my dear friend. Now's the time to expedite elections in your state. I agree entirely that one should strike while the iron is hot.

Rathbani Rajrai-ji, you've echoed my views. The time's ripe for elections. The remaining green kurtawallahs here have no sympathizers. Everyone here is a devotee of our friend Todi, and so our success is assured.

Todi I completely agree with your views. The truth is that I've already begun my own preparations in this regard. The first thing I plan to do is undertake a *rath yatra*,[16] after seeking Rathbani-ji's blessings. Everywhere I travel, I shall thank people for protecting the glory of our faith. I'll tell them to hold their heads high, and to be proud of what they did.

Rajrai So, let the *rath yatra* be known as a journey for honor.

Rathbani Well said, very well said! Rajrai-ji, it's only someone wise as you could've suggested such a thing!

Enter a very worried looking **Police Commissioner**.

Todi Well, what brings you here at this moment? I didn't summon you.

Police Commissioner Please forgive the intrusion, Todi-ji, but I was compelled to come here.

Todi Well, what's compelled you?

Police Commissioner Todi-ji, these days groups of confidantes and sympathizers of green kurtawallahs openly roam the streets. They speak with all kinds of people, and give out all kinds of stories to newspapers and TV channels.

Rathbani We're aware of this. But, on the other hand, our journalists and workers are also on the move, proving false everything that's being claimed. There's no need for you to be worried.

Police Commissioner My biggest worry, Sir, is that these confidantes and sympathizers possess all kinds of passes for visiting refugee camps. There, they gather information about camp conditions and distribute things like blankets, woolens, and medicines. That's why the green kurtawallahs in refugee camps sing their praises.

Rathbani Rajrai-ji, it's time to impose restrictions on the visitors to camps. They're crossing the limit now.

Rajrai You're right. That's exactly what I want. These people, especially the sympathizers, can create a difficult situation since they are internationally well connected.

Todi (*to the* **Police Commissioner**) You can go now. We'll give this matter a thought.

Police Commissioner Todi-ji, I haven't told you the real news yet. It's better to discuss the matter in the presence of these two senior leaders.

Todi All right, quickly tell us your real news.

Police Commissioner Todi-ji, a group of young kurtawallahs has become rebellious. They're holding meetings every day. Through their confidantes, they've established links with people abroad. These young men demand justice. They say they'll rest only after taking revenge. My informers tell me they're planning to attack a big temple of ours.

Rathbani Should that ever happen, rivers of blood shall flow.

Rajrai Rathbani-ji, be a little patient. The first thing you've got to do is to ensure such an eventuality doesn't occur. Then, security measures need to be tightened in the country. Todi-ji, especially in your own state. Get the troublemakers identified and put them in jail. I think I'll leave now. My aircraft stands ready, and I've got to reach the capital quickly. The Lok Sabha[17] is in session, and one has to answer all kinds of tricky questions. Rathbani-ji, when are you arriving there?

Rathbani I'll be there soon. So, Rajrai-ji, namaste!

Todi Namaste, Rajrai-ji! My heartfelt thanks to you for being here to share our happiness.

Rajrai Namaste!

Todi and Rathbani escort Rajrai to the exit.

Curtain

* * * *

Scene Eleven

Considerable time has lapsed. A couple of benches sit in a derelict corner of a public park. A few bushes and flower pots can be seen. Four people—the female guard and a male guard (not in uniform), and the female well-wisher and a male well-wisher—are seen entering and walking toward the benches. They are deeply involved in some discussion which can be heard when they reach the benches.

Female guard After all brutality against the green kurtawallahs of this area, the victory of the ruling party in the assembly polls for another term was a veritable farce.

Male well-wisher This had to happen. In fact, most of the minorities were either driven away from their villages, or pressured to change their faith and way of life.

Male guard Survivors and inmates of refugee camps refused to participate in the elections to vent their anger. The long-drawn saffron campaign to poison the minds of the majority was successful. Todi is a blot on his name.[18]

Female well-wisher So you think kind and democracy-loving people no longer live here?

Male guard No, I don't mean that. I've recently met people sad and upset over the brutal incidents, and they've done everything they can to help the minorities. They've given shelter to many green kurtawallahs, saved their lives, escorted them to safer places. But the number of these good samaritans is so small that election results were not impacted on. The recent attack on the big temple in this area also saddened these samaritans. What do you have to say about this?

Female well-wisher Rathbani-ji responded immediately to the attack by saying that it was done at the behest of the enemy across the border. But I have a different take on it.

Female guard What's that?

Female well-wisher Right now there are thousands of young men here who belong to the green community, who've lost everything in the carnage. They've seen their parents and siblings being killed before their eyes. Their businesses have been destroyed. They're homeless, with no relatives, no jobs, no ... They seek revenge for what's been done to them, and care not about their lives. In the refugee camps, you must've seen their obsessive anger. I believe the temple attack was planned by people like them.

Male guard This is most unfortunate. It paves the way for more such things to happen in the future.

Female well-wisher No, I believe it was simply a spur-of-the- moment reaction.

Female guard Even then, such episodes shouldn't be overlooked. We've got to try hard to rehabilitate such people, to transform their anger into something creative and constructive.

Female well-wisher I agree. We've got to plan for their education and employment.

Male guard You're right; very little has been done about these young people.

Female well-wisher One good thing is that some reputed folks from the majority community are taking keen interest in the centers that the minorities have set up for the welfare of children orphaned in the pogrom.

Male guard But a more significant thing is that the party has lost in the recently held parliamentary elections!

Male well-wisher Hope also emanates from the new enquiry committee's interim report. It states that those burnt alive onboard that ill-fated train were not all sadhus and holy men; there were common people, too. The report also states that the "green kurtawallahs" did not set fire to the coach from outside; rather, the fire started from within the coach, and may have been accidental.

Female guard It seems facts were distorted for the success of a well-conceived game plan.

Male well-wisher The fact is that perceptive people thought along these lines, but there wasn't enough evidence to support this view. That's why the new report is so significant. It's taken the wind out of the sails of the saffron party.

Female well-wisher The wind's been taken out of the sails of Rajrai's personality, too. When the crown fell from his head, his own party men declared him useless. Rathbani is very vocal these days, but I've heard that many upcoming young leaders in his party want to get rid of him.

Male well-wisher (*laughing*)

The tussle and chaos in his party is really amusing! An interesting play can be written on the current situation!

Female well-wisher Well, why don't you write the play? But don't forget that thousands of "green kurtawallahs" are still languishing in jails.

Male guard Yes, it's an important issue. Moreover, many homeless and helpless survivors of the pogrom are yet to get compensation. (*To the well-wishers.*) You'll have to help us.

Female well-wisher We'll do everything we can for all this.

Male well-wisher Duties are endless. It's time to eat something. I'm really hungry.

Come on, it's on me. Let's go eat in a good restaurant.

Engaged in conversation, all four exit.

Curtain

* * * * *

Scene Twelve

*The same as Scene One. An empty expanse. A faint bluish light
gradually shines, and small stars seem to twinkle occasionally. Echoes
of soul-stirring music are heard. A long line of lightly made-up children
makes an appearance. They are dressed as angels in flowing robes of
white, and wear silver crowns. On their wings, silver stars glint. Their
gentle and fluid movements convey their innocence. They spread out on
the stage in a semicircle, and raise their hands in supplication to God.*

Angels (*singing*)
Praise to the Almighty, glory to the Creator,
He who made the universe, He who designed the heavens,
Praise to the Almighty, praise to the heavens' Creator.

Enter **Satan**, *dressed as in the opening scene. His earlier bravado,
however, is missing.*

Praise to the Almighty, praise to the heavens' Creator.

What a planet He created, and what heavens!

Satan (*to the* **angels**) Still singing the same old hymn? Aren't you
aware that earth is no longer what it was? It's no longer the enchanting
place that poets and artists celebrated in their works. Even the heavens
have changed. They no longer possess the serenity that'd inspired
countless creative souls.

Angels (*singing*)
From every corner gleams the glory of God,
In it are bathed Earth's particles,
Each phenomenon has He forged,
He's the architect of all Creation.

The **angels** *dance in a semicircle.*

Satan Which universe do you speak of? Just look down from Heaven's
serene heights and see what's happening below? There's no order to
speak of, only chaos. Earth is now a killing field, a stage where evil
triumphs.

Angels (*singing*)
From every corner gleams the glory of God,
In it is bathed Earth's each particle,
Beginning and end is He,
Eternal is His magnificence.

Satan What magnificence?

Suddenly a blinding radiance fills the stage. The music rises to a crescendo. The **angels** *move backstage, stand in a semicircle, and continue singing.* **Satan** *stands in a corner.*

The voice of God Satan, don't argue with the angels! What they say is true, but it's beyond your comprehension. Just say what you've come for. What has taken you so long to return?

Satan Almighty, I seek your forgiveness. I would've been here earlier were it not for an interesting turn of events on earth. Never in my wildest dreams could I have imagined the scenes of killing and murder, looting and pillaging, rape, and violence that I saw there.

The voice of God I had commanded you to at least keep the melodrama under control, but you did nothing of the kind.

Satan O, One Above All, my status amidst the drama of death and destruction was that of a mere onlooker. O, Supreme Being, even had I tried, I couldn't have performed better than those fellows. Indeed, they have surpassed me.

The voice of God Hmm, I had to intervene to assist the victims there; I sent down my representatives.

Satan Yes, Supreme Being, I did observe the dedication of the well-wishers and guards there. But these actors reached there when the scenes of horror were beyond all redemption. Also, their resources paled before the planned frenzy of the saffron brigade.

The voice of God You call their frenzy "planned"?

Satan I seek forgiveness, Almighty God, but to allude to Shakespeare, there was a method in their madness.

The voice of God So you've taken to using Shakespeare to suit your arguments!

Satan O Most Beneficent and Powerful, just see it as my old habit of twisting arguments to suit my case. In recent times, my skills have been honed in the company of pretentious, wicked human actors.

The voice of God Stop your chatter and come to Hell's doorway so that I can destroy you.

Satan (*in a very worried tone*) No, no, O Benevolent God, have mercy on me. Allow me another brief return to earth. This is my last plea to you.

The voice of God Why this desire again?

Satan God Almighty, you are omniscient, you know all!

The voice of God Yes, but it's from your mouth that I wish to hear the reason.

Satan O, Supreme Being, you know that a second Satan has been born there. And I ...

The voice of God Shed some more light on this second Satan.

Satan He is going to be crowned now. On this special occasion, I want to be present before my most revered superior, this second Satan.

The voice of God Satan, in the upcoming drama only the likes of Tommy Rapist will be employed. Your status will, henceforth, be that of a servile minion. So remove your crown and cast it away.

Satan *seems to shrink in size, fades away, and a child is seen standing in his place. The words of* **Satan**, *however, should continue to be in the voice of the adult actor who has so far played the role.*

Child Satan (*balancing his crown*) My Lord, you've made me so small. Please allow me to wear this crown. It symbolizes my identity.

The voice of God Your identity stands changed. The emperor of all evil and brutality is now the second Satan. He is in charge of the stage below. And this crown is too small for his head. As his insignificant slave, this crown again sits ill on your head. But I grant you permission to go to earth. You can witness Second Satan's coronation.

Child Satan (*taking off his crown*) Very many thanks, O Supreme Being. You've fulfilled my last wish. I've a lot to learn from his activities.

The voice of God Indeed, a lot to learn. But it won't be of much use since you will be destroyed along with this Second Satan and his cohorts eventually.

Child Satan (*in great distress*) O Lord of two firmaments, will you destroy him, too?

The voice of God Yes, but it will take time. It's true, Satan, that evil now prospers on the earthly stage like never before. But this condition will change. The apocalyptic events are a warning to mankind, especially to those who regard themselves as all-powerful.

Child Satan But, Lord of the Skies, the innocent also perish in these catastrophic scenes!

The voice of God That is, indeed, unfortunate, but the ways of God lie far beyond your comprehension. It's enough for you to know that in the ultimate scene that they didn't script, these self-proclaimed emperors of power shall receive the punishment they fully deserve. Their existence and memory shall be erased forever.

A booming voice But when, my Lord, when?

The voice of God That is a secret for now. The world has to wait for it to happen. Meanwhile, let the human actors continue their struggle for a heartening change in the future …

A joyful melody is heard in the background.

Final Curtain

* * * * *

The end

Notes

1   Kurta/kurti: A loose knee-length shirt worn by men/women in South Asia.
2   Trindents.
3   Skull caps (white).
4   Holy (Hindu) men.
5   An interjection of surprise.
6   Indian sweets.
7   A Hindu address to God.
8   Sticks.
9   Volunteers for a (Hindu) religious occasion.
10   A Hindu ascetic.
11   A sweet-maker/confectioner.
12   *Roti* (homemade bread) and gram (pulses) are modest staples for people in many states of India.
13   The Indian Ocean.
14   A jacket with a mandarin collar, worn and popularized by independent India's first prime minister, Jawaharlal Nehru.
15   Hindu devotional songs.
16   A journey by chariot (the phrase has a Hindu religious-mythical import).
17   The lower house of India's Parliament.
18   "Todi" (pronounced "Tori") is the name of a Hindustani classical *raga* that presents a mood of gentle adoration.

Plays from Pakistan

We Shall Resist

by
Anwer Jafri

Translated from Urdu by **Sheema Kermani**

Characters

The actors, male and female, play more than one role. Roles are to be distributed by the director according to the three "stories" in the play, respectively.

Narrator (Female)

8 Male actors

8 Female actors

The cast of eight male actors include:

Ustad	**Another 2**
Father/Officer	**Mirza**
PA	**Anwaar**
people forming a queue at the	**Brother**
entrance of a government office	**Others**
Actor 1	**Other 1**
Actor 2	**Other 2**
Actor 3	**Other 3**
Actor 5	**Man**
Actor 7	**Other Man**
Actor 8	**Boy**
Chaudhary	**Boy 2**
Fazlu	**Boy 3**
Numberdar	**Salim**
Maulvi	**Police**
Another 1	**Boys**

The cast of eight female actors include:

Girl	**Women**
Daughter	**Woman**
Dadi	**Another 1**
Mother	**Another 2**
Female 1	**Other Woman**
Margaret	**Old Woman**

Prologue

As the stage lights up, an actor is seen casually walking across, humming to himself. Seeing the audience, he is shocked and runs back to the wings.

Voices from offstage

Actor Hey the curtain's up!

Many voices What? (*Faces peep out from the wings and then disappear.*)

Voice Who raised the curtain so early?

Voice It must be time for the show.

Voice Oh come on, so what?

Voice Could they not wait another 10 minutes?

Narrator (*offstage voice*) Come on, all of you—get ready fast. (*Enters, clearing her throat. Unnoticed by her, another female actor follows her.*) Beg your pardon, ladies and gentlemen, terribly sorry, but we certainly didn't realize that this performance would begin exactly at the given time because ...

Girl (*on stage interrupting, giggles*) Hehehehe ... because (*To the audience.*) you yourselves have made the stupid mistake of arriving punctually, so for another quarter- or half- an-hour ...

Narrator (*on stage angrily*) You ... (*Changing tone—faked voice.*) I mean what are you doing here?

Girl My uncle had promised me the role of the Narrator.

Narrator To hell with your uncle (*Again in a faked tone.*). Oh baby sure, sure, of course you can do the role of the Narrator ... but first go and see if all the cast is ready, or not ... and if they are then quickly call them on stage so that we can begin with the necessary introductions and start our *Nautanki*[1] ...

Girl (*looking into the audience*) Hehehehe ... Who are the VIPs amongst them?

Narrator Those sitting in the front rows.

Girl Hehehehe ... And the VVIPs?[2]

Narrator (*irritated*) Kindly go and do as you are told. (*Girl exits.*)

Narrator (*muttering under her breath*) Bloody uncle's niece ... Doesn't even know how an actor should stand on stage, and she wants to act! There is no respect left any more for art and artists! (*Girl re-enters.*). Yes, dear, so you are back! What is the news that you have brought—are they ready?

Girl Hehehehe ... yes, everyone is ready ... hehehe.

Narrator Everyone is ready? Well, then why don't they come? (*Shouting to the actors.*) Do I have to send you all an invitation card? Come on, come on (*All the actors enter.*). So, finally you all are here! Now get on with the greetings (*The whole cast greet the* **Narrator.**) No, no, no, not me, greet them, the audience—they have been sitting here and waiting so long for you all to appear. (*The cast wave at the audience.*) Oho, this is no way to greet them—don't you want to get their applause? Come on now, bow to them, and greet them properly (*The cast bow and greet the audience.*); well that is better! So, ladies and gentlemen, these are the actors of our play today. They will change colors, roles, styles, characters, mannerisms, and perform tricks, and magically transform themselves to show you the wonders of their art. (*To the cast.*) Now that your introductions are over you may go (*They exit.*).(*To the* **audience.**) Let me tell you—just between us—they are hardly real actors; most of them are nephews and nieces of the producer! Well, you yourselves must have got free passes from your aunts and uncles—so, what can one do—this is how it is these days! Isn't it? However, now we will start our play—we will begin from those times, which we are told, were very different from the present. (*To the* **musician.**) Ustad jee,[3] surely you remember which times we are referring to ... (**Narrator** *leaves.*)

Ustad Yes. (*Sings.*)

Alaap[4]

> The times that have gone by
> This is about those times that have gone by
> (*All the* **cast** *enter, singing.*)
> This is about the times that have gone by
> The times that have gone by
> When our spirits were high,
> When our hopes would fly,
> Our journey we were just beginning,
> We were all traveling,
> Our leaders were commendable,

Our people were respectable,
  Our leaders were remarkable.

*The song fades out with the lights. An image of Muhammed Ali Jinnah[5]
fades in on the cyclorama/screen, and a recording of his speech,
delivered to the New Constituent Assembly on August 11, 1947, plays.*

"You are free; you are free to go to your temples, you are free to
go to your mosques or to any other place of worship in this State of
Pakistan. You may belong to any religion or caste or creed—that has
nothing to do with the business of the State ... We are starting with this
fundamental principle that we are all citizens and equal citizens of one
State ... I think we should keep that in front of us as our ideal, and you
will find that in course of time Hindus would cease to be Hindus, and
Muslims would cease to be Muslims, not in the religious sense, because
that is the personal faith of each individual, but in the political sense as
citizens of the State."

*During the projection, and the speech, the set changes and in Scene 1
actors enter, and take their positions. The visual and sound of the speech
fade out—lights fade in to show the setting and characters of Scene 1. A
room in a lower-middle-class home. A family is sitting in the room.*

Scene One

Father And then he said, "Discipline, faith, unity." Ah! What tenor in
his voice—what resonance, what power, *subhanallah*![6]

Daughter Wow! What else did he say?

Father He said—now Pakistan has been created; now we are all
Pakistanis. From now onward, there will be no discrimination on the
basis of religion, caste, or creed. There will be justice for all—there will
be development. Education will be accessible to each and everyone, and
all the people will live together in peace and harmony.

Daughter Wow! Did you yourself hear him speak?

Dadi[7] What have you two been going on about since morning? Let
your father get ready in peace. Don't you ever get tired asking the same
questions over and over again, day in and day out?

Mother *enters.*

Mother Amma,[8] whether she gets tired or not, I like it very much. It

296 Islam in Performance

reminds me of those days when we all used to go to protest marches and demonstrations—there was so much passion and commitment in all of us ... (*To* **husband**.) here is your tea, I am just bringing the *paratha* for you.

Father No my dear, I will have no breakfast today; I got up late this morning—if I sit down for breakfast I will get late for work.

Mother But you must not go hungry the whole day. How can you work the whole day on an empty stomach?

Father I will eat there, if I can find some time.

Dadi You know that eating out is not good for your health—have something at home before you leave. What if you reach office late one day?

Father Amma, out of all the principles you've taught us since childhood, the most important is punctuality. I must go now. Goodbye! (*Exits.*)

Mother People turn up at his office early morning, and by now there must be a long queue of visitors waiting to see him. These are difficult times for everyone, mother.

Dadi If they are already waiting for him, then they can wait a little longer. After all, the common folk are used to waiting for the officer.

Mother Amma, please, at least now you must get rid of this decadent notion of "common folk and officer"—now we are a free nation—government officers are now the servants of the public as they are paid from the public exchequer.

Dadi Oh, I don't understand all these new concepts of yours ...

Narrator (*enters, singing*)

> The journey was just beginning,
> We were all traveling together,
> Our leaders were commendable,
> Our people were respectable,
> Our leaders were remarkable.
> Then what happened afterward?
> Where did this wind blow from?

Scene Two

The reception at a Commissioner's Office. The father of the preceding scene, now "Officer," is sitting at his desk, and is trying to control a crowd of people with documents in their hands: these are applications for a number of different things, including government jobs, licenses and permits, ration cards, and so on. Noise.

Officer Everyone will get their turn. Sir, everyone will get their turn—after all we are sitting here to serve you, but first you must get into a queue. Have you already forgotten what our leader used to say to us? Discipline! This is very strange—it has only been a couple of years since he passed away, but you people have already given up following his teachings. (*Sees a man jump the queue.*) ... Hey, hey Sir, where do you think you are going?

Man I am going to see the Commissioner!

Officer Sure, sure you can see him—but this old lady, here, and all these other people have been here much before you; they are all waiting to see him.

Man I have this note for him.

Officer Note? What note?

Man Yes, this note. The Commissioner's PA gave it to me—I have paid him a good ten rupees for it.

Officer (*turns to the* **PA** *sitting there*) What is going on here?

PA We only follow orders, Sir. Whatever order comes from the top, we can only follow it.

Officer I will not allow this. Did we sacrifice so much for this?

PA Sir, why are you getting excited. Just sit quietly—you will get your share.

Officer Good God! My share be damned! I will complain about you and report this.

PA To whom? To whom will you complain? Sir, you are about to retire in a couple of months—how will you survive on your pension? Have you thought about it? There is still time—make the best of it. These principles of yours! You never know when you may be dismissed from service—you could very well lose your pension as well. (*To the* **crowd**.) Come on, come on—as for this old man, his days are over! Now it is our turn. Yes, yes come, come—ten rupees, ten rupees, and a chit for you—ten rupees.

Officer But ... (*Gets pushed over by the crowd.*)

PA (*addressing another man*) Sir, Sir—Oh, Sir, why did you have to come yourself? Sir, you do not need any note. (*Pointing to an ordinary man in the queue.*) Hey you, move back, make room for the officer— how dare you touch someone in uniform?

Narrator (*enters*) Ahah, you made a big mistake by touching the *Genie* in uniform. Now for the next 50 years this *Genie* will not go back into the bottle. (*Sings.*)

> Hurry and change your color, Brothers,
> Hurry and change your style.
> The same hue doesn't do you any good,
> You must use more guile.
> So hurry up and change your color, Brothers,
> Hurry up and change your style.
> Be on your knees in front of the boss,
> Be angry and rude to the *chaprassi*,[9]
> Massage the feet of the man on the top,
> Abuse the laborers,
> Hurry and change your colors.
> Sing praises of those higher-ups,
> Treat the man on the street with a kick,
> If it fetches what you must have,
> Be sure to call an ass your Dad.
> Hurry and change your color, Brothers,
> Hurry and change your style.

Scene Three

As the song ends, the cast move around the stage, in a circle, in pairs. Some pairs, called "groups," pause by turn as they each approach downstage center and deliver their lines before falling back into position in the moving circle. One group of male actors may double as another group. These groups depict various phases of Pakistan's history.

Group 1 of 2 male actors—representing General Ayub Khan's era[10]

Actor 1 I say that General Sahib did the correct thing.

Actor 2 No, no, not General—Field Marshal, you must call him Field Marshal.

Actor 1 Yes, yes, of course. I was saying that, first of all, by imposing Martial Law he cleansed the society of corrupt officers, and then this wonderful system of "Basic Democracy" ... wah wah ... What a brilliant idea this was ... Ah ... Mr. Chairman ... a ... a ... Your Excellency, Sir ... Before the elections you had mentioned something about a plot of land ... and Sir ... surely you remember ... about the Permit, Sir? ...

Group 2 of 2 female actors.

Female 1 So I said to him, "Do you think our Madam doesn't have enough saris? Yes, yes, if you want to give her something then gift her a diamond necklace ... it would look so good on her ... ." Madam, please if you would put in a word about my husband to Sir *jee*[11] ... a ... a ... please put in a word, and get my husband a transfer to London, please. ... Oh, Madam, you are looking so beautiful ... my God, you are absolutely stunning!

Group 3 of 2 male actors—During the Army action in East Pakistan.[12]

Actor 3 Oh Sir, don't you worry about this. Nobody can dare to touch or harm us. Our friends are well prepared to help us—they (*referring to the US fleet*) have a naval fleet on alert, and ready to come to our aid, if necessary—you just wait and see—our enemies will be taught a lesson that they will never forget—Oh, don't worry about rumors, Sir, people will always spread rumors ... They have nothing else to do.

Group 4 of 2 male actors—Mr. Bhutto's period in the mid-1970s.[13]

Actor 5 Amazing! The entire country's wealth was grabbed and divided amongst 22 families—can there be more injustice? Total exploitation! Actually Islam and socialism are the same—they have the same message—justice, equality, and the end of the class system. Now it is time for the masses—it is the *awami daur*[14]—the rule of the capitalists and feudal lords is over—now, at last, we have a constitution.

Group 5 of 2 male actors—The Zia era.[15]

Actor 7 Good God! Listen to me, the 1973 Constitution was no sacred scripture; it was not made by God that there can be no amendments to it. Right? When there is so much at stake for the nation, when it becomes essential for the sake of the country, then, the "Doctrine of Necessity," has to be applied. Right? General Sahib has promised that within 90

days, he will hold elections. He is a God-fearing man, a true believer—
he will never go back on his word.

Actor 8 Oh, to hell with the elections—I am going to move a
resolution that General Sahib be made President for life—the *Ameer ul
mobineen*[16]—you must let him know that I said this.

Group 6 of 2 male actors.

Actor 1 God bless you, God bless you, Sir. What an honorable and
righteous move! Sir, previously all the department staff had to go
outside to the mosques to say their prayers—now, since the prayer
assembly is held within the office itself, I must say, Sir, the whole
Ministry seems aglow. It radiates purity—has acquired the holiness
of a mosque, Sir. What a great decision … wonderful … Absolutely
wonderful—God bless you! God bless you!

*Group 7 of 2 male actors—After the mid-air explosion of the airplane
which killed General Zia-ul-Haq.*

Actor 3 At last the opportunists and adventurists have been defeated.
They have been annihilated. Now, after eleven years, we can finally
breathe once again. Thank God for the box of mangoes; otherwise, God
forbid, perhaps for another eleven years we …

Group 8 of 2 male actors—General Musharraf's period.[17]

Actor 5 *Array*[18] Sahib,[19] this was no ordinary plunder—they took every
penny out of the country, sucked us dry! We have had it—no democracy
for us—no—not even a single politician is capable enough to give us
democracy—you, Sir, you took the right step at the right time … Your
commando training saved us and our nation … . Had you not been
here … Oh … . One dreads to think about it … . God knows where we
would have been, what would have been our fate!

Scene Four

*The whole cast start running, as if they are chasing someone; they
re-emerge on stage, as if they are being chased; then as two gangs, they
start fighting with each other until they all fall down dead.* **Narrator**
enters.

Narrator On August 11, 1947, while addressing the New Constituent
Assembly of the newly established nation of Pakistan, the founder of the
country, Quaid-e-Azam Muhammad Ali Jinnah, said: "You are free; you

are free to go to your temples, you are free to go to your mosques, or to any other place of worship in this State of Pakistan. You may belong to any religion or caste or creed—that has nothing to do with the business of the State." But today what is happening in Pakistan? In the name of religion, people are being killed. People have been divided into sects; some sects have been declared as minorities, and these minorities are being targeted and victimized. Pakistan is being destroyed in the name of faith—there is blood all around us, there are dead bodies everywhere.

The dead bodies rise and exit. Only one female character stays on stage. **Narrator** *goes to her.*

Narrator Who are you? What is your name? Why did they kill you?

Woman My name was Margaret. I belonged to the Christian community—we lived in a small village in Punjab, where we had been living for generations. I worked in the fields ...

Narrator *leaves. Men and women enter dancing the Bhangra,*[20] *sing a folk song, create a rural scene—while working in the field. Enter Chaudhary,*[21] *with his Numberdar,*[22] *and Maulvi—the three of them oversee the fields.*

Chaudhary (*to* **Maulvi**) Come Maulvi Sahib, see this is all my land. Give it your blessing so that we get a bounteous harvest this season.

Maulvi *prays while casting a lecherous look at the women.*

Chaudhary Hey Fazlu—how are you? And how is your son? Has he got married?

Fazlu Yes Chaudhary Sahib, yes. His wedding was yesterday.

Chaudhary (*looking around*) Where is he? I don't see him.

Fazlu He is home, Sir; he has not come to work today. Chaudhary Sahib, he got married last night only ...

Chaudhary What if he got married last night? Is he the son of a *nawab*[23] that he sits at home? Tomorrow I want to see not only your son, but also your daughter-in-law working here in my fields. Do you understand me?

Fazlu Yes, yes, Chaudhary Sahib—whatever you say ... he will be here tomorrow.

Margaret *goes to the Numberdar.*

Margaret Numberdar *jee*, please, I have a request to make.

Numberdar Yes, what is it?

Margaret I need some money—my child is very ill—I have to buy some medicine for him. I have been working for the last six months, but I still haven't got any wage. Please speak to Chaudhary Sahib, and get me some money. I beg of you—please help me—my child will die.

Numberdar Oh I see. Listen, I think you should ask him yourself.

Margaret No, no, I can't ask him—you please do this for me.

Numberdar Oh, you don't know our Chaudhary Sahib. He is such a generous man; he is very kind. You should ask him. If you ask him yourself, I tell you, his heart will melt, and he will surely help you. Go, go to him yourself.

Margaret How can I talk to him? … No, no—please you do this for me.

Numberdar I am telling you if you ask him yourself, he will give you more than what you want. Go on, go on, trust me …

Margaret Salam, Chaudhary Sahib.

Chaudhary Yes, what is there?

Margaret Chaudhary Sahib, a … a, I need some money. If I can, a … a, if I may, possibly … get five hundred rupees … please?

Chaudhary Five … hundred? What do you need so much money for?

Margaret Chaudhary Sahib, my child is very ill—that is why I am forced to …

Chaudhary Numberdar!

Numberdar Yes, Sahib.

Chaudhary Look up your register—see for how long this woman has been working here. Calculate her wages and tell me.

Numberdar Yes, Sahib. Sahib, she has been working for the last six months—but Sahib, it is your discretion as to how much she should be paid.

Chaudhary Working for only six months, and she wants to be paid already—a huge sum of five hundred rupees? No, no, I am not going to give you so much money. Look, look at Fazlu here—he and his whole family have been working for me for the last sixteen years, and he has never once dared to ask me for such an amount; and you—you have just been here for six months, and you want me to give you so much money? No, no, this is not possible.

Margaret Chaudhary Sahib, I would never have asked you—but my child is very ill. He has a very high fever. I have to take him to a doctor in the city—it will cost me this much money. Had it not been for this, I would never have bothered you. Please, please have mercy on me—I must save my child—please give me this money. I will work for you as long as you like. You can deduct this from my wages. Please—who else can I go to for help?

Chaudhary Enough, enough—I have a very delicate heart. Oh, I am feeling so bad. Wait, I will find a way to help you. Numberdar, come here (**Numberdar** *whispers in his ear.*)

Numberdar You, come here—listen to me (**Margaret** *happily runs toward him.*) Listen, Chaudhary Sahib is saying— (*Whispers in her ear.*)

Margaret What? What are you saying? (*Screams.*) Are you mad? Have you gone out of your mind? How dare you say this to me! Who do you think I am? (*Other women run toward her, and gather around her.*)

Women What happened? What happened? Why are you crying?

Margaret Look at him! I only asked for some money, and he says that I should … that I should …

Fazlu What's the matter?

Numberdar She was demanding money.

A Woman So what? She has worked for it—this is her *right* –she must be paid!

Chaudhary Ah—so—her right? Well, I will tell you all about your rights. Go on—move away, get on with your work.

A Woman Chaudhary Sahib, no one can be as cruel as you! Don't you fear God? You should be more merciful!

Maulvi Sinful woman! How dare you take God's name? May God save us from the Devil! Shameless, you shameless people! Damn you! God forbid!

Numberdar Chaudhary Sahib, you don't know—all of these people are Christians.

Chaudhary What? Christians! Curse on you! You have brought Christian people to my lands! How dare you? Curse on you!

Fazlu What if we are Christians? We have worked on these lands for many years.

Maulvi These people take the name of God but they do not believe in Allah. They are kaafirs—they are infidels.

Numberdar Yes, they are Christians—they are Kaafirs.

A Woman Chaudhary Sahib, you have reaped your wealth through our sweat and blood. Where would you be without us? Your status of a Chaudhary is because of our labor and toil.

Chaudhary Oh, I see, I see—I am going to show you where I am and where you belong. Numberdar, go, go, and get your men from the other village—give these bastards a lesson that they will remember. We will show these people their rights. (**Numberdar** *exits*.) I will break all the bones in your bodies—you ungrateful wretches.

*The **peasants** gather together, and talk amongst themselves.*

A Woman We have had enough of his cruelty.

Another 1 He thinks he can do anything.

Another 2 We will also inform the other villagers about your deeds.

Chaudhary (*to* **Maulvi**) Maulvi Sahib, if they do inform the other villagers about this I will lose face. Do something—think of a way out.

Maulvi Don't you worry. This is nothing. I am here for you. Tell me what you want. You want a "fatwa"[24]—you will get a "fatwa"—you just have to say "yes."

Chaudhary Thank you, thank you, Maulvi Sahib—you are great—this is why I am such a follower of yours. In fact, I have always been a follower of yours. You don't worry at all, this year I will double your share of the crop and I will have it sent to your home.

*The **Numberdar** returns with other men.*

Numberdar I have brought my men, Chaudhary *jee.*

Chaudhary So you have. Well, here are these people. Maulvi Sahib, you tell these good men what these Godless Kaafirs have been saying

Maulvi My Brothers, these people have been blasphemous; they have spoken against our Allah and His Prophet. Peace be upon Him. It is our sacred duty to kill them. They are Kaafirs; they are non-believers; they should not be allowed to live; they are Christians, Kaafirs. You must kill them, burn their huts, put them on fire, kill them—kill the Kaafirs.

All die. Amidst the mayhem and chaos of killing, the **Maulvi** *emerges singing, and others enact the song.*

Maulvi
Haq Allah! Haq Allah, Haq Allah, Haq Allah!
The world sees me as the truthful one, Haq Allah
The world believes in my miracles, Haq Allah,
I am a trader in religion,
Come and see my vocation,
I provide Kalashnikovs and grenades to these believers—
Those who are blind in their faith,
I turn them into suicide bombers.
Though I am myself Satan's disciple,
I sell them the vision of Heaven—
Heaven, where they will get *Hooris*,[25]
Haq Allah, Haq Allah, Haq Allah, Haq Allah.

Scene Five

A man who seems hysterical runs around the stage.

Mirza (*to the audience*) You know—you must know. (*Addressing the* **Maulvi** *as he enters.*) Do you know why I was murdered? You surely know why. (**Maulvi** *shrugs and exits.*) What was my fault? Someone tell me why, why was I murdered? I did nothing wrong—I did not harm anyone. Tell me, someone please tell me. Please. My name is Mirza Abu Ahmed. It was my daughter's wedding (*Music and wedding songs, girls laughing, etc., in background.*) The house was full of the sound of laughter and of music (*Sound of the shehnai.*[26]); everyone was so happy. I had got my daughter's wedding invitation printed in golden letters. Oh, it was such a beautiful card. I took it myself to my dearest friend's house.

*Scene goes back in time—***Mirza**'s *friend* **Anwaar**'s *house.*

Mirza Assalam alaikum,[27] Anwaar bhai.[28]

Anwaar *Array, Array* Mirza, walaikum assalam.[29] Mirza, where have you been these days? Haven't seen you for a long time.

Mirza Yes, I have been very busy. Busy with preparations for Tanno's wedding.

Anwaar Oh get lost, Mirza—I don't want to see you—go home. I am very angry with you.

Mirza *Array* why, why? Why are you angry with me? What's the matter?

Anwaar *Beti*[30] Tanno is getting married and I haven't even been informed? I thought you would consult me before taking such an important decision. Are we not the oldest friends? Am I not like your older brother? Go away. I will not talk to you.

Mirza Oh come on, *yaar*.[31] Yes, Anwaar bhai, I am truly sorry, but it all happened so fast that there was no time to come and talk to you. Come, come now, you can't be angry at such a happy moment in our lives. Come and embrace me.

Anwaar Congratulations, Mirza! I am so happy—happy that my lovely Tanno is getting married (*They hug and embrace.*) Mirza, you must do all to make this a great occasion. Tanno must have the best wedding possible. You know that I would do anything for you—if you need anything from me, please, please tell me. You know that she is like my own daughter.

Mirza Ah, yes, Anwaar bhai—thank you so much, you have always been so kind. Yes, I did want to ask you—remember the loan you had taken from me—well, now I need the money back—you know how much one has to spend on these occasions. So if you could repay that loan ...

Anwaar (*turning cold*) Mirza, you know that these days there is no work—buying and selling is very bad—I will not be able to repay your money at this point.

Mirza Anwaar bhai, I really need the money now—I had saved it for Tanno's wedding, and I gave it to you, if you remember ... on condition that you would return it to me whenever I needed it. And now I do need it back. There's no other option for me. I am sorry, but I really expect you to somehow return that money. I have no one else whom I can ask ...

Anwaar When is the wedding?

Mirza Here is the invitation. I came to invite you, too. See, the wedding is next Friday.

Anwaar I can't possibly arrange the amount by next Friday.

Anwaar's *brother enters.*

Brother Any problem, Brother? You look distressed.

Anwaar (*takes his* **brother** *to a side*) Mirza wants his money back. He needs it for his daughter's wedding.

Brother (*notices the invitation*) What is that?

Anwaar The invitation to his daughter's wedding.

Brother *takes the card and reads it minutely.*

Brother Hmmm … . I see! Now, listen carefully. Let me handle this. Just follow the line I take, and your problem will be over … forever! (*Loudly.*) Oh my God, this is blasphemy!

Mirza Blasphemy? Why? What happened?

Brother Are you not an Ahmedi,[32] Sir?

Mirza Well … yes … but …

Brother Then what is this? (*Waves the invitation before* **Mirza**'s *face.*)

Mirza What? Is there any mistake on the card? Can't possibly be—I checked everything myself, many times over.

Anwaar You, you are an Ahmedi?

Mirza Yes I am—so, so what?

Brother So, who gives you this right?

Mirza What right? What are you talking about?

Brother You have printed "Bismillah"[33] on this card, and you are saying "so what"?

Mirza So—we are also Muslims.

Brother No, you are *not*. You are an Ahmedi, and you cannot do this. You think you can make fun of our religion and get away with it?

Mirza What are you saying? (*Turns to* **Anwaar**.) Anwaar bhai? We have been friends since childhood. We grew up together. How many times we have helped each other—we have shared so much together— how often I have helped you out! How can you say such a thing?

Anwaar Yes yes, you have helped me often—but all that is something else. (*Raising his voice.*) How dare you make fun of our religion? (*At the noise other people enter.*)

Others What's the matter? What's happening?

Anwaar Look at this man, he is an Ahmedi and he has the audacity to have "Bismillah" printed on his daughter's wedding card. How dare he?

Others Yes, how dare he use "Bismillah"? He is a Kaafir. He is not a Muslim: he is an Ahmedi. He is not allowed to do this. This is blasphemy.

Mirza (*to* **Anwaar**) Anwaar bhai, when you took the loan from me, did you not know that I was an Ahmedi?

Anwaar Well yes, so what, that is different. But we will not allow you to disrespect our religion. You will have to pay for this.

Mirza Ah, now I understand. You are creating this whole drama so that you do not have to return my money.

Brother I am telling you he is a blasphemer—he must not be allowed to ridicule our religion.

Others (*hitting* **Mirza**) He is a blasphemer—kill him. He is ridiculing our religion; he is a Kaafir.

Another Yes, this blasphemer should not be allowed to live—kill him—kill him (*They push and hit* **Mirza** *who falls down.*)

Anwaar (*kneeling by* **Mirza**'s *side*) Mirza, Mirza, Mirza. Oh my God. He is dead. What do we do now? They will hang me.

Brother No, no, no. He was an Ahmedi. You need not worry.

Others We will tell them that he spoke against our religion, against our prophet.

Other 1 Yes. He was a blasphemer. He ridiculed our religion.

Other 2 Of course. Don't you worry. No one will touch you.

Other 3 In fact, you have only tried to protect Islam. He was a Kaafir!

(*They walk as in a procession, shouting.*) Kaafir, Kaafir, Kaafir!

The whole cast join in.

Scene Six

A gathering of women and men by a roadside.

Woman Look, look, what is here?

Another Don't touch it! Perhaps it's a bomb!

They all gather around, screaming hysterically.

Another 1 Don't go near it!

Another 2 It may be a bomb!

Woman No, no, look, it is moving. (*She picks up the bundle.*)
This is not a bomb. Oh look, it's a baby.

Other Woman It's a new born!

Another 1 Oh, see how cute it is!

Another 2 But what is it doing here amid the rubbish?

Woman This is a newborn baby. Perhaps thrown away by its mother!

Man Put it back where you picked it up from—this could be dangerous.

Other Man Yes, this comes under the *Hudood*[34] Ordinance.

Woman *Hudood*? What is *Hudood*?

Other Man Leave it there—we will all get into trouble!

Woman But it is alive, how can we leave it here?

Pir[35] (*enters, rising above the rest*) This is the sign of the end of the world—women have become immoral—Haq Allah, Haq Allah!

Woman Who is this?

Other Woman Don't you know who he is? He is a famous Pir Sahib.

Man He is well-known for his amazing miracles.

Other Man Yes, he has many Djinns and spirits in his possession!

Pir (*sings*)

Haq Allah! Haq Allah. Haq Allah, Haq Allah!
The world sees me as the truthful one, Haq Allah.
The world believes in my miracles, Haq Allah,
I am a trader in religion,

They trust my faith,
I give them these baubles,
And fill my pockets with their money;
I make use of their fear,
Ignorance and illiteracy,
And fool these blind believers.
(*Then, he says.*)
How dare you touch this piece of Sin!

Woman But this is an innocent child!

Pir It is a result of sin!

Woman Sin! What sin? It's an innocent child!

Pir No, this is a child of sin. Whoever touches it will burn in Hell. It is born out of an immoral and evil act. It deserves being stoned to death. Ah Muslims, why are you standing thus, and what are you watching? Islam is in danger, and you stand around gaping like idiots? Do you all want the doors of Heaven to be closed on you? Where is your pride and shame? Don't you have any honor left? Come, my Muslim Brothers; this is the time for jihad. Earn your place in Heaven. You will be rewarded—we must eliminate this obscene sign of immorality; we must purge and cleanse our society of this child of the devil. Muslim Brothers, come pick a stone and destroy this evil.

Many shout hysterically and start throwing stones at the child.

Old Woman (*enters*) Wait, stop, stop all this—(*Grabs the child.*) This is my child.

Pir Ahah—so the criminal accepts her crime. She is the mother of this evil. She should be burnt alive.

Man But she is an old woman—she must be at least 80 years old.

Old Woman What difference does my age make? I am *only* a woman. It does not matter how old. I may be ten years old or 80-years old! Yes, this is my child—my granddaughter gave birth to this baby last night, and then died. She was an orphan herself—her parents had died a long time ago. She was barely seventeen—yes, yes, she was a criminal—I am a criminal—all the women in this world are criminals—simply because they are women! Ah, but tell me, can giving birth to an illegitimate child be only a woman's crime?—Can she do this alone, all by herself? Is there no partner in this crime? Who is the father of the child? Tell me—is it someone from amongst you? Yes? Tell me! Is it Haji

Abdul Choudhary, the one who lives in that huge bungalow where my granddaughter used to go to work as a maid? ... Or, is it his son?

As the **Old Woman** *narrates, the following episodes should be enacted.*

Episode 1

Both the father and son would leer at her, and lust for her. She was only a maid servant, doing cleaning and washing. She worked hard and labored all day—sweeping the floors, and washing the dishes. Then, one day when Choudhary Sahib tried to force himself on her, and she slapped him across his face, Choudhary's wife saw this. To prove his innocence, Choudhary charged my granddaughter with theft. She was unable to say anything—and she was sent to the police lock-up.

Episode 2

What happened there? She was in the police lock-up for two days. And what did those so-called guardians of the law do to her in those two days? What did they do to my young innocent girl? Nobody knows what they did ... all that we know is that after she came back from the lock-up, she was a changed person ... she was like a lost child. She would remain quiet; she would not speak; she lost her laughter, her youth; she was like a frightened child; she could not sleep; she would get up screaming at night ... Then, someone said that she was possessed by a Djinn, and that she needed to be exorcised—that Pir Sahib can bring her back and help her, that he was a healer, that he could do wonders.

Episode 3

She was taken to Pir Sahib. He took one look at her and said ...

she was possessed by an *Ifrit*.[36] It was not easy to get rid of him; it took time.

Then, for many days she was kept in his *hujra*[37] and Pir Sahib would exorcise the Djinn out of her—and, finally, she was cleansed, and the evil spirit left her—and last night she died. Before dying, she left behind this baby of hers.

Old Woman You say that my girl and her baby are sinful, that they committed crimes against the law; you accuse them both of being criminals—her crime or her sin was nothing but her helplessness—yes, nothing else. Who is the real criminal? Why don't you go catch him and punish him?

Who is the real culprit, the real criminal?

Is it the Choudhary?

Or the so-called guardians of the law?

Or was it the Pir ?

At this, the **Pir** *starts running, and the others chase him trying to catch him, shouting.*

All Catch him, catch him—don't let him get away!

Scene Seven

A **Girl** *enters, repeatedly looking back anxiously.*

Girl Save me, someone, please help me, save me—don't kill me!

Narrator (*enters, running*)

What's up? Who are you? What is your name? Who are you running from? Tell us what we can do for you.

Girl My name is Pooja Mehra—when I left my office the other day … (**Narrator** *exits.*)

Boys *follow her, singing, teasing her, harassing her.*

Boy Wow, what a piece! Just look at her!

Boy 2 Yes, yes I am looking at her—she is a killer!

Boy 3 Ah, beautiful—where are you off to?—Take us with you.

Girl Let me go—get out of my way. You know I walk through here every day, and every day, you people tease me. Why do you do this? I am just like your sister. How would you like it if someone behaved the same way with your sister?

Boy Sister—ha ha ha—Sister … how can you be our sister? You are a Hindu?

Girl What if I am a Hindu? I am also a human being!

Boy 2 Oh, oh—she is a human being; she is a human being! Did you hear that?

Boy 3 If you want to be our sister, then become a Muslim.

Boy Yes, recite the *Kalimah*.[38]

She sees someone she knows at some distance away, and calls out to him.

Girl Salim bhai, please help me—see these boys are bothering me again.

Salim (*enters*) Why are you all troubling her? Leave her alone!

Boy What has it to do with you? Who is she to you?

Salim She is my sister.

Boy 2 Ha ha ha—Hindu sister of a Muslim brother!

Salim So? So what? She lives in my neighborhood, on my street—I have known her since childhood.

Boy 3 But what is this Hindu–Muslim brotherhood?!

Boy I don't quite understand this.

Boy 2 All sisters have one brother, Salim Brother, Salim Brother.

Salim Stop this nonsense—we are all one—we are all citizens of this country.

Boys (*menacingly*) Oh. So. Unhun …

Boy So, we are all one? Is that so?

Boy 2 Who are one? Hmm. Tell us, who all are one here?

Salim Oh come on—stop this. We are all Pakistanis. Dear friends, come now—don't let's divide ourselves into Hindus and Muslims—let's leave our religions out of this.

Boy 3 Go on, you idiot, go and give this speech to someone else— somewhere else. There is no August 14 *Jalsa*[39] taking place here. (*Starts kicking and pushing* **Salim**.) Go on, get lost, you bastard—telling us what to do, telling us how to behave?

Boy (*joining in*) Who the hell do you think you are—telling us what to do? We will show you who we are. (*Punches* **Salim**.) You son of a bitch, you pig—we will tell you how to divide yourself (*All the boys beat him; the girl shouts for help.*)

Girl Help, help, someone please help!!!

2 policemen—*an* **Officer** *and a* **Constable**—*appear, and stop the boys. Of the 2 policemen, only the* **Officer** *speaks.*

Inspector Sahib, please help me, please save us.

Police What is happening here?—Why are you hitting this man?

Boy Sir, this man was harassing this girl.

Boys Yes, Sir, this man was teasing this poor girl—we were only protecting her.

Police Are you all telling the truth?—Miss, was this man teasing you?

Girl (*shocked*) No, no, Inspector Sahib—it is these boys who were harassing me in the street—this poor man was trying to help me, he was protecting me.

Police (*to the* **boys**) So, you boys are lying to us—the girl says that you all were teasing her!

Boy 3 Sir *jee*, Sir *jee*, come hear, listen to us. (*Confidentially to the* **Police**.) Sir, you don't know this girl. She is that type, you know; we saw them together, you know what I mean? They were going on, here in public, no shame.

Boys Yes, Sir, we swear to you, we saw them with our own eyes. The two were not just holding hands, they were ... you know ... (*One of them whispers in the* **policeman**'s *ear.*) *And, Sir jee, she is a Hindu girl ...* .

Police I see (*to* **Salim**). Well Mr.—what is your name?

Salim My name is Salim.

Police (*to the* **girl**) And what is your name?

Girl My name is Pooja.

Police (*to* **Salim**) And what is she to you?

Salim Inspector Sahib, she is like my sister.

Police Pooja, Salim, Salim, Pooja—do we look like idiots to you? You go around shamelessly in public—and when you get caught ... you say, she is my sister.

Salim Sahib, these boys are lying. They are liars, they are street loafers; whenever any girl passes through here they bother her, they harass her.

Girl Yes, Inspector Sahib—these boys have made my life miserable— every day they harass me.

Police So, you swines, you think you can loaf around in my area?

Boy No, Sir, you don't know who this girl is. She is Pooja—she lives behind the Mandir.[40] (*They offer money to the* **Inspector** *who refuses, but signs to the* **Constable** *to take the money.*)

Police (*aside to the* **boys**) Hmm ... so, what is your plan?

Boy Plan—well there is only one plan.

Boy 2 We have to convert this Hindu girl—to Islam.

Police Ah, right—but I will have the first privilege. (*To* **Salim** *and the* **girl**.) The two of you have been caught red-handed indulging in ...   and these three young honorable gentlemen are witnesses. You are charged with obscene behaviour in public. Constable, arrest this man, Salim!

The **Constable** *handcuffs* **Salim**, *and takes him away. The boys encircle* **Pooja** *who starts screaming.*

Girl Save me, save me, help, help ...

The **Officer** *joins the boys and they surround the girl.*

All men (*shouting*) Hindu, Kaafir, Hindu, Kaafir ...

The whole cast come on the stage and speak, by turn.

1   Who is responsible for all of this?
2   Never does anyone get arrested for doing this.
3   They pull them out of public buses and kill them.
4   They enter our homes and kill us.
5   If we protest, even then we get killed.
6   We are killed on the basis of nationality, religion, and politics.
7   How long is this going to go on?
8   What are they greedy for?
9   What is it that they want?
10   Power, wealth, and position.
11   How many people have to be killed before your thirst is quenched?
12   How much blood must flow?
13   How many people must die?
14   How many dead bodies do you want?

Narrator (*re-enters*) Enough! Enough! We have had enough! But who will stop all this?

Actor 1 I will.

Actor 2 I will.

All We will. (*Asking the audience.*) Will you? Will you, too?

Narrator Yes, we will all stop this! We will all stop this together!

All (*sing*)
These increasing menaces
This shedding of blood
These upholders of religion
These guardians of faith
These waves of hatred
We will stop all of this
We shall resist them.
We are Hindu, Muslim, Sikh, Christian
We are Shia, Sunni, Mirzai
We all are inhabitants of this land
We will stop them.
We are the ones who toil,
We are the workers, the laborers,
We are the ones burdened with pain,
We are the peasants,
But we are full of strength,
We are powerful, full of hope.
We will end this nuisance
We will turn the wheel around
We will stop this
We will change this
We will make a better world
We shall resist …

The end

Notes

1   A folk theater form popular in northern India and some parts of Pakistan.
2   Very Very Important Persons.
3   An expert (here a specialist in music).
4   The opening part of or a prelude to an Indian classical recital (vocal or instrumental).
5   Leader of the Indian Muslim League, and the architect and first Governor-General of Pakistan.

6   Glory be to Allah.

7   Granny (father's mother).

8   Mother.

9   A low-ranking employee in an office.

10 The General was President of Pakistan from 1958 to 1969, and was the first Chief Martial Law Administrator.

11 A form of address of respect suffixed to a name.

12 The reference is to the action taken by the West Pakistan Army to crush the Liberation War in Bangladesh in 1971.

13 Zulfikar Ali Bhutto, the ninth Prime Minister of Pakistan, was also the fourth President. He was executed in 1979 for his alleged involvement in the murder of a political opponent.

14 "*Awami daur*" means "people's era." This was made into a slogan during the populist rule of Z. A. Bhutto in the 1970s.

15 General Zia-ul-Haq, Chief of Army Staff, deposed Bhutto in a bloodless coup, and became the sixth president. He was responsible for initiating the Islamization program in Pakistan.

16 Leader of the faithful.

17 General Pervez Musharaff was the tenth President of Pakistan (2001–8), who seized power through a bloodless coup d'état in 1999.

18 An interjection, proclaiming surprise.

19 A desi Sahib (addressed to, or meant for, General Musharraf himself or any other army officer from Musharraf's era).

20 A Punjabi folk dance.

21 A title bestowed on a *zamindar* (landlord) during colonial times.

22 Assistant.

23 Colloquially used to mean a rich and snobbish person.

24 A legal ruling, or directive, issued by an Islamic scholar.

25 Beautiful female inhabitants of heaven, given to men who go to heaven for their virtuous work on earth.

26 A South Asian oboe, played at celebrations and concerts.

27 An Islamic greeting on meeting a person.

28 Brother—an intimate address to a male friend or acquaintance.

29 Said in response to "Assalam alaikum."

30 Daughter.

31 A colloquial word for "friend."

32 Ahmedi, or Ahamediyya. The Ahamediyyas (also known as Mirzais) view themselves as propagating the pristine values of Islam after the teachings of their self-proclaimed messiah, Mirza Ghulam Ahmad.

33 An invocation, meaning "In the name of Allah," used by practicing Muslims at the beginning of an undertaking.

34 Hudood Ordinances occasioned major changes to the existing laws of Pakistan, especially on sex-related crimes (*zina*) and theft (*sariqa*), which were widely perceived to be inhuman because they included such punishments as amputation of limbs, flogging, and death by stoning.

35   This term is generally used for a highly religious person.
36   An evil creature of the underground in Islamic mythology.
37   A kind of guesthouse.
38   The words of purity one must say to become a Muslim.
39   August 14 is the Pakistan Independence Day; "*jalsa*" means "celebration" here.
40   Hindu temple.

Watch the Show and Move on

by
Shahid Nadeem

Translated from Urdu by **Shuby Abidi**

Characters (in order of appearance)

Narrator	Oppressed Persons (OP1, 2, 3, 4)
White-clad Men (WM1, 2, 3, 4)	Audience (another woman)
Black-clad Men (BM1, 2, 3, 4)	Woman 2
Hawker	Spectator 1
Poet	Spectator 2
Mother (an old woman)	Spectator 3
Woman	Spectator 4

Why try to catch a flying arrow?
Why grieve the others' grief?
Why jump into someone else's fire?
Why not just mind your own business?
What if a woman is being sold in the marketplace?
What if her modesty is outraged in public?
Well, you just enjoy the play,
Only watch the *tamasha*,[1] and move on.
What if a robbery is being committed somewhere?
What if an explosion's about to take place?
None of it all, really your business.
Just watch the show and move on.

If you see atrocities being inflicted on others,
If you see a crime being committed before you,
Or a poor person being beaten black and blue,
Turn a blind eye like everyone else.
Just watch the show and move on.

This world is only a show
Changing now and then,
Just go on watching,
Do not trust anyone.
Be a mere creature, not a human.
Watch the show and move on.

Narrator Ladies and Gentlemen, Brothers and Sisters, the play we are going to stage today is only a play. It has no connection whatsoever with any reality, with our lives, or with our problems. Any similarity between our characters and any living personality is a matter of pure coincidence. I am the Narrator of the play, Ravi, and you are the audience. My job is to narrate the story and connect the scenes, and your job is just to watch it all. If you like the show, applaud; or just watch it and go away. The purpose of this opening is to discourage you from finding, even by mistake, any semblance of reality in the play.

So, my dear audience, come let's start the play, and give the characters a chance to put on their performance. Give me an opportunity to be the Narrator, and you become the audience.

During this time, four men in black dress and masks come to the foreground of the stage and install a wooden cross, and prepare a noose for hanging. They check the noose for its strength. As the **Narrator** *exits, the* **black-clad men (BM)** *bring some white-clad men* **(WM)** *to* *the arena, hidden behind a black curtain from the audience, except for their white turbans. The* **WM**, *when the black sheets are taken off them, should appear white from head to toe—white hair, white eyebrows, white robes, white long beads in hand, and white turbans on their heads. They sit on the stools (or boxes) at the back and close their eyes. They chant loudly, in the manner of traditional Buddhist chanting, to the loud beat of a big gong. The* **BM** *wait in silence, but menacingly.*

White-clad Men (WM)

(*they chant*)

> We are the Chosen ones.
> We have left the worldly ways.
> We must purify all those
> Who are full of filth, in and out.
> May Paradise be promised for the true believers
> And the infidels be consigned to Hell.
> Haq hoo (*He is the True One*).

The **WM** *open their eyes and see the audience. The* **Narrator** *enters.*

Narrator   Let me introduce the characters of the play. Well, those who are intelligent enough may have already guessed that the men in white symbolize goodness, benevolence, and virtuosity. Those in black stand for evil, and for all the tension it embodies.

The **WM** *stare at the* **Narrator***. The* **Narrator** *smiles timidly, and moves away.* **WM1** *looks at the audience aggressively, sizes them up, and addresses them in a hysterical manner.*

WM1   Brothers from the same faith. The human being is Allah's supreme creation. (*He recites a verse from poet Iqbal.*[2])

It's better to be a human being than an angel,

But the task is much harder.

Blessed are you all

Allah sent the Holy Prophet and

Revealed to him the Sacred Book.

Congratulations to you all on being born humans.

Praise be to all.

Black-Clad Men (BM) (*all together, to the audience threateningly*) Applause, Applause.

WM2 But friends, being of the same species, have you ever realized how lucky you all are? But then it is a huge responsibility to live as God's Chosen. To do justice to being God's vicegerents is tough indeed, a huge challenge.

BM (*all together repeat in an aggressive style*) A challenge, a challenge, indeed.

WM3 Dear folks, we who share the same language and the same skin color know that devilish forces have ever sought to spoil lofty human efforts. The agents of evil have entered our lives, and are constantly trying to erode our faith and honesty.

BM (*all together*) Honesty, faith, honesty, faith.

WM4 Citizens and people from my community! Be prepared to combat the evil forces all the time. If you succeed here in this world, the world, hereafter, shall be yours. But if you hesitate or succumb to greed or any kind of temptation, then destruction and repentance will be your destiny in this life and beyond.

BM (*all together*) Destruction, repentance, destruction, repentance.

The tone of the **WM** *gradually suggests warning. During the conversation, the* **BM** *imitate the* **WM** *in words and action. They jump, praise, dance around the noose, and then stand to attention. After the speech is over, the* **WM** *come toward the stools, and the* **BM** *move toward the audience.*

BM1 (*like a salesman*) Ladies and gentlemen, the noose is ready!

BM2 It is strong and durable.

BM3 It is very loyal.

BM4 It is quite scary.

BM (*all together*) The noose is ready.

The **BM** *move back, and the* **WM** *address the audience.*

WM1 It is extremely necessary that humanity is protected from evil and negative forces.

WM2 It is necessary that the identity of our religion and community is kept away from the conspiracies and influences of other religions and communities.

WM3 It's our duty to sacrifice everything to keep our faith and belief pure and pristine.

WM4 In order to protect one's community if one has to incur loss of life and property even then there's no harm.

*The **WM** move backward. The **BM** sing.*

BM (*all together*)

> The noose is ready. It's quite scary.
> For its sake, one neck's necessary;
> Question of a neck.

*The **WM** stand on the stools and lecture.*

WM1 It's better for society to sacrifice individual interests in favor of collective interests.

WM2 The world is more content to ignore the interests of the minority for the majority.

WM3 It is natural, and also justifiable to suppress the minority's creed for the enforcement of the majority's.

WM4 It is only for the welfare of society that the obstacles put on the road to progress must be removed.

*At this time, the **BM** go down to the audience to search for someone who might be taken captive. They catch one.*

BM1 He thought he would escape us ...

BM2 Where will you go?

BM3 The trial will be held, and justice will be done.

BM4 Neither the sin nor the sinner will be pardoned.

All the people present there freeze. A hawker enters and reads out some headlines from a newspaper, which are about inflation, poverty, exploitation, etc.

Hawker Newspapers, papers, papers. Today's breaking news.

1 Inflation has badly hit the public.
2 People are craving for a single crystal of sugar. Have no other option but to buy it for 120 rupees a kilo.
3 The prices of mutton, vegetables, and fruits have soared too high.
4 The government has failed to control the demon called Inflation.

Newspapers, papers, papers.

The **Hawker** *leaves. A* **Poet**, *who looks more like a beggar, enters.*

Poet Prices have soared so high,

Prices are touching the sky.

With no money for pulses and flour,

How to buy veg that's so rare?

Sweetness in sugar is gone,

Mangoes even dearer than gold.

And in the name of mango

What's being sold?

Mango seeds, the seeds of mangoes.

All this you find in today's newspapers.

The **Poet**, *lost in himself, walks away. The* **BM** *continue their investigation.*

BM (*All together.*) Tell us, what do you do?

BM1 Tell us, what is your name?

BM2 What's the color of your skin?

BM3 What's your caste?

BM4 Who is with you?

BM1 Who supports you?

BM (*all together*) Say, say, speak up, speak, speak …

The oppressed weak person is tossed from one side to another. The **WM** *are busy worshipping.*

BM3 How much money do you have in your pocket?

BM4 Number of cattle in your field?

BM1 How much land do you own?

BM2 We have the right to take your land.

BM3 Our circle of action is narrow.

BM4 Something of yours may be mine.

BM (*all together*) Speak, speak, speak!

The **BM** *bring the* **Oppressed Person** *before the* **WM** *who make a sign and cast a charm on him. He wants to say something but doesn't get a chance. Following the signal from the* **WM**, *the* **BM** *carry him toward the noose.*

Oppressed Person (OP) For God's sake, don't do this to me. It was only a petty land dispute. The charge is false, and I am innocent. I haven't insulted anybody. How can a man like me dare to do anything like this?

The voice of the **OP** *gets drowned in the chanting of the WM,* "Hang him ... hang him."

The **BM** *hang the person. Silence prevails for some time after the hanging. The* **WM** *come and stand among the audience. The* **BM** *throw out the dead body. The* **Narrator** *enters.*

Narrator (*embarrassed*) I did mention earlier that it was just a drama. The characters and incidents are all fictitious. The incident, which occurred a while ago, was also imaginary. It is not even remotely connected to reality. It's all made-up. If I were a character in the play, then I would have tried to change its direction. But I am only a Narrator; my job is to narrate the series of events and not to change them. And you! You all are just the audience. So watch the play. (*He goes away.*)

WM1 My friends, how can we allow you to assail our dignity, modesty, reputation, and goodwill? How can we afford to remain quiet?

WM2 My friends, it's a question of our existence. It is a matter of our honor. It's an issue of our self-esteem.

WM3 Friends, we should eliminate the real enemies of our society, and religion. Otherwise, we will indirectly destroy ourselves.

WM4 Friends! One who doesn't respect our Holy Book, one who doesn't follow our curriculum, one who doesn't agree with our beliefs, one who doesn't conform to the signs of God, should be crushed.

The **BM** *catch hold of another person* (**OP2**).

BM (*all together*) Profession? Income, skin color, religion, community, group? Consider every person who belongs to another caste and community to be a disbeliever. Sign this declaration. You are laughing again? Is it a joke? Do you want the passport?

BM1 Oye ... where is your card? Take it out right away.

BM2 Check the color.

BM1 It's black.

BM2 I doubted it right in the beginning.

BM1 Come on, Brother, move ahead.

They take the person to the arena. The **WM** *sit on the stools. The* **Hawker** *walks through and loudly reads out the headlines from the last edition of a newspaper, which are about peace, robbery, murder, and other things.*

Hawker Newspapers, newspapers, papers. Today's breaking news. Across the country, incidents of violence have increased. People are forced to confine themselves to their houses. Fear looms large all over. In Faisalabad, a minority colony was burnt down. Seventeen individuals were burned down to ashes. The Peshawar blast shocked everybody. Newspapers, papers, papers.

After this the **Poet** *reenters, croons the verses of Bulleh Shah[3] and moves out. The* **BM** *continue their interrogation of* **OP2**. *During this time the* **WM** *play a musical chairs-like game, using the stools.*

BM1 Nobody can escape us.

BM2 Nobody can hide from us.

BM3 We'll hunt down our enemies.

BM4 No blows go to waste.

BM1 Tell us, who is your Prophet?

BM2 Tell us, who is your God?

BM3 Tell us, where is your Book?

BM4 Tell us, where is your answer?

BM (*all together*) Tell us, tell us.

The **BM** *toss* **OP2** *from this side to that side, and present him to the* **WM**. *An old woman emerges from the audience. She tries to talk to the* **WM**, *but they turn their back on her.*

Mother For God's sake, please leave my son alone. He's innocent.

BM (*all together, jokingly*) Innocent?

Mother My son has never hurt anybody. He respects everybody.

BM (*all together*) Respects everybody?

Mother It is a false accusation.

BM (*all together*) False accusation?

Mother Why don't you listen to me? Why don't you speak? For God's sake, for the sake of humanity, do something.

BM (*all together, mockingly*) For the sake of humanity!

Mother For the sake of justice and truth.

BM (*all together*) For the sake of truth!

Mother Don't play with my son's life. For the sake of God, for the sake of your God.

BM (*all together*) For the sake of God, for the sake of your God!

They push out the mother, and protect the arena. The **WM** *get up and dance. They walk around the captive. They get up on the stools, appear to charm the captive, and then speak.*

WM (*all together*) For peace … for tranquility.

For discipline … for law.

For religion … for community.

For faith … for belief.

Hang him … hang him.

Blow off the head … blow off the head.

The captive is hanged. The **BM** *start chanting. Silence. They watch the actions of the audience, signal to the* **WM**, *and then go and sit on the stools. The* **WM** *come forward and address the audience in a friendly tone.*

Mister, don't worry a bit. Leave the matters of collective interest to our discretion. Come, we are going to present a program for your entertainment.

The **WM** *wear black goggles, with "lotas"*[4] *in their hands, using them as mobile phones, while pretending to be watching the moon. They go to the corner and try to spot the moon, and talk over the phone. They agree on something and sing.*

Let's go and play with the moon.
With closed eyes let's see the moon.
Half a moon is all the moon.

Up and down, let's find the moon …
Let's go and play with the moon.
It's evening but where's the moon?
Let's go out in the night,
And find the moon.

They go back and stand on stools. One woman walks across. The **BM** *take notice of her, and speak in a rakish manner among themselves, "dissecting" her physical appearance in a manner that gradually gets nasty. The* **WM** *stealthily watch the "drama," and get busy worshipping.*

BM1 Brothers, today the moon has risen this side and not on the other side.

BM2 But unlike ever it is a full moon.

BM3 Whatever you are, I swear by God, you're just too beautiful.

(*Sings the first two lines of a song from a Bollywood movie.*)

Chaudwee kaa chand ho, ya aaftab ho,
Jo bhee ho tum khuda kee kasam, lajawab ho.[5]

Woman What are you doing? Let me pass.

BM1 Take my life, sweetheart, what is a "pass"?

Woman Shame on you, don't you have mothers and sisters at home?

BM2 They are at home. They don't loiter in public places and markets.

BM3 I have mothers and sisters, but there is the need of a beloved.

Woman You all are shameless. (*Addresses the* **WM**.) Why don't you stop them?

WM1 Don't talk to us, lady. You are a stranger.

WM2 Means you are improper to us.

WM3 Rather, you are non-human to us.

The **BM** *block her way, harassing her. The woman again addresses the* **WM**.

Woman You guys claim to be the custodians of society. Representatives of moral conduct and goodness. Can't you all see what is happening under your nose?

WM1 We can't see anything.

WM2 Something needs to be done.

WM3 It's a question of the dignity of our religion It's a question of our dignity..

WM (*all together*) Stone them to death.

*The **WM**, however, become an obstacle for any outsider who wants to go any farther. The **BM** try to control the woman, and drag her away. They come back, bringing one more person, **OP3**, with them, and begin the investigation.*

BM1 Why do you wear a cap across the head?

BM2 Why is your beard so short?

BM3 Why do you wear the sacred ring on this hand?

BM4 Why is your wife angry with you?

BM1 Why is your moustache below your lips?

BM2 Why do your armpits have a lot of hair growth?

BM3 Why is your head bald?

BM4 Why do you clean yourself beneath your underwear?

BM1 Why do you have such a big tummy?

BM2 Why are you so overweight?

BM3 You seem to be a slimy person.

BM4 You appear to be a conspirator.

BM (*all together*) Tell us, tell us, tell us.

*OP3 is quickly hanged. The **BM** catch another person, **OP4**, and present him before the **WM**. The proceedings of the court start.*

WM1 You try to mislead children.

WM2 You try to teach the illiterate.

WM3 You try to teach them science.

WM4 You are taking them in the wrong direction.

WM1 You are spoiling the progeny.

WM2 You place the Cross inside the mosque.

WM3 How could you dare commit such sacrilege?

WM4 How could you dare do something like this?

WM1 You all talk about justice.

WM2 You all talk about sagacity.

WM3 Let's teach him a lesson.

WM4 Let it be a deterrent for others.

The **WM** *take* **OP4** *toward the noose and put the noose around his neck. Then they go back and stand with their faces turned toward the wall. The captive takes the noose from his neck and addresses the audience.*

OP4 I am just an ordinary teacher. I am an only son of a hardworking poor father. I was born in a slum. Poverty and fear was part of my childhood. I was taught to live in fright and caution. I was told that I was a third-class citizen, with no rights, and that my loyalty to the land is dubious. I am an Untouchable.[6] Untouchable, untouchable.

BM/WM (*all together shout suddenly*) Hang him, put him on the gallows.

OP4 I am a common man, an ordinary teacher. I find happiness in teaching children. Innocent and pure children, free from all sectarianism and hatred. I would narrate the stories of flowers, fruits, and lovely animals; I would explain them good conduct; and my heart would leap up when I saw them happy and excited. Yes, I taught them happiness— told them about the awe-inspiring universe created by God. I also wanted that they embraced a scientific attitude, took my country ahead, and put it on a par with the other developing nations.

WM/BM Enemy of religion …

Enemy of faith.

Enemy of honesty.

Enemy of trust.

OP4 It was my fault that I used to think, I used to feel and I used to love. All this was most intolerable to them. Especially to him who wanted my job for himself, and to him who used to leave his cattle in my school grounds to graze. To those whose career thrived on hatred and communalism. They spread so much hatred for me that all the flowers around withered away. All the trees went up in flame. All the colors faded. Only the colors of hatred and death remained.

The **BM** *tighten the noose around the person's neck. The* **WM** *sing and dance.*

WM (*all together*)

> Let's become the judges and the jury.
> Let's become the Hajjis,[7] and the *namazis*.
> Come, let's weigh every human being.
> Let's measure everyone's faith and integrity.
> Let's smear their face with the ink of death.
> Let's become the judges and the jury.
> Let's get into their minds and terrify them,
> Let's become the judges; let's become the jury.

The **BM** *hang* **OP4**. *Then they take away his dead body. Silence. The scene changes.*

There's a market where the **BM** *are selling human organs and limbs in hawkers' baskets and the* **WM** *are the customers. The conversation takes place quickly, but in a normal way.*

BM1 It's fresh stuff.

WM1 Is it?

BM2 It's absolutely authentic.

WM2 It is difficult to distinguish between authentic and inauthentic.

BM3 It's right from the store, Sir.

WM3 The market is on fire due to inflation.

BM4 Order us, what can we show you?

WM4 Show me some hands.

BM1 See this … take it in your hand and see.

WM1 Hope it's not stale?

BM4 Oh no, it's one-hundred percent fresh, dear; it all gets sold off immediately. It can be easily cut and sliced.

BM3 For sure. See these fingers. These are the fingers of Laila.

WM3 They appear to be the ribs of Majnu![8]

BM4 Oh no, respected Sirs. It's very tasty. Just pick up the fingers and see …

WM4 Oh-ho ... Don't you finger me ...

BM1 Just see these legs—tender, delicate, and light.

WM1 I think these feet are heavy.

BM2 Oh no, Sir, they are so delicate that they get sullied as you put them on the ground.

WM2 What use are these feet for me?

BM3 Take full legs then.

WM3 But full legs will be too much for me?

BM4 You can keep them in the freezer, Sir, for a feast.

WM4 And if the legs get tangled then?

BM1 How about a fresh and crispy neck, Sir?

BM2 Run, the Big Boot[9] is coming.

Chaos ensues. All run away. When they come back, they are in their old form.

BM1 Issues of peace and security are serious matters.

BM2 The virtuosity of the virtuous is in danger.

BM3 The wealth of the wealthy is not safe.

BM4 The jobs for the jobless are uncertain.

WM1 But even in these circumstances there are people who are living in luxury!

WM2 They are having all the fun.

WM3 They are making portraits.

WM4 They are writing poetry.

*The **BM** catch hold of another person from the audience, bring him to the stage, and start the enquiry.*

BM1 You write poetry?

BM2 You tell stories of love and lust?

BM3 You play with words and rhymes!

WM1 Tell us, what is your name?

WM2 Tell us, what is your work?

WM3 How much do you have in your wallet?

WM4 And how much in the bank?

WM1 Tell us, whose side are you on?

WM2 And who is on your side?

WM (*all together*) Tell us, tell us, tell us.

They torture the **Poet** *and bring him close to the noose. The* **BM** *start chanting. All freeze, and then the* **Poet** *addresses the audience.*

Poet

I am not a warrior.

I am not a revolutionary,

I am not a rebel,

Neither am I on any mission.

I am simply a poet.

A poet who renders emotions into words.

One who gives expression to love.

WM (*all together.*) A rebel! A revolutionary! A sinner!

Poet Is it a sin to express, through the God-gifted tongue, beauty and melody in the smallest ions of the universe created by God?

WM (*all together*) It is a sin, it is a sin.

Poet Is it a sin to question?

WM (*all together*) It is a sin, it is a sin.

Poet Is it a sin to dream?

WM (*all together*) It is a sin, it is a sin.

Poet Is it a sin to think?

WM (*all together*) It is a sin …

Poet Is it a sin to speak?

WM (*all together*) It is a sin …

The **BM** *wildly dance and hang the* **Poet**.

Narrator (*enters*) You all must be thinking where the hell the Narrator had vanished to. The Narrator's presence is very important; otherwise, the story breaks down. Just as old alcohol needs a new label, and cheap gifts require nice wrappers, a simple or ordinary play needs the glib tongue of the Narrator to be a success. Take this drama for example. The incidents it relates are not interesting as such. Such unrealistic, intolerable, and crude things abound in it! How can these gory incidents provide a healthy entertainment? It is better to watch a television drama. At least, it is deeply rooted in our real lives and deals with real issues.

The **BM** *laugh.*

Seriously, targeting of teachers, social workers, poets is very sad. But let me make it clear that I am neither a teacher, nor a social worker, and thank God, nor even a poet. Friends, why should I put my hand in the fire? Why shouldn't I live my life peacefully? Do you all agree with me? You can speak; don't worry. There is no danger here. At least here nobody can tease or scare the audience and me. Both you and I are vital part of the performance. Can a play be staged without the audience? Am I wrong?

Audience Yes, you are wrong …

Narrator What do you mean?

Audience Whatever is happening in the drama is the order of the day, it happens around us. How can we remain quiet?

Narrator See, Madam, you are unnecessarily poking your nose into it.

BM (*all together*) The nose will be slashed off.

Narrator This case is of no concern to you.

Audience It is of grave concern to me. I'm a member of the society where such atrocities are occurring.

Narrator Are you from a foreign country?

Audience No.

Narrator Are you from a minority group?

Audience No.

Narrator Then you must be a communist?

Audience No, not at all.

Narrator Are you an opposition leader?

Audience Let them be damned.

Narrator Hope you are not a poet.

Audience Neither a poet nor anything else of that sort.

Narrator Intellectual?

Audience No.

Narrator From the media?

Audience God forbid!

Narrator Now I understand you must be related to that teacher.

Audience No, not at all. I am nobody's relative.

Narrator Hmmmm …   you must be an agent of CIA, RAW,[10] or Mossad.[11]

Audience I am no agent.

Narrator What's your problem then? Why are you spoiling my play?

Audience It isn't just your play. I am also a part of it. I am the audience.

Narrator Then behave like an audience. In this script the audience just witnesses the play. They don't interfere in it.

Audience I've seen enough of this show. I can't be a silent spectator any longer.

Narrator If you are so fond of acting, then why don't you come for auditions and seek the director's permission?

(*To the audience.*)

Ladies and Gentlemen! Just explain it to her. Why can't she remain quiet like you all? When she has not suffered any losses herself, why does she behave thus?

Audience When a fire spreads all around you, how long can your house remain safe? If not today then certainly tomorrow will your house be engulfed by that fire!

Narrator If you keep arguing like this, the fire will then catch you right away; you don't have to wait till tomorrow.

BM (*all together*) What is your address, lady? We'll arrange for it right now.

Audience (*to the* **people**) Do you think whatever is happening is right? Is it appropriate to kill in the name of faith? Is it right to burn down the houses of people who follow some other prophet? Is it right to ban speaking, writing, and thinking—all in the name of religion? Speak. Why are you quiet? Why have you shut your mouth?

BM (*all together*) We have the key to open it.

Narrator Ladies and Gentlemen! My dear audience, don't pay attention to her lecture. She is definitely an agent, at least of our rival theater group.

Audience How long would the drama last?

BM (*all together*) It will take a lot more time. We have booked this place for two hours.

Audience How long will the play go on in the name of religion, in the name of community and group?

Narrator Just look here, lady! You want to lead me to my destruction, don't you? See, the punishment for deviating from the script is very stringent. I'll have to suffer the capital punishment! The writer will throw me out of the script. It means the end—death. (*Mimes slashing the neck to suggest death.*)

Audience I don't care for such a script. I am a human being and not a puppet dancing to the tune of others.

BM (*all together*) If you don't dance that way, then you won't be left in a position to dance at all, lady.

Narrator (*in a changed tone*) May God have mercy on us. The atrocities that we are committing, or those that we are allowing, will, for sure, be accounted for. We'll have to answer for doing injustice to mankind. God's wrath will befall you, surely.

During this time, the **BM** *forcefully bring the audience member over to the arena. The* **WM** *dance. They sharpen the knives. The* **Narrator** *runs away scared.*

WM1 Whatever has been written is irrevocable.

WM2 Changes to what has been said are not permissible.

WM3 Deviation from the given verdict is not allowed.

WM4 It is useless to fight with the destiny that's been already shaped.

The audience member is hanged. Her throat seems to have been slashed, as well, with a knife.

BM1 (*with the blood-smeared knife*) Any other worshipper of truth?

BM2 Any other claimant to rights?

BM3 Any other flag bearer of justice?

BM4 Any damned admirer of his mother?

BM1 Anybody else who dares to speak, think and feel?

BM2 Who else desires to play a role in *our* drama?

BM3 If there is one, let him or her come out in the open.

BM4 (*laughs*) Nobody. How can there be anybody else? Everybody loves to live.

BM1 Who doesn't value one's own wealth? Who doesn't worry about one's own house?

BM2 Who doesn't want the well-being of one's wife and children?

BM3 Come, friends! Let's start the drama again.

BM4 Consider this interference as an interval for more hangings. (*They laugh.*)

BM (*to the* **WM**) Come on; present an entertaining program.

The **WM** *sing a song side by side and gesticulate. Their actions are all very shabby.*

WM (*all together*)

> If women become leaders,
> The community's doomed.
> If the head's covered with *dupatta*,[12]
> If the economy's in control,
> One feels good.
>
> If there's a check on thought,
> If people are deaf and dumb,
> If hanging's done in public,
> Everyone will be afraid of God.
>
> All musicians are lamenters.
> All art is vulgarity.
> He is our culprit,

Whoever is a non-Muslim;
Who trades in profanity,
He's a false hero.
(*They go back to the stools*.)

Woman 2 (*enters*) Has anybody seen my son? He must be 15-years old now. He is tall, handsome, and young. He was in a green-colored *sherwani*.[13] He had gone to Jama Masjid[14] to attend a lecture. I don't know what it was on. He had gone there with great interest after taking a bath. I don't know who hosted the religious meeting. Announcements had been on loudspeakers since early morning. My son was fond of going to public meetings. Now, he would listen to the sermon of one priest; then, he would listen to another's, and then he would compare both to a third one. When he came back, his eyes were red with anger, and he was ready to kill anybody. Burning with anger and hatred, he was ready to kill … . The riots took place, but I still don't know who benefited from them. Bullets were fired; everything was put on fire, houses were burnt. Married women became widows, and children orphans. The speakers spat venom at each other. They vitiated the whole atmosphere with so much hatred and intolerance that it was difficult to breathe. My son got separated from me in this chaos. Whenever any announcement of a religious meeting is made or a riot breaks out, I go there, thinking my son might also be there. Meetings take place, speakers shout, bullets are fired, blood flows. Maybe my son sees the clouds of smoke and rushes in there. If you see my son just tell him that his mother travels from city to city in search of him. I beseech you to convey my message to him. Just tell him that he should come back to his mother.

BM1 Mother, why are you here?

BM2 Go, go, women are not permitted to come here.

BM3 Women are not allowed to go anywhere.

BM4 Especially old ladies and mothers, go, go move away.

They send her away. The **Hawker** *enters and reads aloud the headlines.*

Hawker Bloody brawl between the Jamali and the Jalali. Provocative statements against the Hilal community and the well-wishers of the Dhalis. The Iqbalis have demanded the Inkaris to be declared as nonbelievers.[15]

Communal clashes have crossed all limits.

Today's headlines …

The **WM** *read newspaper and get excited. They sit together and address the audience. The* **BM** *join in. The* **Hawker** *gets scared and runs away.*

WM1 Jamalis, your dignity has been challenged.

BM1 Why are you quiet? Are you shameless?

WM2 Dhalis, if you remain quiet then you'll be a sinner to God.

BM2 And God takes good revenge on those who sin against Him.

WM3 Jalalis, sacrifice your life for your faith.

BM3 And if your life is so dear to you, then take away the life of one from the opposite camp.

WM4 Hilalis, assemble in the mosque and show your power.

BM4 Prove that you are worthy of your faith.

WM1 Attend the meetings, strengthen the hands of the true.

BM1 And destroy the power of the false.

WM2 Tie the shroud around your head and come.

BM2 And take with you whatever weapons you have.

WM3 This is a war between right and wrong.

BM3 This is the war between Islam and non-Islam.

WM4 Victory be yours.

BM4 Victory be yours.

The **BM** *walk down to the audience and try to provoke them. Chaos and confusion. The* **Narrator** *comes into the arena and tries to control the situation.*

Narrator Ladies and gentlemen, don't worry. The play has gotten a little out of control. The characters have become emotional. Actually, the issue is such that everyone becomes emotionally charged.

BM1 Murder them.

WM1 Put everything on fire.

BM2 Destroy everything.

WM2 Put an end to everything.

BM3 Attack.

WM3 Move ahead.

BM4 Let's raise a slogan in the name of God.

WM4 ALLAH HO AKBAR[16] ...

The characters hysterically run among the audience.

Narrator I request the characters to get back to the arena.

WM1 But we need one more character.

BM1 In order to take the play ahead.

WM2 For initiating the court case.

BM2 For delivering the verdict.

WM3 For hanging him.

BM3 Speak up. Is there anybody willing to be hanged?

WM4 Speak up. Is there any character willing to act in the drama?

BM4 Speak.

Narrator We are arranging for it, Friends; we have established contact with the playwright. He is writing one more hanging scene ... the first page is with me. Please come here ...

BM1 No, we want the whole right now.

BM2 We want prey.

WM1 We want blood.

WM2 We want a scapegoat.

BM3 We require a body for exhibition.

Spectator 1 Why don't you listen to what the Narrator has to say? We are not a part of the play. We have come to watch it.

BM4 You are speaking a lot. You are our prey.

Spectator 2 He is not your character. He has come to watch the drama. He lives in Waynpuray.

WM3 He should be hanged.

Spectator 1 You are wrong.

Spectator 2 At least you people shouldn't try to cross the limit.

WM4 Good, your number comes next.

BM1 Instead of one, hang the two together.

WM1 We'll save money.

Spectator 3 It's enough, stop this melodrama. Leave us now.

Spectator 4 We can't tolerate it any longer. Things have crossed the limit.

Spectator 1 Go back to the arena. You won't get any character from here.

Spectator 2 Get out.

Spectator 3 Get lost.

Spectator 4 Go away!

All Spectators Out, out.

The **BM** *and* **WM** *get anxious; and frightened by the noise of the audience, they go back to the arena. They discuss things together. The* **Narrator** *tries to control the audience.*

Narrator Ladies and gentlemen! You are getting too emotional now. In order to recast the characters in the play, you have various tricks. You can order the playwright to make changes to the script. The director can be pressurized. If the problem persists then a case can be framed against the owner of the hall. If the issue goes out of control then the play can be banned. The cast can be put behind bars. The hands of the playwright can be chopped off. The director can be stoned to death. Why are you all so worried? Rest assured, the audience is safe.

The **BM** *and* **WM** *consult each other. Then they come and stand near the* **Narrator***. He looks shaken. But on seeing a smile on their faces, he also starts smiling.*

Narrator Just see, I had told you that everything would be alright!

WM1 Brothers of Islam, the situation is really worrisome. This rowdiness and chaos in an interesting and peaceful drama will not be tolerated.

BM1 We are sorry that the play was interrupted.

WM2 Your pleasure was spoilt. It was really bad.

BM2 You must be of the opinion that the drama should go on.

WM3 By turn new characters should be hanged.

BM3 If the play stops then what would be left in life?

WM4 Reality is much more bitter and painful than this drama.

BM4 It is better to see others being hanged than to bear witness to one's own capital punishment.

WM1 Hanging in public is a pleasure indeed.

BM1 We have found out a solution.

WM2 We have got a clue to the conspiracy.

BM2 The person responsible for all our problems …

WM3 The culprit of all the chaos in the play …

WM3 This Narrator, catch him!

BM4 He should definitely be punished for his actions.

WM4 … punished for his action.

*They (all **BM** and all **WM**) try to catch the **Narrator**. He resists.*

Narrator What do you say? What are you doing? You are the characters in the drama and I'm your Narrator. You are attacking *me*! I'll ask the playwright and get you hanged upside down. I'll get a new scene written in which you'll be deskinned. For God's sake, please leave me. All this is not there in the script.

BM (*all together*) The script is that which is acceptable to us.

WM (*all together*) Your writer is a fool who gives shelter to wolves.

Narrator (*to the audience*) Please help me. The case is really going out of control. You all know I'm your Narrator, *only* a Narrator. I've nothing else to do with this drama. I have not played any role ever. I was never fond of acting. I am a peace loving, law abiding, and pious citizen. I have never tried to interfere in others' matters. I keep to my work only. I am a coward and opportunist, who sees everything, but doesn't say anything. A citizen who doesn't do anything. I should not be subjected to this cruelty. Should this be my end? For God's sake, please save me. For the sake of God and the Prophet. For the sake of community and society. For the sake of humanity …

*The **WM** start chanting. The **BM** catch the **Narrator** and drag him.*

All of them brutally murder the **Narrator**.[17] *He squirms, shouts, and appeals. In the end, he dies. The* **WM** *and* **BM** *address the audience with blood-smeared knives in their hands.*

BM1 Ladies and gentlemen, the span of the drama will be shorter next time.

WM1 But don't worry, the play will be performed again for your entertainment.

BM2 It will start again for sure.

WM2 It will travel from one city to another, from one village to another.

BM3 In every mosque, in every lane shall it be held.

WM3 You are welcome to continue watching the play.

BM4 But you must only watch it and then move on.

WM4 Otherwise, remember the fate of the Narrator.

ALL (BM *and* **WM)** Goodbye and goodnight.

The end

Notes

1   A fun-filled show here. "Tamasha," in its traditional performative context, means a form of Marathi theater, with a lot of singing and dancing.
2   A famous Urdu poet and politician who is credited with the vision of a separate homeland for a large number of South Asian Muslims, eventually to be called "Pakistan."
3   He was a famous Punjabi Sufi poet and humanist.
4   A kind of small water vessel with a spout.
5   *The full moon, or the sun, are you?*
     Whatever, by God, you are incomparable.
6   In the traditional Hindu caste hierarchy, the "Untouchables" occupy the lowest rung. Called "Dalits" in modern India, they are now officially protected by way of additional privileges accorded to them in various walks of life. The status of the "Untouchables" is very different in Pakistan, however, since they are a minority within a minority and, therefore, generally discriminated against by the majority religio-cultural community. The "lowly-born" Muslims and Christians are also treated as "Untouchables" in Pakistan.
7   People who have successfully completed their pilgrimage to Mecca.

8 Laila and Majnu are star-crossed lovers of an Arabian legend.

9 Certain laws under Sharia mandate severe punishments, which may also include amputation of body parts, depending on the gravity of the crime committed. And such punishments are graphically described in the body of Islamic laws: chopping of finger tips or full fingers, amputation of a whole hand, right or left, cutting off the head by the sword, death by hanging, and the like. In the present grotesque scene, the vendors are selling various parts of the human body, which simultaneously reminds one of the mass killings (sacrifice) of animals, small and big, on the occasion of Eid. The pavements are full of blood flowing from makeshift slaughterhouses, and also of body parts of slaughtered animals discarded by customers. The Big Boot here refers to the routine police raid to arrest the unauthorized meat sellers doing brisk business on the eve of the Islamic festival.

10 Research and Analysis Wing, an intelligence agency of India.

11 An intelligence agency working for the protection of Jewish communities.

12 A long strip of handcrafted cloth worn by many Muslim (and also Hindu) women in South Asia.

13 A long full-sleeve, loose-fitting shirt worn by many Muslim (and also Hindu) men in South Asia.

14 The main mosque of a town; the place of gathering for Eid, or Friday prayers.

15 These are the names of local (and often rival) communities, or political parties in Pakistan.

16 "Allah is Great."

17 The seventh killing in the play.

Notes on Contributors

Shuby Abidi (PhD) is Assistant Professor of English at Jamia Millia Islamia, New Delhi. She did her doctoral dissertation on novelists of the Indian diaspora. Co-editor of the journal *The SPIEL Journal of English Studies*, she has published many articles on Pakistani and diaspora literature in reputed journals. Abidi has also translated several short stories by Munsi Premchand. Her areas of interest include: diaspora studies, feminist literary theory, Indian writing in English, third-world literature, and translation.

Ameena Kazi Ansari (PhD) is Professor of English at Jamia Millia Islamia, New Delhi. Her areas of specialization include: modern British fiction, Canadian literature, Australian literature, Greek drama, translations studies, and literary criticism. She has published several books, including *English–Canadian Literary Canon: Emergence and Development* (2003), *Translation/Representation* (co-edited, 2008), *Indian English Women Poets*, (co-edited, 2009), and *The Complete Short Stories of Premchand*, vol. 1 (co-edited, 2010), and also articles on diaspora literature, Canadian literature, Commonwealth literature, Partition literature, and Premchand's stories. Ansari has translated several significant works, including "Munni of Bangali House" (Urdu short story, "Bangali House ki Munni", 2004), and *Partitions* (Kamleshwar's Hindi novel, *Kitne Pakistan*, 2006).

Bina Biswas (PhD) is former Professor of English Communications and Language at an Engineering College, affiliated to Jawaharlal Nehru Technical University, Hyderabad. A translator, critic, poet, fiction writer, and editor, she has specialized in Tagore studies. Biswas has authored several books, including *Tale of the Missing Shoe and Other Stories* (2012), *Breeze in the Old Building and Other Stories* (2013), *Forest Flowers* (a collection of poems, 2013); and co-authored *Bombcase Baxi and Cleo: Detectives Extraordinaire* (2014). She has also translated Naseer Ahmed Nasir's Urdu poems into English, *A Man Outside History* (2014), Mahesh Dattani's play, *Final Solutions*, into Bengali, and co-translated *Meghnad Vadh Kavya* from Bengali into English (forthcoming). Biswas has recently co-edited a volume of essays, *Dattani Plays: Staging the Invisibles* (2015). She is also CEO of Rubric Publishing, India.

Sayantan Gupta is a consultant gynaecologist by profession. He has acted in more than fifty plays and directed about a dozen. Gupta has also written plays, some of which have been successfully staged. A poet and lyricist, he has published many poems, and had several of his lyrics in Bengali put to music. He writes short stories and novels, too. His publications include: *Where the Rainbow Ends* (2011), *The Unclaimed Luggage and Other Stories* (2013), *The Abode of Kings* (2013), and *Sayantan Gupta's Poems on Love* (2014). He is the co-author of *Bombcase Baxi and Cleo: Detectives Extraordinaire* (2014), and co-translator of Michael Madhusudan Dutt's *Meghnad Vadh Kavya* (forthcoming). His novel, *In Pain You Are Mine*, was published in 2015.

Syed Shamsul Haq (1935–2016) is one of the most renowned Bangladeshi writers. In an illustrious writing career spanning over five decades, he has written poetry, fiction, plays (mostly in verse), and essays. His poetical works include: *Ekoda Ek Rajye* (Once Upon a Time in a Kingdom, 1961), *Birotihin Utsob* (The Ceaseless Festival, 1969), *Opor Purush* (The Other Man, 1978), and *Kobita Samagra* (Collected Poems, 2007), in three volumes. He has written more than thirty novels, including: *Anupam Din* (Best Days, 1962), *Neel Dangshon* (The Blue Sting, 1981), *Smritimedh* (Massacre of Memory, 1986), *Stabdhatar Anubad* (Translation of Silence, 1987), *Shreshtho Uponyas* (Best Novel, 1990), *Megh O Machine* (Cloud and Machine, 1991), and *Brishti O Bidrohigon* (Rain and the Rebels, 1996). Haq's most celebrated plays are: *Payer Awaj Pawa Jai* (*At the Sound of Marching Feet* in this volume); *Nuruldiner Sara Jibon* (The Entire Life of Nurul Din), *Ekhane Ekhon* (Here, Now), *Khatta Tamasha* (Bitter Jokes), and *Judhha ebong Judhha* (War and War). He has been honored with numerous awards—such as the Bangla Academy Award (1966), Ekushey Padak (1984), Nasiruddin Gold Medal (1990), Swadhinata Padak (2000), and the National Poetry Honour (2001). Syed Haq has also translated some of Shakespeare's plays.

Anwer Jafri is among the most senior theater practitioners and human rights activists in Pakistan. A playwright, set-and-light designer, and director, he has worked on several major theater productions. His work has been performed in Bangladesh, Germany, India, Iraq, Nepal, and the US. He has also directed a number of music videos and documentaries, and has written and directed many award-winning plays for television.

Sheema Kermani is a prominent theater practitioner and activist for women's rights and peace and is based in Karachi. A trained classical dancer and choreographer, she brings her social and political experience into her performances. Having founded Tehrik-e-Niswan, in 1979, a cultural action group with a mission to create greater awareness about women's rights and social issues, Kermani, as its artistic director, continues to develop performances for the stage, and often takes plays to backward and low-income areas. Her group has mounted over one hundred productions at home and abroad, some landmarks in Pakistan's theater history. Kermani has also acted in a number of popular TV plays and serials. In 2005, she was nominated one of the "1,000 Peace Women from across the Globe" for the Nobel Peace Prize. A founding member of the Pakistan–India People's Forum for Peace and Democracy (PIPFPD), Kermani has taken active part in the peace activities of the organization. Her co-edited volume, *Gender, Politics and Performance in South Asia*, was published by Oxford University Press, Pakistan, in 2015.

Abhishek Majumdar is a playwright and theater director based in Bangalore. He is the artistic director of the Indian Ensemble. His plays, performed in India and abroad, include *Rizwaan* (2009), in English and Urdu); *An Arrangement of Shoes* (2010); *Afterlife of Birds*, *Harlesden High Street* (in verse), *Waterlines* (all 2011); *The Djinns of Eidgah* (2012); and *Kaumudi* (2014). Majumdar is a recipient of the Hindu MetroPlus Playwrights Award (2008), TFA Playwrights Award (2009), Royal Court International Playwrights Residency (2011), and the Special Jury Award at the International Film Festival of Kerala, southern India (2012). An alumnus of the London International School of Performing Arts, he has received the Charles Wallace Trust Fellowship, Inlaks Scholarship, Lispa Scholarship, and the Robert Bosch Arts Grant. He is a member of the Young Vic Directors Network, London, was a visiting scholar at New York University, Abu Dhabi Campus, and was at the Lincoln Center Theater Directors Lab in 2012.

Shahid Nadeem is an acclaimed Pakistani playwright who has been at the forefront of the campaign for human rights and justice in the country, since the 1960s. Imprisoned by various military regimes, and exiled for a period of time, he was adopted by Amnesty International as a prisoner of conscience. Since his return to Pakistan, in 1988, he has served as executive director of Ajoka Theatre, and has written and directed plays on a wide range of human rights themes, including political corruption, gender violence, minority sufferings, and resistance to terrorism. His plays have been translated into several languages, including English, and their popular appeal proves the broad-based support that democracy and human rights enjoy in the Muslim world. Nadeem was a Getty Research Institute/International Pen Fellow in 2001, and National Endowment for Democracy Fellow in 2013–14. He received the President of Pakistan's Pride of Performance award in 2009. A collection of his plays in English was published by Oxford University Press, Pakistan, in 2008. Ajoka's *Dara*, written and directed by Nadeem, premiered in Lahore in 2010, and has been performed in Pakistan and India. Adapted by the National Theatre, UK, the play opened there on January 20, 2015.

Masum Reza is a popular award-winning playwright and scriptwriter for television and film in Bangladesh and abroad. He was commissioned to write for Bangladesh Television in 1996, and then started writing screenplays for feature films, promos, and scripts on development issues. Reza's important stage plays in Bengali include: *Nityapurana* (2000)), *Araj Charitamrita* (2001), *Baghal* (2010), *Jol Balika* (2012), *Kuhokjal* (2014), and many others. Reza's plays have been produced by different theater ensembles in Bangladesh, and have toured several cities in India, Egypt, and the US. Notably, Reza's street play *Kaklash* was staged by more than 200 theater groups in Bangladesh, and played a vital role in the anti-military rule movement in 1986. He has received numerous awards for his work in theater, including the Meril-Prothom Alo Critic Award (best television playwright; for *Modhu Moira*), Cultural Reporters Association of Bangladesh Award (best stage playwright; for *Nityapurana*), Bangladesh Film Journalists Association Award (best stage playwright; for *Araj Charitamrita*) and, most recently, the Bangla Academy Sahitya Puroskar. Reza is also a theater activist and holds key positions in organizations such as Desh Natok, Dhaka; TheatreFolks, Oxford; and the International Theatre Institute (ITI), Bangladesh Chapter.

Ashis Sengupta (PhD) is Professor of English at the University of North Bengal, India. Recipient of the Olive I Reddick award (1995), he has published numerous essays/chapters on South Asian drama and theater, modern American drama, and African American literature in journals/ edited volumes, including the *Journal of American Studies*, *Comparative American Studies*, *Journal of American Drama and Theatre*, *Hungarian Journal of English and American Studies*, *Indian Literature*, *DLB: South Asian Writers in English*, and *Miller and Middle America*. *Mapping South Asia through Contemporary Theatre*, edited by Sengupta for Palgrave Macmillan (2014), has been hailed as the first cross-national study of theater in the region. His areas of research include: race and ethnicity, gender and sexuality, nation and nationalism, religious studies, and diaspora. Sengupta was a Fulbright American Studies Institute fellow in 2002, and a Fulbright visiting professor in 2006. He also visited Malaysia and Sweden as guest lecturer in 2003 and 2009, respectively.

Zahida Zaidi (1930–2011) was a distinguished poet, dramatist, and critic. She authored more than 30 books in Urdu and English, and translated the works of Chekhov, Pirandello, Beckett, Sartre, Ionesco, among others. Her noted works include: *Beyond Words* and *Images in a Broken Mirror* (English poetry collections, 1979 and 1980, respectively), *Inquilab Ka Ek Din* (Urdu novel, 1996), *Kyunkar Us But Se Rakhun Jaan Aziz* (Urdu play, 1997), *Burning Desert* (English play, 1998), and *Shola-e-Jan* (Urdu poetry collection, 2000). Zaidi also directed and produced plays from the West and India, both in English and Urdu. A Cambridge graduate, she taught at Lady Irwin College and Miranda House in Delhi, as well as at Women's College, Aligarh, before joining the Department of English, Aligarh Muslim University, in 1964. For her significant contribution to Urdu literature, Zaidi received many prestigious awards, including the Uttar Pradesh Urdu Academy Award, Bihar Urdu Academy Award, West Bengal Urdu Academy Award, Imtiaz-e-Mir from All India Mir Academy, Hum Sab Ghalib Award, and Kul Hind Bahadur Shah Zafar Award.